Twayne's Filmmakers Series

Frank Capra

Frank Capra at the peak of his career
1939

Frank Capra

CHARLES J. MALAND

University of Tennessee

NEW YORK

Twayne Publishers

1995

Frank Capra

Published in 1980 by Twayne Publishers,
A Division of G. K. Hall & Co.

Copyright © 1980 by G. K. Hall & Co.

Printed on permanent/durable acid-free paper and bound
in the United States of America

First Printing, December 1980
First Printing (pbk.), February 1995

This is a revised reprint of a hardcover edition
originally published by Twayne Publishers.

Library of Congress Cataloging in Publication Data

Maland, Charles J
Frank Capra.

(Twayne's theatrical arts series)
Bibliography: p. 192–94
Filmography: p. 195–211
Includes index.
1. Capra, Frank, 1897–   2. Moving-picture produ-
cers and directors—United States—Biography.
PN1998.A3C265   791.43'0233'0924 [B]   80-22299
ISBN 0-8057-9273-2
ISBN 0-8057-4501-7 (pbk.)

Contents

About the Author

Preface to the Paperback Edition

Preface

Acknowledgments

Chronology

1. Backing into the Movies (1897–1926)   19

2. Learning the Craft (1927–30)   39

3. Making It (1931–35)   63

4. "The Ecumenical Church of Humanism" (1936–41)   89

5. Capra and World War II (1942–45)   117

6. *It's a Wonderful Life:* The Masterpiece (1945–46)   131

7. Declining Fortunes (1947–Present)   155

8. Conclusion: In the American Grain   175

   Notes and References   187

   Selected Bibliography   192

   Filmography   195

   Index   212

The Author

CHUCK MALAND is a Lindsay Young Professor of the Humanities and a member of the English Department at the University of Tennessee, where he teaches courses in film studies, American literature, and American studies. He also chairs the Cinema Studies Program.

Professor Maland's other writings include *American Visions: The Films of Chaplin, Ford, Capra and Welles: 1936–1941* (1977) and *Chaplin and American Culture: The Evolution of a Star Image* (1989). The latter won the Theater Library Association award for writing on film in 1990. He has also published widely on film and its relationship to American culture in such journals as *American Quarterly*, *Cineaste*, *Film and History*, *Film/Literature Quarterly*, *Film Quarterly*, *Historical Journal of Film, Radio, and Television*, and *Post Script*.

He lives with his wife, Nancy Klein Maland, and his son, Jonathan, in Knoxville, Tennessee.

Preface to the
Paperback Edition

IN THE LATE 1970s Warren French asked me to do a concise one-volume overview of the career of Frank Capra. A Sicilian immigrant who began working in movies during the silent era, Capra became so well known by the late 1930s for his comedy-dramas about archetypal American heroes and for his active involvement in the movie industry that his picture appeared on the cover of *Time* magazine. Because of my interest in American films and their relationship to American culture, I happily accepted the assignment and had the good fortune to spend three days talking with Capra about his work in March 1978. After I researched Capra, saw all his films available then—some could only be screened at the Library of Congress—and wrote the book, *Frank Capra* was published in 1980.

Since the original publication of the book—marked by the emergence of cable TV, videotapes, and laser discs—interest in Capra's films among filmgoers has remained high. Surely holiday viewings of *It's a Wonderful Life* became a ritual for many families in the 1980s. Because the legal owners of the film amazingly failed to renew copyright on the film in the 1970s, *Wonderful Life* entered the public domain, making it easy and cheap to show. The results, however, were both good and bad. On the positive side, it introduced hundreds of thousands of viewers to the remarkable film. On the other hand, this saturation around Christmas on a small screen also tended to dull the film's effect and peg it as just another Christmas movie, like the ubiquitous *Miracle on 34th Street*. This is unfortunate, because I believe that *Wonderful Life* is, from a formal, historical, and ideological perspective, a crucially important American film, as I try to explain in Chapter 6, the only chapter devoted to a detailed reading of a single film.

Besides public popularity, Capra and his films have also received considerable formal recognition since the publication of *Frank Capra*. In 1982 Capra received the American Film Institute's Life Achievement Award. In 1986 he was one of nine artists to receive a National Medal of the Arts from the president of the United States. After the U.S. Congress passed the National Film Preservation Act in 1988 to recognize films that are "culturally, historically, or aesthetically significant," three Capra films have been added to the list as of 1995: *It Happened One Night, Mr. Smith Goes to Washington* and *It's a Wonderful Life*.

So Capra's films still command our attention. This paperback edition retains the basic structure and argument of the original edition. Blending formalist, auteur, and cultural analysis, I aim here, as in 1980, to provide readers with a general overview of Capra's work, placed in the context of the American film industry and American cultural history between 1920 and 1960. However, I have updated and revised the book to correct errors and draw on new information that has surfaced since 1980. Some of that new information emerged when Capra donated his papers in 1981 to Wesleyan University in Connecticut. The Frank Capra Archive at Wesleyan contains a wide variety of materials covering many facets of the filmmaker's career. They include such documents as production memos, scripts, letters, and telegrams by and to Capra, press releases, photographs, newspaper clippings, and reviews. Organized by Curator Jeanine Basinger and her staff, the Frank Capra Archive offers much to Capra scholars.

A number of important critical works in the past decade have drawn in part on information from the archive and contributed to our understanding of Capra and his films. I'd like to highlight four: Raymond Carney's *American Vision: The Films of Frank Capra* (1986); Jeanine Basinger's *The "It's a Wonderful Life" Book* (1986); Charles Wolfe's anthology, *"Meet John Doe": Frank Capra, Director* (1989); and Joseph McBride's biography *Frank Capra: The Catastrophe of Success* (1992).

Carney's critical study, which connects Capra to a tradition of American visionary romanticism and is marked by insightful close analysis, argues convincingly that Capra, struggling for artistic achievement within the studio system, became what Emerson called a "representative man" in American culture. Capra's films, in Carney's words, "can be read as his spiritual autobiography, his ongoing reflections on the predicament in which he found himself as he made them and in which so many other Americans find themselves in their daily lives in the imaginative force field of American society" (xii).

Basinger's *The "It's a Wonderful Life" Book* serves as a valuable companion to the film. Opening with Basinger's production history of the film, the book also includes Leonard Maltin's interviews with James Stewart and the cameraman Joseph Biroc, the text of the short story on which the film is based, commentary on the early scripts of the film, the shooting script, and a section called "Frank Capra at Work," which offers readers a captivating look at Capra's working and revising methods through his handwritten notations, some of which are reproduced. (Basinger was also involved in producing the Criterion Videodisc on *Wonderful Life*, which includes the film on CAV format and a supplementary "videobook" on the film.)

Charles Wolfe draws on the Capra Archive and other archival sources for his anthology on Capra's fascinating failure, *Meet John Doe*. His introductory essay, "*Meet John Doe*: Authors, Audiences, and Endings," provides a useful history of this troubled production. It is particularly helpful in tracing the script changes and variant endings of the movie. The collection also includes the continuity script, parts of the variant endings, reviews, and recent critical essays on the film by Richard Glatzer, Nick Browne, and Dudley Andrew. (Wolfe is also the author of the valuable bibliography of Capra's life and films, *Frank Capra: A Guide to References and Resources* [G. K. Hall, 1987], which will be useful to students of Capra's films for a long time).

McBride's ambitious and painstakingly researched biography portrays Capra's career as a "catastrophe of success." Although McBride provides much new information about Capra, some of it helpfully correcting inaccuracies in Capra's autobiography, at times he seems to work overtime to debunk Capra. I also believe the biography contains an unresolved tension: McBride often reads Capra's films autobiographically while also claiming that Capra's films owed more to his screenwriters than Capra admitted. It's hard to hold both positions. However, McBride's basic premise runs parallel to my own perspective that Capra, like many American artists, was haunted by what William James called "the Bitch-Goddess Success" and carried within himself tensions and contradictions of his culture. McBride's biography is sure to generate more discussion about Capra.

All of these works helped me as I revised and updated *Frank Capra*, and I'd like to thank each of the authors for their commitment to scholarship and their passion for American movies. Their works, along with many others on Capra written since 1980 by such analysts as Neal Gabler, Robert Ray, Kaja Silverman, and Robert Sklar attest to the vitality of Frank Capra's films in our times. As we approach the centenary of the cinema, it is clear that Frank Capra's films remain central to the history and cultural dynamics of American movies.

Preface

"THE PROOF of a poet," wrote Walt Whitman in the preface to *Leaves of Grass*, "is that his country absorbs him as affectionately as he has absorbed it." Judging from the popularity of Frank Capra's films, especially those made between *It Happened One Night* (1934) and *It's a Wonderful Life* (1946), Capra was surely an important artist. His affectionate portrayal of America led film director John Cassavetes to comment, "Maybe there really wasn't an America, maybe it was only Frank Capra." In a number of his films in the 1930s and 1940s—*It Happened One Night, Mr. Smith Goes to Washington, Meet John Doe, It's a Wonderful Life*—Capra did create a vivid picture of American life, animated by a skillful control of film comedy and a consistent moral vision. Though Capra's fortunes as a filmmaker declined in the 1950s—a time hostile to his optimism—his moral vision lives on. Richard Dreyfuss, when asked recently what kind of films he would like to work on, replied: "I would love to update the Frank Capra ethic."[1] His readers, many of them frequent college campus moviegoers, knew what he meant.

I first encountered Frank Capra's films systematically at a week-long festival of his films at the University of Michigan in Ann Arbor in 1973. I remember being impressed by the structural and thematic similarities of the films, as well as the enthusiasm of the audiences. Nevertheless, some of the buoyantly optimistic endings seemed stretched to me, and the overt patriotism of *Mr. Smith Goes to Washington* and *Meet John Doe* were out of place in an America poised between Vietnam and Watergate. Yet I knew the films had been very popular in their era, and, as a student of American films and American culture, I resolved someday to explore in greater detail Capra's development as a filmmaker and the relationships between his films and the culture in which he lived and worked.

This study represents my way of keeping that resolution.

Though the auteur approach provides the structure for this study—the main focus will be on the thirty-six feature films directed by Frank Capra—it will not be the only focus. In the past decade it has become apparent that by studying the recurring stylistic and thematic patterns of a director's work, the pure auteurist critic may neglect several important areas of inquiry. He may first tend to simplify the greatest films of the director, discussing instead only those elements of a masterpiece which recur in other films. Second, he may forget that Hollywood feature films are made within an institutional structure at a particular moment in history for large audiences. It is very difficult to explain the development and significance of Capra's films without connecting them to the evolution of the American film industry and the contours of American cultural history in this century. Finally, the auteur critic may forget that film is a collaborative art and thus ignore the contributions of others in the films of a particular director. To neglect the differences between a film like *The Bitter Tea of General Yen* (1933), written by Edward Paramour, and *It Happened One Night* (1934), written by Capra's favorite collaborator, Robert Riskin, would be to ignore perhaps the key reason that the films are so different. In general, I agree with Robin Wood's suggestion that a critic "should be able to draw from the discoveries and perceptions of each theory, each position without committing himself exclusively to any one." What Wood calls "synthetic criticism" seems most useful in studying Capra's films. [2]

The structure of the book indicates how this approach will be worked out. Because Capra's films are so closely related to the American cultural experience in the 1930s and 1940s, a chronological approach seemed imperative. Chapter 1 discusses Capra's early life, some of the formative elements of his artistic sensibility, and his work in films until he was fired by Harry Langdon in 1927. Capra learned his craft as a filmmaker in his early years at Columbia. His first three years at Columbia, when he directed over a dozen films, provide the basis for Chapter 2. The third follows Capra's growing recognition as a filmmaker, culminating with the extremely successful *It Happened One Night*. During these years Capra's collaboration with Robert Riskin helped cement his position as a major force in Hollywood. Chapter 4 will examine the cultural mythology of Capra's films at his peak, focusing on the five films between *Mr. Deeds Goes to Town* (1936) and *Meet John Doe* (1941). Capra made war with film during World War II, and the fifth chapter will examine the "Why We Fight" series and Capra's role in helping to make them. *It's a Wonderful Life* (1946) is Capra's favorite film, Jimmy Stewart's favorite performance, and one of the landmarks of American film. Chapter 6 will focus entirely on its structure, style, and theme, and on its position as the culmination of Capra's work. Capra's fortunes as a filmmaker declined quite noticeably after *It's a Wonderful Life*, and Chapter 7 will examine the films, both feature length and documentary, he made between *State of the Union* (1948) and *A Pocketful of Miracles* (1961), in an attempt to understand the decline and to assess the achievements of these later films. The final chapter judges Capra's place in American film history and suggests how his films rest squarely in the traditions of American cultural history and narrative art.

As an epigraph to his autobiography, *Name Above the Title*, Capra wrote, "There are no rules in filmmaking, only sins. And the Cardinal sin is dullness."[3] One might add that a potential sin of prefaces is dullness, so let's end here and move on to ask our first question: what kind of man was Frank Capra and what are some of the formative factors to discuss if we are to understand his films?

CHARLES J. MALAND

University of Tennessee

Acknowledgments

THIS BOOK results in part from the kindness of many people. My thanks must first go to Frank Capra for his films and his cooperation on this project. His willingness to talk with me about his films and his life helped me understand both more fully.

For providing research facilities and assistance I would like to thank the following institutions: the American Film Institute Library in Beverly Hills; the University of Southern California Film Archives; the Motion Picture Sections of the Library of Congress and the National Archives; and the library staffs at Lake Forest College and the University of Tennessee. For additional films, I am grateful to Audio-Brandon Films, Paramount Pictures, and especially to Kit Parker Films for making available a number of Capra's early Columbia films. For stills, I thank Movie Star News, the Museum of Modern Art, and Bill Hamilton.

A grant from the Hodges Fund helped support the original research. I am also grateful to my English Department colleagues, my department head, Allen Carroll, and the university for their support of my work.

Three film historians and critics have contributed so much to my understanding of American films that I must thank them for their fine work: Garth Jowett, Robert Sklar, and Robin Wood. Though this list isn't complete, I'd also specifically like to thank Charles Affron, Charles Behling, Nick Browne, Neal Gabler, Lauren Rabinovitz, John Raeburn, and Rick Shale for assisting me in various ways while I was thinking about and writing this book. Thanks, too, to Frank Beaver and Mark Zadrozny for making the paperback edition possible.

Finally, I would like to thank Nancy Klein Maland and J. T. Maland for providing a small yet loving community of support. For that, and much more, I dedicate this book to them.

Chronology

1897 Frank Capra born in Bisacquino, Sicily, May 18.

1903 Immigrates to United States with family, settles in Los Angeles.

1916 Father dies in machinery accident.

1918 Graduates with a bachelor of science degree from Throop College of Technology (later renamed California Institute of Technology). Enlists in army, is assigned to the Presidio at Fort Point in San Francisco Bay, and is released on December 8 after the end of the war.

1919 Unable to find engineering job, lives in California and travels in the Southwest for next three years doing odd jobs, including selling books and photographs door-to-door.

1922 Directs first film, *Fultah Fisher's Boarding House*, in San Francisco.

1922– Works as developer and printer in lab, prop man, editor for
1925 Bob Eddy, gag writer for Roach's *Our Gang* comedies, then for Mack Sennett. Marries Helen Howell in November 1923.

1926 Directs *The Strong Man* (Harry Langdon).

1927 Directs *Long Pants*. Fired by Langdon, directs *For the Love of Mike*. Divorces Helen Howell.

1928 Joins Columbia Pictures as a director. *That Certain Thing, So This Is Love, The Matinee Idol, The Way of the Strong, Say It with Sables, Submarine, The Power of the Press*.

1929 *The Younger Generation, The Donovan Affair, Flight*.

1930 *Ladies of Leisure, Rain or Shine*.

1931 *Dirigible, The Miracle Woman, Platinum Blonde*.

1932 Marries Lucille Reyburn. *Forbidden, American Madness*.

1933 *The Bitter Tea of General Yet, Lady for a Day*.

1934 *It Happened One Night, Broadway Bill*. Son, Frank, Jr., born.

1935 *It Happened One Night* wins five major Oscars. Capra elect-

ed president of Motion Picture Academy. Son, John, born.
Self-doubt and illness lead Capra to "committed" filmmaking.

1936   *Mr. Deeds Goes to Town.*

1937   *Lost Horizon.* Daughter, Lulu, born.

1938   *You Can't Take It with You.* Son John dies of blood clot on the
brain. Capra's picture appears on the cover of *Time.* Elected
president of Screen Directors' Guild.

1939   *Mr. Smith Goes to Washington.* Capra and screenwriter
Robert Riskin leave Columbia and form Frank Capra
Productions.

1941   *Meet John Doe* (released by Warner Brothers). Mother dies.
Son, Thomas, born.

1942   *Arsenic and Old Lace* completed (released by Warner
Brothers in 1944).

1942–   Serves in armed forces. Assigned first to the army's
1945   Morale Branch (later called Special Services), where he is
involved in the "Why We Fight" series and a number of other
War Department documentary films. Later named commanding officer of the Signal Corps' Special Coverage
Section in charge of organizing photo teams to cover the war.
Awarded Distinguished Service Medal by Gen. George
1945   Marshall in 1945.

1945   Forms Liberty Films, an independent production company,
with Sam Briskin, William Wyler, and George Stevens.

1946   *It's a Wonderful Life.*

1948   *State of the Union.* Liberty Films sold to Paramount.

1950   *Riding High* (remake of *Broadway Bill*).

1951   *Here Comes the Groom.*

1952–   Serves as a U.S. delegate to the 1952 International
Film Festival in Bombay. Involved in making a series of four
science documentaries for Bell Telephone (released between
1956 and 1958).

1959   *A Hole in the Head.*

1961   *A Pocketful of Miracles* (remake of *Lady for a Day*). During
the filming, Capra begins to have cluster headaches, which
persist periodically until 1971.

1962–   Involved in a number of unrealized film projects.
1971   Visits Soviet Union as State Department representative in
1963. For the Martin-Marietta Company, makes *Rendezvous
in Space*, a promotional film shown at 1964 New York World's
Fair. Works on autobiography.

1971   Publishes *Name above the Title*. For the next decade is active as speaker and participant at film festivals around the United States.

1977   Travels to Italy, including a visit to Bisacquino, for eightieth
1971   birthday celebration.

1981   Receives honorary doctorate from Wesleyan University. Donates his papers to the Wesleyan Film Archives.

1982   Receives the American Film Institute's Lifetime Achievement Award.

1984   Lu Capra, the director's wife of 52 years, dies on July 1.

1986   Receives, along with eight other artists, a National Medal of the Arts from President Ronald Reagan.

1991   Dies on September 3 at age 94.

1

Backing into the Movies (1897–1926)

FRANK CAPRA was an auteur long before the auteur theory. Advocate of the "one man, one film" approach to film at least two decades before Truffaut's essay "La Politique des Auteurs" appeared in *Cahiers du Cinéma* in January 1954, Capra worked himself into a position of power at Columbia Pictures by consistently making successful films in the late 1920s and early 1930s, helping to transform Columbia from a fledgling movie company into a major studio. In so doing, he became a powerful and prestigious member of the Hollywood film community in the late 1930s, serving as president of both the Motion Picture Academy of Arts and Sciences and the Screen Directors' Guild, appearing on the cover of *Time* magazine in 1938. His name was also familiar to moviegoers in the late 1930s, in part because his name appeared on the credits of his movies *before* the title. Few directors in the 1930s earned that right.

When viewing Capra's films from the 1930s, one senses a firm hand guiding both the film style and narrative. One suspects the hand is Capra's. The suspicion is reinforced when one meets him. In March 1978 Capra visited the small midwestern college where I was teaching, and for three days he participated in the usual film festival activities on campus: visiting classes, answering questions after screenings, and holding sessions on film in general and his career in particular. The man who emerged from those sessions combined a number of qualities. About five feet five inches tall, medium build, bald headed, and moustachioed, Capra talked and gestured with animated enthusiasm about movies. His face lit up

Photo (left): Harry Langdon in a characteristically elfin pose

when he told stories, many of which were funny, all of which were
well told (like Mark Twain, Capra knew that *how* to tell a story is
as important as *what* the story is about). He usually seemed a happy,
even serene, man, as optimistic as Jefferson Smith about the pos-
sibilities of human beings. Occasionally, however, another side of
Capra emerged. Once, a well-heeled woman at an informal session
tried to dominate Capra's attention. Her questions revealed that
she knew nearly nothing about Capra's films, yet she presented
herself as something of an authority on Capra and Hollywood movies. After tolerating the woman's pretensions for a time, Capra
issued a sharply effective yet subtle denunciation, then turned his
attentions elsewhere. It seemed plain that the man was not simply
sweetness and light. Even at age eighty-one he knew precisely how
to defend himself. If Capra's behavior displayed some contradictions—perhaps "tensions" is a better word—it's fitting, for though
the endings of his films are always bright, certain dark forces in his
best films threaten completely to overshadow them. Despite what
critics claimed in the 1950s, Capra is not a Pollyanna.

If we find traces of Capra's films in his personality today, we can
find the roots of them in his early years. For those directors like
Wyler and Cukor who are more interested in translating properties
into effective films than in developing their own social visions, examining their early lives can become somewhat pointless. But because Capra came to see filmmaking partially as a moral
responsibility—a vocation that leads to instruction as well as entertainment—and because he was able by the 1930s to choose his
properties and work closely with his screenwriter, it's essential to
look at his background and experiences to see how they influenced
the social vision he developed.

Born May 18, 1897, to Salvatore and Sarah Nicolas Capra, Frank
Capra was the sixth of their seven children (and the third son). He
spent his first six years in Bisacquino, Sicily, a village about thirty
miles from the seaport town of Palermo. Capra's oldest brother,
Ben, had immigrated to the United States when Capra was still an
infant, and when Capra was six his parents decided to leave for
America themselves, taking the four youngest children with them.
Capra himself remembers the trip: being sick on the boat trip,
traveling cross country on a train, eating only the food his father
could manage to purchase at infrequent station stops. Clearly
Capra's status as an immigrant is one of the most important influences on his character.

The Capra family came to America, settling in Los Angeles, in the midst of the second great wave of American immigration, to which Italians contributed a large number. Before 1917 over 6 million Italians had come to America, more than a sixth of that country's population. Palermo, the Capra family's starting point, was one of three major expatriation centers in Italy during the period. Since Capra makes constant reference to his peasant background in his autobiography, it might be useful to look at why so many southern Italians came to the United States and who actually came.

Historians of American immigration discuss the "push" and the "pull" theories of who came to America.[1] The push theory suggests that the immigrants were pushed from their countries because of poverty, starvation, and lack of alternatives in their own countries. The resulting immigrants to America, this theory posits, were the most demoralized, poor, and hapless members of their societies. The "pull" theory, on the other hand, suggests that immigrants were pulled to the United States (or whatever country) by the lure of potential riches and increased opportunities. According to this theory, the immigrants were among the most hard-working, ambitious, and future oriented of their class.

Evidence from southern Italy indicates that the pull theory is the more accurate hypothesis. Though Sicilians were often disparaged by United States immigration officials in this era, the United States consul to Palermo during peak immigration years said that Sicilian emigrants were among "the more frugal, thrifty, and energetic of the class."[2] In addition, emigration was highest from those areas (including Palermo and its surroundings) where land was relatively dispersed. In other areas, where a few large landowners dominated, members of the lower class tended to develop a working-class solidarity and to remain in their homelands. In Capra's region, however, the lower classes sought to own their own land, stressing individual achievement and social mobility instead of class solidarity. Capra's father, who owned his own house, had some sheep, and later was to buy a fruit orchard in California after saving enough money, exhibited the aspirations toward proprietorship and individual advancement described by the pull theory (NATT, 3, 8–9).

Salvatore Capra's son—partly of necessity, partly by choice—was as ambitious as many other children of first-generation American immigrants. The family did need financial help from the children, and Frank did his part by hauling newspapers on the streets of Los Angeles. While in high school, he worked at other part-time jobs,

including janitorial work and guitar playing. Besides helping his
family financially, he decided that getting an education was a pre-
requisite for making it in America. Thus, after graduating from
Manual Arts High School, he enrolled in Throop Polytechnic (later
the California Institute of Technology) in September 1915. Here he
added more jobs—waiter at the campus dorm, night engineer at
the Pasadena Power and Light Plant—and with the help of schol-
arships and loans graduated with a B.S. in chemical engineering in
June 1918 (NATT, 6–10).

If all of this sounds like a Horatio Alger story, it's understandable.
Critics often use the phrase to describe Capra's rise from poor
immigrant to major director. Capra himself cultivates this at times
in his autobiography. In the preface he writes: "I hated being poor.
. . . I wanted out. A quick out." John Ford's introduction to the
book claims that "Frank Capra is an inspiration to those who believe
in the American Dream." Even in the first chapter Capra includes
a daily timetable of rigorous activities, reminiscent of our first
Horatio Alger hero, Ben Franklin, and our foremost fictional embodiment of the American Dream, Jay Gatsby. The success myth
is a powerful one in America, and Capra has clearly been affected
by it.

But Horatio Alger, however popular his books were, never wrote
a great book. Capra, while also popular, directed at least one masterpiece (*It's a Wonderful Life*) and a number of other lasting films,
and I'd like to suggest he did so in part because his life experiences
were in many ways quite *unlike* the Alger myth and because they
taught him about the extreme complexity of what constitutes success
in America.

Let me digress for a moment to elaborate on this theme. Though
Capra did rise from obscurity to importance in Hollywood, what
strikes me is how uneven his rise actually was. Rather than looking
at Capra's career as a parabola rising steadily until the end of World
War II, then gradually declining as his fortunes as a filmmaker
tapered off, I'd prefer to describe his career as a series of wavy and
at times jagged rises and falls. Capra did enjoy some striking successes, but surprisingly often those successes were quickly undercut
by personal disappointment or disaster. Shortly after winning a
freshman scholarship at college, Capra was stunned by the news
that his father had been killed in a machinery accident at his recently
purchased lemon orchard. The family lost the farm, and Capra had

to get loans for school expenses to help support his family. On the rise again, he received his bachelor of science degree and enlisted in the army with grand expectations. But his assignment to teach ballistics kept him in California for the duration of the war. After his release from the army, he could find no work as an engineer after working so hard to get an education. Capra enjoyed a great success as director of two popular Harry Langdon features; yet Langdon fired him without warning, a matter that we will look into further. After the ecstasy of winning a string of Oscars for *It Happened One Night,* Capra became both physically ill and psychologically overwhelmed with self-doubt. Several years later, on his way to the preview for *You Can't Take It With You*—which would soon earn Capra another Oscar as best director—he was summoned to the hospital to find his young son John dead from an unexplained blood clot. This pattern of rise and fall continued throughout Capra's career. Wealth, prestige, and success were all tremendously appealing to Capra, but his experience taught him how transient and—judged from another scale of values—how unimportant they really were. The constant flux of Capra's experience—the firm achievements and abrupt disappointments—had something to do with his ability to convey convincingly not just the triumphs of heroes in his films but also the agonies, despair, and self-doubts which plague the most fully realized Capra heroes. One need only recall Mr. Deeds hunching on a bed at the mental institution, Mr. Smith nearly weeping with despair on the floor of the Senate, or George Bailey contemplating a jump from a bridge on a snowy winter night to gauge how Capra's experiences affected his art.

So Capra's status as an immigrant and his roller-coaster experience led both to a strong desire for success and recognition and to a complex realization of how transient such achievements can be. Both of these aspects of Capra's life helped to form him into the man and artist he became. Though he retained his optimism, Capra could not do so without maintaining a strong will. He also needed to be able to affirm life, as comedy does, in spite of the dark forces, both in society and in man, that threaten to disfigure it.

As mentioned above, Capra found himself an unemployed chemical engineer after his release from the army in 1919 and also suffering with abdominal pains for several months after. Between the time of his recovery and 1922, when he directed his first film under unusual circumstances, Capra bummed around the West and Southwest, working at various jobs. Reports vary about what Capra actually did do during this time. Capra himself remembers "hopping freights, selling photos house-to-house, hustling poker, playing guitars" (NATT, 17). Richard Griffith wrote in 1951 (and Andrew Bergman repeated) that Capra worked as an extra in some Harry Carey Westerns (of which I can find no evidence), worked in fruit orchards, and sold wildcat stock during these years.[3]

This period of somewhat undirected wandering is important for at least two reasons. The first is that it was during this time that Capra learned something about dominant American attitudes, values, and behavior. Talking with Richard Glatzer about these years, Capra recalled that he "got a real sense of small towns, got a real sense of America. I found out a lot about Americans" (FC, 31). Moving outside of Los Angeles, roaming around and observing people and their environments with care, Capra accumulated experiences that would both help present common Americans convincingly in his movies and understand something of what his audiences would like and dislike.

The wandering years also provided Capra with some of his first experiences at telling convincing stories to audiences. One of his jobs during this time, he told me in an interview, was selling a fourteen-volume set of books by Elbert Hubbard door-to-door.[4] His pitch was superb. The potential buyer learned that Capra, orphaned at age seven, was working one day picking rocks from a field when a kindly man relieved him of his backbreaking work and took him to his nearby home. The man was a bookbinding artisan and taught Capra the trade so well that Capra made books not just with his hands, but with his head and heart as well. Slowly Capra would reveal that he was (for $125) trying to give people the opportunity to have these finely made books in their homes. He wasn't trying to sell anything, only to *place* all the books so that he could return to the home of the man—none other than Elbert Hubbard—and make some more of the wonderful inspirational books. Capra told me the story so well I almost bought a set for myself. Since Capra told a similar story to Geoffrey Hellman for a *New Yorker* article in 1940 (FC, 7–8), I tend to believe that this period was a time when Capra began to sharpen his storytelling abilities.

Capra ended his wanderings and began his film career in San Francisco in 1922, under circumstances that can only be called bizarre. Answering a newspaper column which mentioned the establishment of Fireside Studios, Capra convinced Walter Montague, a Shakespearean actor turned movie producer, that he was from Hollywood and would consider directing the film during his "vacation" in San Francisco. As Capra described their encounter in his autobiography, it's hard to decide who is the bigger huckster, for neither knew much about how to make a film. Nevertheless, Capra convinced Montague to have him direct the film, hired a cameraman friend who wouldn't divulge his fabrication, and chose nonprofessional actors who wouldn't realize his lack of experience. The result was Capra's first film: *Fultah Fisher's Boarding House.*

The film is based on Rudyard Kipling's "The Ballad of Fisher's Boarding House." The poem, first published in *Departmental Ditties* (1886), contains eighteen six-line stanzas and is set in a rough bar in Calcutta (Kipling lived in India when he wrote it). It concerns a fight between Hans, "the blue-eyed Dane," and Salem Hardieker, a "lean Bostonian," over the attentions of Anne of Austria, one of the barroom women. Their quarrel leads to a knife fight, Hans is killed, and Anne of Austria loots a small crucifix from Hans's neck in the last stanza, reinforcing the poem's portrayal of brutal behavior in a sordid environment.

For a man who had little experience in moviemaking, Capra showed some talent in making the film. He begins by framing the story: the first shot of *Fultah Fisher's Boarding House* is of a well-dressed man sitting by a desk reading the poem, as is the last shot. From this start, Capra moves into the poem itself, introducing the three main characters. Throughout the film, stanzas from the poem are superimposed over the action. One of the film's best moments occurs during the fight when a Kipling line—"A dance of shadows on the wall/ A knife-thrust unawares"—appears on the screen. With it, Capra includes a long shot of shadows of the scuffling men on the wall. While we see the shadows of Hans and Salem, the shadow of a third man, Luz, approaches and stabs Hans in the back. Capra cuts to Anne moving toward the felled Hans, while Luz in the background grabs his gear and sneaks out. Besides these particular touches, Capra for the most part exhibits a good intuitive grasp of how to change camera distance and camera angle (he uses one high angle shot of Salem and Hans scuffling on the ground). Once he violates the rules of Hollywood continuity editing, which state that the camera should always stay on the same side of an imaginary straight line when filming an action (the 180° system). Capra violates this by showing a long shot of a man being shoved down to the right, then cutting to a medium shot of the same man falling to the left and rear of the frame. In addition, he might have emphasized Luz a little more, preparing the viewer more successfully for the fatal stab. Nevertheless, the narrative flowed quite well for a starting filmmaker, and by the time Capra directed again several years later, he'd learned to avoid the technical mistakes he made here.

The most significant detail about the film in terms of Capra's whole career is the ending. Instead of concluding with Anne's theft of the charm, Capra altered the work he adapted. Just as he was to do with many other literary properties—*You Can't Take It With You* and *State of the Union* are good examples—Capra changed the story to make it fit his perspective. In the film, Anne takes the crucifix from Hans's neck, as she does in the ballad, but then stands holding it in a medium shot for a short time. Then, in a close-up, with tears in her eyes, she presses the charm to her face. Experiencing a conversion, Anne throws off her necklace, takes off all her rings, then turns and walks away, up the stairs, presumably to a new and better life. From there we cut back to the man reading the poem and the conclusion of Capra's first film. Like Orson Welles's *Hearts of Age,* it's unspectacular filmmaking but surely interesting in the light of the director's later achievements.

Montague was able to get the film released by Pathé in 1922, and according to Capra, it brought in more than double Montague's production costs of $1,700. It even earned some positive reviews— one review thought it a movie with "dignity, beauty, and strength"— and Capra began to develop a yearning to learn more about the movie business (NATT, 24–30).

About the time Capra was involved with his first film, movie audiences were enjoying Erich von Stroheim's *Foolish Wives,* another D. W. Griffith film, called *Orphans in the Storm,* a new star named Rudolf Valentino in *Blood and Sand,* and a fascinating documentary film about Eskimo life called *Nanook of the North.* In spite of his modest success Capra knew the directing offers would not start flooding in from Hollywood. Wisely he took another route, resolving to learn as much about filmmaking as he could by starting at the bottom.

Thus from 1922 to 1926, when he directed his next film, Capra worked at a wide range of movie jobs; this was a formative phase which helped him as a director at least as much as the years of wandering around the Southwest at the very start of the 1920s. Capra's first job was working at a small film lab in San Francisco run by Walter Ball. There he not only developed, printed, and dried film, but also edited some of the newsreels, amateur documentaries, and advertising footage that came in for development. Since editing is one of the keys to the art of film—"the foundation of film art is editing," wrote Pudovkin in the introduction to *Film Technique*—and since many of Capra's films contain particularly effective editing, the importance of this experience should not be minimized.

After Capra had been with the lab for about a year, Ball acquired the job of processing the daily rushes of a Hollywood comedy director named Bob Eddy, who had been shooting near San Francisco. While viewing some footage at the lab projection booth, Eddy asked Walt Ball if he knew any prop men available for work. Ball suggested Capra, and Capra became a prop man for a time, learning another dimension of moviemaking. When one sees the attention to props and the set in films like *Mr. Smith Goes to Washington* or *It's a Wonderful Life*, one suspects that, in his work as a prop man, Capra began to understand how props can be used for creating laughs and for enriching the formal intentions of a film.

From prop man Capra moved on to edit full time for Eddy's slapstick comedies, drawing and improving upon his experiences at the Ball film lab. After cutting three of Eddy's films, Capra was promoted to become Eddy's gag writer, and the editor and prop man moved to another stage of his film education. After several months in this capacity, Capra was introduced to Bob McGowan, a director of *Our Gang* comedies for the Hal Roach Studios. Here Capra worked for six months writing gags for these silent comedies. The roots of the visual humor in the Capra films—Elly Andrews diving from her father's yacht in *It Happened One Night*, for example, or Long John and the Colonel playing catch with an imaginary baseball in *Meet John Doe*—reach back to these days as a writer of visual gags. Though Capra's comedy would become deeper and richer, he never forgot what visual humor could do to satisfy and amuse audiences.

Yet after six months with McGowan, Capra became restive. He still ultimately wanted to become a director. Since McGowan forbade writers on the set, Capra decided to move on in late 1924 and took a job as a gag writer at Mack Sennett's Keystone Studio. Sennett had been renowned as a producer of film comedies for over a decade. Like Roger Corman today, Sennett seemed especially able to recognize new talent. He gave Chaplin his first movie contract, and at Keystone in 1913 and 1914 Chaplin first developed his tramp character and became an overnight sensation. Also members of the Sennett family at one time or another were Fatty Arbuckle, Buster Keaton, Charlie Chase, and Raymond Griffith. When Capra first joined Keystone as a gag writer, Sennett not long before had hired another whose name was soon to be uttered for a short time with Chaplin, Keaton, and Lloyd, a name that helped elevate Capra to his first place of distinction as a film director. That name was Harry Langdon.

We don't know precisely when Capra began writing gags for Langdon shorts at Keystone, since credits were often not given to gag writers. Leland Poague believes that it could be when Harry Edwards directed his first two-reeler (*The Luck O' the Foolish*, September 1924); McBride suggests it was in *All Night Long* (November 1924), which Capra coscripted without credit (McB, 146).[5] Though the starting point of the collaboration is not clear, we do know several details about the Capra-Langdon relationship. We know first that Capra was credited with Arthur Ripley as the scriptwriters for a Langdon two reeler, *Plain Clothes*, released in March 1925 (Edwards directed). We know that the same three collaborated with Langdon on at least two more two-reelers, then followed Langdon when he left Keystone for First National. There, we know, Capra worked with Langdon on his first feature film, *Tramp, Tramp, Tramp*, learning about budgets and time schedules for the first time. We know that Edwards quit after that film, and that Capra finally became a director, doing *The Strong Man* (1926) and *Long Pants* (1927). Finally, we know that at the end of *Long Pants*, Langdon and Capra had a falling out and Capra was dismissed by Langdon, whose career quickly declined.[6] Before discussing Capra's contributions to Langdon and the two features, it is important to say a few words about silent feature film comedy, the genre within which Langdon and Capra were working.

Capra won his first chance to direct a feature-length comedy at a time when the form was nearing its peak. William K. Everson voices the critical consensus when he writes, "There can be no doubt that the comedy film, especially in the mid-1920s, formed one of the richest and most unique aspects of the American film."[7]

Though several varieties of film comedies were common during this era—situation comedies, sophisticated marital farces, romantic comedies—the dominant form in both quantity and quality was the comedy revolving around a single male comic persona. Most observers agree that Langdon is, with Chaplin, Keaton, and Harold Lloyd, one of the four major comics to work in the form.

These comic persona films have their roots in Chaplin's early days at Keystone (1914–15), though studios discouraged them from making feature comedies until Harold Lloyd released *Grandma's Boy* in 1922. (Chaplin had made *The Kid,* about sixty minutes, in 1921, but then backed off to making shorter comedies, not returning with a comic feature until *The Gold Rush* in 1925.) Buster Keaton followed with *Our Hospitality* in 1923—he would do eleven more features before sound—and the form was becoming established. Nearly all of the films focus on the comic persona trying to make his way in the world, often trying to win the affections of a woman, always encountering difficulties along the way.

Each of the top four—Chaplin, Keaton, Lloyd, and Langdon—developed a unique persona. Chaplin possessed the grace of a ballet dancer and sought from his audience both gentle laughter and pathos. More than the other three, he needed to be loved—both by his lover and by his audience. Keaton was a stern-faced pessimist, methodically and skillfully going about his business. More acrobatic than graceful, Keaton also understood better and experimented more with cinematic form. Harold Lloyd was probably the most consistently popular of the four, perhaps because his persona sought constantly to succeed through hard work and determination—and made it, thus fulfilling the fantasies of many moviegoers. Langdon was probably closest to Chaplin, an innocent childish man, eternally optimistic, even when circumstances negated the optimism. Capra himself understood well Langdon's character in relation to the others, describing it in this way: "Chaplin depended on wit to get himself out of trouble, Harold Lloyd on speed, and Buster Keaton on pure stoicism. But Langdon's character had the mind of a child, and a very slow child at that."[8]

Of the four, Langdon's period of popularity was the shortest, lasting only from the release of his first feature, *Tramp, Tramp, Tramp* (1926), through his third, *Long Pants* (1927). Significantly, Chaplin did not appear during these years: *The Circus* (1928) was his first film after *The Gold Rush* (1925). Because Capra directed the two most successful Langdon features and because Langdon's career quickly declined after he fired Capra, some observers have suggested that Capra made Langdon, thus attributing all of Langdon's success to the director who understood, indeed developed, the Langdon persona. Others have defended Langdon and warned against overemphasizing Capra's contribution, so that a critical quarrel has been established.[9]

Though no final answer to the Langdon-Capra controversy is possible—Langdon has been dead since 1944—to say that Capra had nothing to do with Langdon's success is as great an oversimplification as to say that Capra "created" Langdon. In trying to define the authorship of *The Strong Man* and *Long Pants*, we are really dealing with what Leland Poague termed "complimentary multiple authorship" (p. 122). Langdon himself had certain physical attributes (pale complexion, chubby hands and cheeks) and abilities (timing, gestures of hesitation) without which there would have been no films. Capra's contributions, it seems to me, were largely stylistic and narrative: he made the films interesting and engaging visually, and, particularly in *The Strong Man*, he placed the hero in a narrative framework that would recur in later Capra films. Judging from the two Capra-directed Langdon features, I would suggest that Capra's contribution was greater in *The Strong Man*, where the first distinct hints of the Capra hero appear. And, though I don't have evidence to substantiate it, I'd also suggest that one of the reasons for the friction between Langdon and Capra on *Long Pants* may have resulted from Capra's uneasiness about the character Langdon was playing. To sum up, it seems fairest to say that while Capra contributed significantly to Langdon's success, he didn't "create" Langdon's persona.

The Strong Man, the first feature film Capra directed, is probably Langdon's best. Capra came to the film well prepared, already experienced as editor, prop man, gag writer, and, to some extent (from his work with budgets, time schedules, and the like on *Tramp, Tramp, Tramp*), producer. The resulting film manages successfully to unite three elements within the narrative: visual comedy, a romance, and a clear conflict between forces of good and evil. Though it will not be possible to segment every film in this study, a segmentation of *The Strong Man* will give an indication of how skillfully the narrative is constructed. The central characters are Paul Bergeon (Langdon), a Belgian soldier; Zandow, a German soldier who becomes a strong man after the war; Lil, a New York woman of the streets who plants money on Paul; Mary Brown, an American girl Paul corresponds with during the war; Parson Brown, her father; and Mike McDevitt, the villain. The film contains five segments, each containing one or more key actions and locations:

1. Belgium: Soldier Paul is captured.
2. New York: Paul and Zandow arrive at Ellis Island/Paul searches for Mary on streets of New York/Lil tries to retrieve money she plants on Paul/Paul at Madame Browne's Art Studio/Paul and Zandow prepare to leave New York.
3. Cloverdale: Town corruption, conflict between Parson Brown and Mac set up/Brown and reformers march down Main Street/Mary introduced.
4. Paul and Zandow on the road: Paul struggles to shake his chest cold.
5. Cloverdale: Paul arrives in town with Zandow/Paul encounters Mary by accident/Paul performs, then helps to destroy the forces of evil/after time passes, Paul and Mary are together, the town reformed.

The first of the three central narrative strands in *The Strong Man* is visual comedy, the staple of silent comedy. Capra, just promoted from the position of gag writer, combined with the other gag writers on the film and with Langdon's performance to make a very funny picture, consistent with the childlike innocence of the Langdon persona. While fighting in World War I, Paul tries to protect himself by using a slingshot and shooting such things as crackers and crushed onions. Paul arrives at Ellis Island with a life preserver and a canoe paddle, which leads to comic results. When dealing with "Lil" in New York, Paul (1) gets his foot caught in a spittoon; (2) carries Lil backwards up a stairway, then up a stepladder at the top of the stairs, a gag repeated in *A Hole in the Head* (1959); and (3) gets chased around Lil's room when she tries to retrieve her money. His uncertainty and embarrassment when he encounters the nude at Madame Browne's Studio is amusing. First he steps toward the model to cover her, then bolts toward the outside, knocking down a wall divider and falling on the stairway as he scuttles out.

The two most accomplished and extended gags in the film are of Paul trying to control his cold while on a bus and of Paul putting on a strong-man performance, leading eventually to the destruction of the town's corruption. The first scene—much of which is taken in a single long take of several minutes—shows Langdon's skill as a pantomimist. His red nose prominent on an otherwise white face, Paul struggles to control a cold. After fumbling with some pills tied in a handkerchief and some Smith Brothers cough drops, Langdon rubs camphor on his chest. Putting a cough drop on a spoon, he inserts the spoon into his mouth, swallowing the cough drop. He then pours medicine into the spoon. Fearing the taste, he hesitates, then suddenly sneezes, spraying the medicine all over the man sitting next to him. The man angrily tears off a bandage taped to Harry's chest. The topper to the gag comes when Harry mistakes a jar of limburger cheese for his camphor and rubs his chest with it. A title announces Paul's pleasure: "My head's clear. I'm beginning to smell." The other riders summarily throw Paul out of the bus onto a hill, but the bus turns a sharp curve and—with timing reminiscent of Keaton's best work—Paul rolls down the hill and back into the bus through the roof.

In the final scene, comedy arises primarily through Paul's incongruous attempts to be a strong man. Wearing a costume much too large—it looks like a set of decorative winter underwear—Paul timidly steps on stage, nearly tripping and falling. When he can't budge a 400-pound weight, he does a little comic dance. After falling through a hole in the stage, he places a bottomless pail over the hole, drops two cannonballs through the pail (and hole), then lifts the empty pail into the air. When Paul drops the pail, pigeons fly out from his baggy pants. Paul refuses to do the cannon shoot, and the crowd complains and then gets hostile. Challenged, Paul goes into action, defending Mary, her father, and the forces of good by throwing bottles, opening a plug on a barrel, and kicking it down into the crowd after the barrel empties. Flying through the air on a trapeze, Paul ends the party by pulling a stage backdrop over the crowd. The topper here is a chain-reaction visual gag. Paul shoots a small barbell from the cannon, which hits Mike McDevitt in the head. McDevitt topples out of a window into a garbage can. The lid falls, revealing a sign: "Dump trash here." The gag men and Langdon himself were working in top form in both sequences.

Besides the successful comedy, the film develops a romance between Paul and Mary Brown, the blind daughter of Parson Brown (Chaplin was to use a blind heroine with great effectiveness in *City Lights* five years later). The romance is guided in part by Paul's extreme shyness, and in part by the pathos inherent in Mary's blindness. Because the romance begins with their love letters to one another during the war, neither knows the other. Their meeting is sensitively presented by Capra. Paul leaves the drunken Zandow to fetch water. When he sees Mary, he becomes terribly nervous but fakes self-assurance. He introduces himself. Mary weeps because she fears he will reject her because of her blindness. In a long shot Capra shows her struggling and stumbling by a tree. Paul in the background realizes she's blind. As she sits on a bench huddling by the tree, Paul stands motionless, frozen in a new awareness. Immediately, Capra avoids their uncomfortable first moments and fades to a medium shot of the pair together by the tree. After pantomiming his experiences with Lil, the Broadway hustler, Paul nervously plays with his hat, which Capra would repeat with Jimmy Stewart as Jefferson Smith over a decade later. Finally, with a shy but deliberate and almost noble gesture, Paul innocently kisses Mary's hand. The scene is done with a gentle delicacy, preparing the way for Paul's defense of Mary—he gets into the climactic brawl because someone threatens to bring Mary into the saloon—and the concluding shot of him and Mary walking serenely down the street together.

The third strand of the narrative—the clear moral struggle and conflict—was already present in *Fultah Fisher's Boarding House* and would be a persistent dimension of Capra's films in the 1930s. Malcolm Lowry, whose sister played Mary Brown in the film, described that conflict well in a letter to his sister upon seeing the film again in 1952. Like Capra's later films, Lowry wrote, *The Strong Man* mines "that apparently inexhaustible gold mine of the American consciousness of decency and wisdom against the forces of hypocrisy" (FC, 48).

As in Capra's later films, that struggle between decency and hypocrisy was clearly drawn. When we first see Cloverdale, a title tells us it was once a "peaceful little border town." Capra follows it by idealized images of a sleepy, harmonious small town: people rock on their porches and dutifully attend Parson Brown's church. Another title tells us that things have changed: "Certain interests had found it ideally located for a defiance of law." In one of the best scenes in the film, Capra economically suggests the change in the town. The first shot shows cars filling the previously empty main street. A truck is filled with cases of bootleg liquor, this during

Prohibition. The town hall has become a saloon called the Palace
Music Hall. Cutting inside, Capra constructs a montage of images
to suggest change and decadence that reminds one of George Bailey
returning to Pottersville in the dream sequence of *It's a Wonderful
Life*, made two decades later. From a chorus line, Capra cuts to
two women in grass skirts, a close-up of beer spigots filling mugs,
and a birds-eye shot of a spinning roulette wheel. Moving out, he
shows a series of shots indicating a general breakdown (at least from
Parson Brown's perspective) in human morality: loose women sit
on men's laps, people fight, a man shoves his wife away from him,
a brother tries to persuade his sister to leave the saloon. A title
sums up the thrust: "Justice and decency had fled before the new
law—money."

The embodiment of evil and leader of the new Cloverdale is Mike
McDevitt, the proprietor of the Palace. In one shot after the "montage of depravity," McDevitt confronts Parson Brown, telling him
to give up. In a title Mike reiterates his perspective: "Money speaks
louder than you do." Failing to buy off Parson Brown, McDevitt
leaves to Brown's condemnations. Standing on the porch, the parson
gathers the respectable townspeople around him, urging them to
have faith, proclaiming that the walls of Jericho are ready to fall.
The inspired group marches down Main Street singing "Onward,
Christian Soldiers" (its words are superimposed on the screen).
When one of the town toughs sitting on the curb says, "You
know. . . I wish I'd led a cleaner life," a nearby friend berates him
for being taken in by "Holy Joe." The scornful McDevitt calls Brown
a "Psalm-singing idiot" and threatens to feature Mary as the main
attraction in the Palace.

But the walls of Jericho do not tumble until later in the film when
Paul becomes the town's Joshua. Though his reason for fighting is
more romantic than moral—Paul springs into action when a drunk
says he wants Mary in the saloon—Paul sends McDevitt into a
garbage can and the Parson proclaims a miracle.

The film's final sequence neatly unifies all three strands of the
narrative. A title assures viewers that "again Cloverdale becomes
quiet." Children play ball on Main Street. The Palace is transformed
into the Cloverdale Community Hall. And, in a situation that echoes
Chaplin's *Easy Street*, Paul—now a constable—walks down the
street with Mary at his side. Though Paul trips over a rock and loses
his belt when getting up, Mary helps him stand, then they walk off
again, Paul contentedly twirling his nightstick.

The mixture of romance, comedy, and moral conflict in *The Strong Man* clearly foreshadows the quality of Capra's films in his major period of the late 1930s, with two fundamental differences. The visual comedy of *The Strong Man* would, of course, be supplemented by verbal comedy in Capra's talkies. But a more important distinction involves the moral conflict. The side of good in *The Strong Man*, represented by Parson Brown, is more genteel, more small-town respectable elite, than Capra's later democratic, vernacular films. Whereas Paul provided the comedy and romance in *The Strong Man* and Brown the moral perspective, by the late 1930s Capra would often invest all three elements in one character, a Deeds or a Smith. Perhaps *The Strong Man* reflects its era. Parson Brown does seem to embody the white Protestant values of what George Santayana called the "genteel tradition." Though these values had been challenged by more cosmopolitan elements of the younger generation from World War I on, they still held some credence among traditionalists. Not until the stock market crash and the early worst years of the Depression was the validity of this value structure fundamentally questioned and altered in the minds of the dominant culture. The new synthesis of values, a product of the late 1930s, relates closely to Capra's films of that era, but that is a subject to be taken up later. At this point, it is important to note that the narrative of *The Strong Man* clearly resembles Capra's later films in spite of certain important differences.

The next Capra-Langdon collaboration, *Long Pants*, was made under more difficult circumstances than *The Strong Man*. As Capra tells the story, Langdon began to believe critics who were proclaiming his genius after *The Strong Man*, which had made some ten-best-films lists for 1926. Tensions grew throughout the making of the film until a conflict at the end of shooting led Capra and Langdon to dissolve their relationship (NATT, 68–70). Both Capra and William Everson suggest that the source of the conflict was that Langdon and Arthur Ripley disagreed with Capra about the screen character Langdon was to portray. Capra saw Langdon's persona as a "man-child whose only ally was God." In contrast, Ripley held a blacker outlook on life, more suited, according to Everson, to "the anarchistic comedies of W. C. Fields, and, much later, the *film noir* thrillers of the 1940's."[10] The tension between these two visions of Langdon's character are evident in *Long Pants*, making it a less unified, less successful film than *The Strong Man*, despite some strong scenes.

The central characters are Harry Shelby (Langdon), Bebe Blair, and Priscilla. Harry is first introduced as the Boy, an adolescent who dreams about romance he's read of in books and waits restlessly for his first pair of long pants. He's *literally*, not figuratively, a child at the start of the film. Bebe, first introduced as the Vamp, is an evil yet alluring woman from the city, accused of and then jailed for smuggling dope. Nevertheless, she excites Harry's romantic imagination and lures him away from Priscilla, whom his parents expect Harry to wed. The structure is quite different from *The Strong Man*. Instead of moving from war to city to small town, then helping reform the town, here Harry moves from the harmonious small town to the corrupt city, returning when he realizes Bebe's real self does not coincide with his image of her. The film's final shot, a medium close-up of Priscilla and Harry's parents happily surrounding him upon his return, suggests Harry has returned to the place he belongs.

Capra's notion of Harry as an innocent, in particular a *romantic* innocent, is deeply embedded in parts of the film. The first shot is of books in the romance section of a library and of a hand pulling *Great Lovers, Mark Antony and Cleopatra,* and *Don Juan* from the library shelves. Only at home in the attic do we see the boy Harry wearing short pants. Harry's innocent romanticism is also stressed in a dream sequence, in which he imagines himself dressed like a soldier in cape and full regalia, climbing a trellis to his lover's balcony. When Harry later waves at two girls through a window, one says, "Little boys should be seen and not heard." When Harry first sees Bebe, he's reading *Desire Under the Elms*. Even after he leaves to help Bebe escape from jail, Harry exhibits an extreme naiveté about the ways of the world. On one level, he follows Capra's conception of the Langdon persona.

On another, Harry plays Ripley's concept. In his famous essay "Comedy's Greatest Era," James Agee observed a "sinister flicker of depravity about the Langdon character."[11] This is Ripley's Langdon, and it comes out strongest, oddly enough, in perhaps the funniest sequence of the film. In it, Harry takes Priscilla, his new bride, into the forest with plans to murder her and rescue Bebe from jail. Before shooting her, he must clear leaves away where Priscilla would fall. When she plays hide and seek with him, Harry loses his gun in the leaves, picking up and aiming a gun-shaped stake. When he finally finds the gun, he is halted by a "No Shooting" sign. After various other difficulties, Harry finds himself with his hat over his eyes, pulled to the ground by a rope trap hooked to a tree. Though the scene is funny, deriving from the frustrations Harry encounters, it's also totally out of character. The innocent child-man would not murder another person, nor would he help a woman escape from jail and follow her to the corrupt city, as he does later in the film. In the middle of the film, Ripley's Langdon dominates. Not until Harry finally realizes he's been had—a title has Harry telling Bebe, "Why I'm surprised. My goodness. I'm sorry but we must part. I'm through"—does Capra's Langdon return. The tensions in the Langdon persona finally make *Long Pants* a failure.

Though Capra worked with considerably less freedom in the Langdon films than he would later at Columbia—he was an employee of Langdon after they both left Sennett—he nevertheless played an important part in the making of Langdon's most successful features. In both *The Strong Man* and *Long Pants*, Capra provided an unobstrusive and clear directorial style, keeping the camera out of Langdon's way. *The Strong Man* was as much a Capra film as a Langdon film, exhibiting narrative characteristics which Capra would return to and perfect later in his career. The tension between Langdon and Capra, which led to Capra's separation from Langdon after *Long Pants*, is evident even in the narrative of the film as an uncertainty about the Langdon persona itself.

So in 1927 the ambitious thirty-year-old Sicilian-American had already in one sense made it. He'd entered the movie business by accident, become fascinated by it, and methodically learned the business as lab man, editor, prop man, gag man, and director. Yet he also had to live with disappointment: on the verge of his greatest successes, about the time the movie industry was wondering about adjusting to the talkies and America was riding on a wave of speculative prosperity, Capra was out of work, having marital problems, broke, and unsure of his future. It would take the unlikely person of Harry Cohn to give him his next, perhaps greatest break.

2

Learning the Craft (1927–30)

IN THE PAST three decades, as the cost of making movies has climbed and the number of films produced each year has dwindled, it has become very difficult for film directors to gain experience directing feature films within the industry. Costs are too high, failures too costly. Many experienced directors (Lumet, Penn, Pollack, Altman) learned their craft in television. Some younger directors (Coppola, Scorsese, Lucas, DePalma, Spike Lee) went the film school route. But when Frank Capra was seeking to establish himself in the late 1930s, it was still possible for a director to school himself in filmmaking by working on B pictures. And that is just what Capra did: after finding a job with Columbia Pictures in 1928, Capra directed fifteen feature films in less than four years. During this time he polished his visual and rhythmic sense while at the same time successfully making the transition to talking pictures. At this writing ten of these fifteen early Columbias are available for viewing at film archives or from film distributors, some just recently made available thanks to the effort of Kit Parker Films. Since few of these films have had wide circulation in recent years, this chapter will attempt to provide concise, accurate comment on the ten available films with only brief references to the lost films. At the same time we will note how Capra gradually mastered film form during these formative early years at Columbia.

After being fired by Langdon, Capra found himself persona non grata in the film industry. For four months in 1927 he went without work, and then First National offered him a job to direct a feature in New York called *For the Love of Mike*. It was a story about an orphan, raised by three men, who goes to Yale, rows on the crew,

Photo (left): Capra with Bessie Love on the set of The Matinee Idol *(1928)*

and almost agrees to throw a race for gamblers to whom he's in-
debted. But he doesn't, his team wins, and Mike wins the love of
Mary, played by Claudette Colbert in her first screen role. The film
was not well financed, which contributed to its relative failure at
the box office. It is now lost. Back in Hollywood, Capra still had
trouble finding work as a director and was forced to go back to
Sennett as a gag writer for twelve weeks (NATT, 73, 76).

About the time he returned from New York in August 1927,
Capra was given divorce papers by Helen Howell Capra, whom he
had married in 1925. Capra himself admits in the autobiography
that when he began directing for Langdon, his job dominated his
every attention and his marriage suffered. Since he had no income
when the papers were served, Capra agreed not to contest the
divorce if Helen would agree not to ask for alimony. That agreed
upon, the divorce was granted, and the second blow to Capra's ego
landed: no job, now no marriage (NATT, 67, 77). The man who had
been riding on the crest of a wave after *The Strong Man* now
floundered underwater.

Yet after several months as a gag writer, Capra was offered another
chance to direct, this time for Harry Cohn's Columbia Pictures, on
Hollywood's "Poverty Row." The company began in 1920 as CBC
Film Sales, started by three former Universal employees: Harry
and Jack Cohn, and Joe Brandt. They had initially been funded by
a loan from A. H. Giannini, president of Bank of America, successful
self-made Italian-American who would later serve as a model for
the banker-hero in Capra's *American Madness* (1931). By January
of 1924 CBC assumed the name of Columbia Pictures, and in 1926
Harry Cohn persuaded his partners to buy a small lot with three
stages on Gower Street in Hollywood.[1] Capra joined Columbia at
an opportune time: Columbia then made only cheap B pictures,
and Capra could learn his craft without anyone's having to risk huge
sums of money. In addition, Capra had the gumption to tell Cohn's
aide, Sam Briskin, that he would accept the job only if he had
control to write, direct, and edit his own films. Since Capra agreed
to work cheaply under those guidelines ($1,000 per film) and since
the notoriously crass Cohn liked Capra's brash self-confidence, the
deal was made. Thus, at the time the Hollywood studio system was
becoming increasingly centralized and directors were losing much
of their creative control, Capra won an unusual power to make films
as he saw fit. As long as the films made money, Capra was all right
(NATT, 77–80).

Immediately, Capra began to make films at breakneck speed: six weeks per film—two for writing, two for shooting, two for editing. By the end of 1928, Capra already had seven credits, including one of Columbia's rare A pictures *(Submarine)*. Though it would be a mistake to claim too much for these sixty- or seventy-minute features—this was apogee of silent film art in America, the year of Murnau's *Sunrise*, Vidor's *The Crowd*, Ford's *Four Sons*, and Chaplin's *The Circus*—the ones available for viewing today do have their merits and are particularly interesting in light of Capra's later development.

Capra's first two films for Columbia, both available today, are silent comedy/romances: *That Certain Thing* and *So This Is Love*. The first film concerns a romance between the wealthy A. B. Charles, Jr. (Ralph Graves, whom Capra had worked with at Sennett), and Molly Kelly, a poor Irish girl who works at a hotel cigar stand. When Junior leaves to marry Molly, his father, A. B. Charles, Sr.,—owner of the ABC Restaurant Chain—disowns him, mistakenly believing Molly to be a golddigger. Newspaper headlines, as they do in many Capra films, make their private actions public: "A.B. Charles, Jr., DISINHERITED BY IRATE FATHER: Cigar Girl's Dream of Wealth Shattered." Without money, Junior digs ditches for a time. When he overhears fellow workers complaining about the skimpy ham sandwiches at his father's restaurants, Junior decides to start a box-lunch business. Thanks in part to Molly's shrewd business sense and organizational ability, the firm flourishes while Dad's business suffers. At the end, A. B., Sr., buys the Molly Box Lunch Company for $100,000, names Junior the general manager, and blesses the marriage of Junior and Molly. By proving herself a good capitalist, Molly wins her husband in this reverse-role Horatio Alger comedy.

Capra clearly uses his *Our Gang* gag-writing experience in this first Columbia feature. In the opening sequence, Molly washes her young siblings in the bathtub. When they get water on the floor, it leaks through the ceiling of the apartment one floor below. There a woman, upon seeing the wet carpet, berates her dog for misbehaving. In addition, Capra's experience with Langdon is evident: the structure of the narrative is a comedy-romance similar to the Langdon comedies, except that Capra does not have a comic persona of Langdon's stature and hence relies more on the romance and a success story than on comedy.

The style of the film is generally functional and unobtrusive silent filmmaking, though a couple of effective touches stand out. Capra uses associative editing skillfully when making a transition from Molly working at her cigar stand to the offices of A. B. Charles, Sr.: shot of Charles's aide buying cigars from Molly, cut to close-up of a cigar box opening, cut to a long shot of the senior Charles. Titles are also imaginatively used: when Junior gets his idea for his business, the title—"BOX LUNCHES!"—starts in medium-sized letters and grows large when the camera moves closer. When Molly whispers to Junior, the letters are very small. When Molly nervously begins to negotiate with Senior, her words are lettered in jagged lines.

The story itself finds echoes in later Capra films, though he really hadn't yet developed a personal vision. Like *Ladies of Leisure* the film features a rich hero and poor heroine; that structure would shift in many of Capra's most successful films: Stew Smith, Peter Warne, Dan Brooks, Longfellow Deeds, Jefferson Smith, John Doe, and George Bailey all emerge from lower- or middle-class roots. A few of the later Capra heroines, especially Anne Schuyler and Ellie Andrews, are upper-class characters who either democratize and win the hero (Ellie) or refuse to change and lose him (Anne). *That Certain Thing* also exploits a popular topic at the time—box lunches—just as *American Madness* used bank runs; *It Happened One Night*, auto camps; *Mr. Deeds*, unemployment; *You Can't Take It With You*, corrupt munitions industrialists; and *Meet John Doe*, domestic fascism. Finally, A. B. Charles, Sr., is a forefather of Alexander Andrews in *It Happened One Night*: the father who opposes the impending marriage of his child, then gives in, the archetypal parental obstacle that occurs so often in Shakespeare's comedies (*Midsummer Night's Dream*) and tragedies (*Romeo and Juliet*). Though the romance is handled in an extremely simple way, *That Certain Thing* is overall a pleasant, funny film.

So This Is Love, recently recovered in France from a 35mm nitrate print, works less well. It concerns Jerry McGuire, an aspiring clothes designer who works in a tailor shop and is in love at a distance with Hilda Johnson, a clerk at Green's Delicatessen. Hilda, though, secretly loves a bullyish boxer named Spike Mullins. After Jerry takes Hilda to the Boxers' Ball and Spike steals her away, Jerry vows to learn to box and win back Hilda. Soon after, Jerry gets his chance when Spike's scheduled opponent is injured and withdraws. Hilda, now in love with Jerry, feeds the hungry and overconfident Spike a huge meal, ending with mounds of ice cream and a huge cigar. Of course, the food takes effect and Jerry knocks out Spike after a few rounds. The last shot is a long shot of Hilda embracing the battered but ecstatic Jerry. *Rocky*, clearly, is not very original.

Released about five weeks after *That Certain Thing*, *So This Is Love* seems somewhat rushed. Spike Mullins is well characterized visually with his dandified clothes and omnipresent toothpick, and Capra nicely undercuts Hilda's potentially oversentimental look early in the film by having an egg break in her hand. Generally, however, the gags are somewhat stale: two fat men vie for space at the boxing match, a third man constantly gives the Bronx cheer, a boxer wearing only a towel keeps getting interrupted in a lockerroom hall by Hilda. Capra followed this film with three silent B pictures: *The Matinee Idol*, *The Way of the Strong*, and *Say It with Sables*. The first and third are lost, the second recently rediscovered in Denmark. In his autobiography, Capra says he was dissatisfied with the mixture of romance and comedy in *The Matinee Idol*, and that in the next two films he experimented by downplaying comedy and experimenting with "heavy drama." The results, he felt, were "dismal" because he did not know how to sustain dramatic conflict (NATT, 85–86).

Following these five features, Capra was unexpectedly given an opportunity to direct his first A film, *Submarine*. It will be discussed below with two later Capra films that imitate its structure: *Flight* (1929) and *Dirigible* (1931). Capra's next film, starring Douglas Fairbanks, Jr., was *The Power of the Press*. Though the film is not presently available for viewing, Capra described it as "a gangster movie about the power of the press to unearth gangsters when the police can't find them" (FC, 25). The film is significant for at least two reasons. It is Capra's first film in which a newspaper reporter plays a prominent role, something repeated in *Forbidden*, *Platinum Blonde*, *It Happened One Night*, *Mr. Deeds Goes to Town*, *Meet John Doe*, and others. It's also Capra's last all-silent film, released in October 1928.

By that time silent movies were already on the way out. About two years earlier Warner Brothers had released their first talkie, *Don Juan* (on August 6, 1926, in New York). A year before *The Power of the Press*, on October 6, 1927, *The Jazz Singer*, starring Al Jolson, premiered. The film was a striking success, more known

today than *Don Juan* in part because of Jolson's presence, in part
because so many more theaters were wired for sound by the time
it was released, thus giving so many more people a chance to see
the film. The phenomenal success of *The Jazz Singer* sent studio
heads scrambling back to their studios, anxious to get a piece of the
action.

The next year Hollywood studios were deciding about whether
to adapt to sound and, for the most part, making the transition.
Though only fifty-five theaters were equipped with sound-on-film
systems at the start of the year, over a thousand were a year later.
During 1928 about eighty feature-length talkies were made, about
30 percent coming from Warner Brothers. By 1929 nearly all of the
studios, including Columbia, had switched or were switching to
sound.[3]

Capra's first talkie, *The Younger Generation*, is more accurately
one of the curious by-products of the transition years: a part-talkie.
These films were often conceived as silent films, then partly adapted
to sound by having several sequences shot with dialogue. This was
the case with *The Younger Generation:* the film featured a recorded
musical score running throughout the film, interrupted several
times by scenes using recorded dialogue. Though Capra and Columbia would have preferred to make an all-talking film, Capra
recalls that since sound stages and equipment were at such a pre-
mium, Columbia had to settle for shooting the dialogue sequences
all at once, then mixing them with the silent ones.[4]

The most striking thing about *The Younger Generation*, however,
is not the sound track. Rather, the engrossing story and the visual
presentation stand out above all else. The narrative, based on a
story by Fanny Hurst, focuses on the choices confronting second-
generation Jewish-Americans. The central characters are Morris
Goldfish, his sister, Birdie, his parents, Julius and Tildie, and
Birdie's boyfriend, Eddie Lesser. Opening in the Lower East Side
in New York, the film sets up the conflict in the opening sequence.
From childhood, Morris is an ambitious businessman, shrewd and
ruthless in his work, anxious to escape his ethnic origins. On the
other hand, Birdie prefers to stay near her roots: she's in love with
Eddie Lesser, a poor but talented musician and aspiring songwriter.
In this conflict Tildie supports Morris (she believes her husband is
too lazy), while Julius sides with Birdie. Wealth does come to Morris: he rises from his father's secondhand store to an import shop

on Fifth Avenue, changes his name to Morris Fish (disguising and repudiating his roots), and moves his sister and parents into an opulent new home on Park Avenue, complete with butler. Both Julius and Birdie are miserable away from the DeLancey Street community. Eddie and Birdie marry, and when Eddie is sent to jail, wrongly convicted for a bank robbery, Morris throws Birdie out, saying that their parents never want to see Birdie again. In the next two years Morris destroys Birdie's letters to her father, who becomes even more miserable away from his daughter. Julius does not see Birdie until, on his deathbed, he calls for her. When she arrives with Eddie and her year-old son, Julius wakes, smiles in contentment, and soon after dies. Tildie, beginning to feel the emptiness and loneliness of her new life, refuses a trip to Europe with Morris and moves back to DeLancey Street to live with Birdie, Eddie, and her grandson. Unable to convince them all to live with him, Morris is alone at the end of the film, hunched dejectedly and alone before his fireplace, a very un-Capraesque ending.

The visual style of that ending suggests how Capra was developing as a filmmaker. The fireplace is in a spacious, elegant room which seems larger because it is sparsely furnished. Windows covered with Venetian blinds are on the wall to the right of the fireplace. Capra chooses a long shot directly facing the fireplace as the last shot of the film. Morris, his back to the camera, sits with sagging shoulders on a bench in front of the fireplace. Light streaming through the blinds casts prisonlike shadows over him. On his shoulders rests an old shawl his father had worn in an earlier scene, composed almost exactly as this final shot. Visually, Capra is able to connect the emotional coldness Julius felt earlier in the film with Morris's loneliness at the end. This scene illustrates that the former gag writer was also gradually learning how to sustain drama in his films.

The Younger Generation reminds one of Abraham Cahan's novel, *The Rise of David Levinsky*, which focuses on the tension between ethnic community values and individual achievement. Instead of embodying that tension in one character, as Cahan did in *David Levinsky*, Capra externalizes the conflict. Birdie and Julius adhere to community values; Morris, to individual achievement; while Tildie converts from a strong adherence to the success ethic to a realization of the importance of family and community. These conflicts of individualism versus the community, wealth versus human fulfillment, modern versus traditional values, are skillfully developed in *The Younger Generation* and later become common structural dichotomies in Capra films, even though his settings and characters significantly change. It is interesting that Capra, an immigrant himself, should have done so sensitive a study of the conflict and tensions of immigrant life more than forty years before such similar films as *Godfather I* and *II, Hester Street*, and *Lies My Father Told Me*. Discovering this early Columbia film was one of the greatest pleasures of my research.

Following *The Younger Generation*, Capra directed his (and Columbia's) first all-talking film, a murder-mystery called *The Donovan Affair*, shot almost entirely indoors, which is available only in a sound version without the sound track at the Library of Congress. It is unfortunate that a complete version is not available, because Capra has written that, as he worked on it, he began to have "a true understanding of the skills of my craft: how to make the mechanics—lighting, microphone, camera—serve and be subject to the actors" (NATT, 105). Following *The Donovan Affair*, Capra—now working at the slower pace of about three films a year—directed *Flight*, the second of a trilogy of films starring Ralph Graves and Jack Holt that began with *Submarine* and ended with *Dirigible* (1931). Looking at these three films together gives one a good idea of Capra's preoccupations and development in the last gasp of silent films and the start of sound.

These films might be called the "*Wings* trilogy," because they clearly seem part of a cycle of films begun by Paramount Pictures' *Wings*, a popular war film which celebrated masculine friendship above all other values. *Wings* was enormously popular: it played continuously in New York for eighteen months after its release and won the Oscar for best film in 1928, beginning a series of similar films including *Dawn Patrol* (1930) and the three Capra films.[5] Like *Wings*, the three Capra films combined two elements: a love triangle consisting of a woman and two male friends, and action footage related to a war or potential disaster. In the Capra trilogy, the friendship of the males is tested when one falls in love with the wife or girlfriend of the other. In each film the male friendship transcends the conflict arising from competition for the woman's favor and their bond of friendship survives both the woman and the dangerous action. Finally, each film is based on some topical subject: *Submarine*, on two submarine disasters in the mid-1920s; *Flight*, on

United States involvement in Nicaragua in 1928; and *Dirigible*, on Commander Byrd's expeditions to the South Pole.

Submarine, the first of the trilogy, is also the least successful. As a celebration of adventure-loving male friendship above all other human relations, it presents a social vision quite foreign to Capra's own perspective. A friend aptly described *Submarine* as a Howard Hawks movie directed by Frank Capra. Part of the reason for this odd tension is that Capra was assigned to the film after shooting had begun. Replacing another director on his first big-budget film, Capra had no part in developing the story and consequently had to work within the framework of a script given to him.

That script concerns the friendship of Jack Dorgan, a deep-sea diver, and Bob Mason, his telephone man. Separated from his friend when Bob is assigned to a submarine, Jack marries a dance-hall girl named Bessie. Unaware of who she is, Bob meets Bessie at the Palais Ballroom and has a brief affair with her when Jack is on a mission. When Jack learns of the fling, he banishes Bob from his house. Soon after, Bob's submarine is damaged in an accident, falling to the ocean floor. Though Jack is the only diver able to go deep enough to rescue the crew, he initially refuses to because of his grudge against Bob. When he learns that his wife initiated the affair, however, he relents and saves the crew. At the end of the film, Jack's wife is back at the bar, using her standard line to entice the attentions of another unwary sailor, while Jack and Bob walk cheerfully together along the beach.

Submarine has a number of flaws. The narrative depends on Jack discovering Bob's affair, and the discovery is both forced and unlikely. Capra ingeniously used a tiny model of a diver being lowered with a string toward a model submarine so he could get an underwater long shot during the climax, but the model looks like just that—a model. Finally, Jack's wife is too obviously evil and the men too obviously blameless to make the story any more than puerile.

Despite these flaws, Capra did manage to tell the story economically and skillfully. As with the use of the fireplace setting in *The Younger Generation,* Capra uses visual repetition when he shoots Bessie three different times at the same table in the Palais Ballroom, giving Jack, then Bob, then another sailor the same line. He includes a visual montage to evoke a 1920s party atmosphere, double exposing images of dancers, a singer, and a dance band, ending with a shot of dancing feet, then dissolving to a broom sweeping the same floor to suggest the passage of time. Though the film is silent, it was originally released with a sound track. Included were sounds of whirring plane motors, door knocks, hissing oxygen tanks in the submarine chamber, and taps on the submarine when Jack reaches it, though a New York reviewer complained that the sounds weren't well synchronized.[6] More effective is his use of intercutting. Learning a lesson from D. W. Griffith, Capra moves at the end of the film among three locations: the submarine crew in a chamber quickly losing oxygen, the floating barge directly above the sub, and Jack's slow descent toward the embattled crew. The accelerated pace of the editing skillfully helps build the suspense. Though working on a film whose story wasn't well adapted to his interests, Capra did do what we could call a workmanlike, professional job.

The film did well, and Capra followed it a year later with *Flight*. This time he wrote the story with Ralph Graves, and the Jack Holt and Graves characters are more interesting, the female lead more sympathetic. The film uses two topical issues to build a story. It opens by having Lefty Phelps (Graves) copy Roy Riegles's wrong-way run following a fumble recovery in the 1929 Rose Bowl. It also, by portraying the attempts of the Marine Flying Corps to put down a rebel uprising in Nicaragua, exploits American military involvement there. Though Marines had been in and out of Nicaragua since the 1910s, in 1928 they returned to put down turmoil stirred up by a leftist group led by Sandino (Lobo in *Flight*). Marines helped squelch the conflict but did not entirely pull out until 1932. When *Flight* was released, the issue was still fresh in people's minds.

The central preoccupations of *Flight* are Lefty Phelps's attempts to prove himself after his wrong-way run and the competition between Lefty and Panama Williams, his flight instructor, for the love of Elinore, a nurse. Lefty joins the Marine Air Corps but loses his nerve and crashes on his first solo flight. Sympathetic, Panama takes Lefty along to Nicaragua as a mechanic. Lefty, serving as gunner of a plane during combat, is shot down. When Panama rescues him, Lefty hops in the plane and pilots it while under fire from Lobo and his men. Later, he even lands the plane at the marine base, though one landing wheel is damaged. The film closes with Lefty following in Panama's footsteps as a flight instructor and married to Elinore.

Elinore is much more sympathetic than Bessie in *Submarine*. Early in the film Panama—portrayed as excessively shy with women—loves Elinore and contemplates proposing, though Elinore isn't interested. She meets and admires Lefty. In Nicaragua (Elinore has followed to help provide medical care) Panama plays Miles Standish, asking Lefty to propose to Elinore for him. He does, but Elinore professes her love for Lefty. As in the other two films in the trilogy, tensions arise between the male friends, and Panama refuses to help search for Lefty when he crashes. When he learns from Elinore that Lefty did not betray him, however, he sheds his romantic notions and leaves to search for Lefty. In the end, the woman is not an outcast, as in *Submarine,* but happily married to the hero, and the male friendship also survives.

Flight challenges the notion that early talkies did not move. Particularly in the aerial shots in Nicaragua, exciting action footage is combined with skillful use of the sound track. When the Air Corps attempts to save the besieged Marine infantry, Capra cuts between aerial shots and ground shots. Accompanying the aerial shots are noises of the plane hum and machine-gun fire, while battle footage from ground level is combined with gun shots and appropriate battle sounds. The scene is intercut much as the rescue in *Dirigible*—the infantrymen are out of ammunition, using only bayonets, when the planes first arrive—and the effective editing of sound to accompany the rapidly shifting images suggest that Capra and his technicians were quickly solving the problems posed by the introduction of sound. For a film released in 1929, *Flight*—and especially the battle sequence—contains a kinetic quality absent in most early talkies.

Like *Submarine, Flight* has its problems. The crashes are clearly done with models, making it hard to understand how Lefty and Roberts survive their crash. It's also difficult to accept Lefty's heroics in the plane near the end of the film. Though the plot demands that he must overcome his fear and prove himself, it's unlikely that under fire Panama would let the unproved Lefty pilot the plane. These narrative puzzles weaken *Flight.* A year and a half later, in *Dirigible,* Capra shows more control of story and film style.

The main characters in *Dirigible* are more fully realized, more complex, and closer to Capra's mature vision that those in the first two parts of the trilogy. Graves plays Frisky Pierce, a talented but arrogant flying ace who seeks headlines above all else. Holt is Jack Bradon, an old navy buddy of Frisky's who has become committed to flying dirigibles, a less spectacular but more steady mode of air transportation than Frisky's airplanes. Finally, Fay Wray plays

Photos: (top) from *Submarine*, Ralph Graves and Jack Holt with feathered friend in their bunkroom; (bottom) from *Dirigible*, the crash of Frisky Pierce's plane as he attempts to reach the South Pole

Frisky's wife, Helen. Early on, we learn that Frisky has been home only two months in their two years of marriage and that Helen, though she loves Frisky, is terrified of his reckless heroics.

The story concerns the attempt of the scientist Rondelle, assisted by Jack and Frisky, to reach the South Pole. As Leland Poague has pointed out, the film is structured around three attempts to reach the pole.[7] The first two fail. First, Jack Bradon's dirigible is downed in a thunderstorm along the Atlantic coast shortly after departure. The second attempt fails when Frisky crashes his plane, unable to clear a mountain near the Pole. Only the third attempt—Bradon's rescue of Frisky and his men with the dirigible—succeeds, and it does so because the final attempt is aimed not at achieving glory, making headlines, or winning a race to the pole but at saving human lives.

The film follows some conventions established in the earlier two films. The crash of the dirigible during the storm, dramatically shot in low-key lighting with rain falling and wind howling, parallels the submarine and airplane accidents in the earlier films. Likewise, the struggles of the crew who go down with Frisky, including the painful death of McGuire, echo struggles and deaths (Skip in *Submarine*, Roberts in *Flight*, both of whom die in Graves's arms) in the earlier films. But in *Dirigible* the quest and the love triangle are much more skillfully integrated than in the earlier films. When Frisky insists on going on the second expedition in spite of Helen's protests, Helen writes a note for Frisky to open upon reaching the pole. It reads: "Frisky, when you read this you will be all over the front page again, but maybe there will be room for this. I will be in Paris getting my divorce and begging Jack Bradon to marry me. I'm tired of being married to a headline." Though Helen does spend time with Jack after Frisky leaves, Jack—who respects humans over glory—will not betray Frisky in spite of his friend's arrogance. Thus, after he saves Frisky at the film's climax, he makes up a response when the chastened Frisky asks him to read Helen's letter. In Jack's version, Helen's letter reads, in part: "I love you and adore you and hope you'll come home safe to me." The central conflict of the story—Frisky's irresponsibility and search for personal glory versus Jack's combined sense of responsibility and concern for other human beings—is resolved in favor of Jack. In the film's last sequence Jack is fittingly honored as the hero in a parade down Fifth Avenue while

Frisky and Helen—reunited—look on from a balcony overlooking the parade.

Dirigible succeeds over the earlier two films in part because Capra worked with a screenwriter, Jo Swerling, who had had some experience in dramatic construction as a playwright in New York. *Dirigible* avoids the worst narrative improbabilities that flawed *Submarine* and *Flight*, thanks in part to Swerling's talents. The film also succeeds on a stylistic level: the dirigible accident is presented effectively, as are the crash of Frisky's plane, the survival efforts of Frisky and his crew in the simulated Antarctic tundra, and the tension involved in the rescue. All suggest Capra's growing confidence in the film medium. Finally, the thematic concern over the moral issue of what constitutes true heroism is considerably clearer and more sophisticated than a male-buddy film like *Submarine*. Starting by imitating the successful *Wings*, Capra was, as the "*Wings* trilogy" indicates, both mastering the film medium and beginning to learn how to weave a clear moral perspective into his films.

After *Flight* was released in 1929, Capra collaborated with Jo Swerling on five films in the next three years. In addition to *Dirigible*, Swerling received screenplay credit for *Ladies of Leisure*, *Rain or Shine*, *The Miracle Woman*, and *Forbidden*, the subjects of the rest of this chapter. (*Platinum Blonde*, released before *Forbidden*, will be discussed with the other early 1930s Riskin-Capra films in the next chapter.)

Ladies of Leisure, a talkie based on Milton Herbert Gropper's play *Ladies of the Evening*, presents character types from the 1920s in 1930. As in *That Certain Thing*, the main characters are the son of a wealthy businessman and a middle-class woman who is accused of being a golddigger. Unlike it, *Ladies of Leisure* is a dramatic film, focusing on the effects an idealistic artist has on a hardened woman. Early in the film, Jerry Strong (Ralph Graves) is clearly alienated from the dissipation of leisure-class life in New York. He meets Kay Arnold (Barbara Stanwyck) on the road after leaving a penthouse party in New York. Struck by her beauty, he hires her as a model. When he tries to paint her, he finds that instead of conveying hope, she seems to be "covered up," creating an aura of bitterness, cynicism, and despair, while he wants to recreate the radiant hopefulness he saw in her face on their first meeting.

Gradually Kay begins to be converted from cynicism to hope (she tells Jerry's mother that she feels like she's been cured from a long bout with consumption). Jerry's father, a railroad magnate upset with Jerry's "unpractical" artistic leanings, is convinced that Kay is a golddigger. Even Jerry's mother, though closer to Jerry, is suffused with class bias and offers to pay off Kay so she'll abandon Jerry. Because she loves Jerry enough to worry about how much marriage would ruin his relationships with family and friends, Kay agrees to go to Havana with Bill Standish, Jerry's drunken friend. The melodramatic climax shows Kay's roommate trying to contact Jerry about Kay, then Jerry's attempts to reach Kay before the boat sails. He fails, but we learn via a newspaper headline that Kay unsuccessfully attempted suicide by jumping from the ship. In the last scene, Capra tracks from Kay's feet to her face then pulls back to reveal her hospital bed, then Jerry, who tells Kay she has nothing to worry about.

The relationship between Jerry and Kay, at the center of the film, is an early formulation of something Capra would return to again and again in the next decade: a cynical heroine converted to hopeful idealism by a vulnerable yet idealistic hero. Yet, as I mentioned above, *Ladies of Leisure* uses the stereotypes of the 1920s: a young, wealthy, alienated hero like Jerry would not work in the popular iconography of the 1930s. Capra still had not learned that the embodiment of social values in his films needed to be a common man if he expected broad moviegoing audiences to respond—as he wanted above all else. Though Jerry's character is clearly drawn and Kay's beauty is skillfully highlighted (one back-lit, soft focus close-up of Kay by Joseph Walker, when Kay lies on a bed beside a window covered with raindrops, is breathtaking), *Ladies of Leisure* could never thrive at the box office when the country was becoming increasingly aware of how severe the crash really was.

Capra returned to comedy after *Ladies of Leisure*. Though film historians have on occasion called *Rain or Shine* Capra's only musical, it is in fact an adaptation of a popular Broadway musical in which the songs are all removed. The play starred Joe Cook, a popular and talented Broadway comedian, and so does the film. Two others from the Broadway cast—Tom Howard and Dave Chasen—also played in the film. About the time he was finishing *Ladies of Leisure* Capra boasted to a friend that he was so confident of his filmmaking skills that he could make an entertaining film using the phone book as a script (NATT, 122). With a story not much more ambitious than the phone book, Capra showed what he meant in *Rain or Shine*.

At the center of the film is Joe Cook as Smiley Johnson, a talented circus acrobat, juggler, and comic who has turned down offers from Barnum and Bailey. Cook, a small, slight man with a mouth and grin almost as wide as Joe E. Brown's, provides expert juggling, ball walking, and tight-rope walking in the course of the film. He's also a good verbal comic, especially when talking a gullible old bumpkin named Amos K. Shrewsbury into becoming a partner for the circus, then confusing him with non sequiturs whenever A. K. questions his investment.

The story hangs loosely around Cook and is mainly preparation for a climactic circus tent fire at the end of the film. Unlike *Ladies of Leisure*, the romance here is clearly secondary. Bud, the son of a rich father, is in love with Mary, the daughter of a circus family who has taken over the show after her parents died. But their romance is unresolved at the end of the film. The climactic tent fire begins when the audience riots, responding to a strike of circus workers led by the opportunistic ringleader. In the ensuing mayhem, an overturned popcorn wagon starts a fire, and Smiley heroically saves Mary from the blaze. The fire creates the spectacle of the film— a huge circus tent is actually burned down, which Capra catches effectively in long shots—a spectacle that reminds one of the conclusion of *The Strong Man* and looks forward to the dirigible accident in his next film, *Dirigible,* and the fire in *Miracle Woman.* The how of *Rain or Shine* easily surpasses the what.

After *Dirigible* Capra again worked with Barbara Stanwyck in *The Miracle Woman.* Based on a play by John Meehan and Robert Riskin—the latter would soon become Capra's most famous collaborator—the film was again scripted by Jo Swerling. Loosely patterned after the life of the flamboyant woman evangelist Aimee Semple McPherson, *The Miracle Woman* is a fascinating failure, starring Stanwyck in a role of converted cynic remarkably similar to the role she would play ten years later in *Meet John Doe.*

The Miracle Woman opens with a Bible verse on a title: "Beware of false prophets which come to you in sheep's clothing" (Matthew 8:15). Another title explains that the film is "offered as a rebuke to anyone who, under the cloak of religion, seeks to sell for gold, God's choicest gift to Humanity . . . FAITH." In the opening sequence

Photos: (top) Jerry Strong (Ralph Graves) and his father critically examine his painting in *Ladies of Leisure*; (bottom) the cynical Hornsby works on a pensive Florence Fallon (Barbara Stanwyck) in *The Miracle Woman*

Florence Fallon (Stanwyck), the daughter of a minister who has just died after being falsely ousted by his congregation, takes the pulpit for what was to be her father's farewell sermon. Though she excoriates the congregation for their ingratitude and hypocrisy—Capra shoots her from a low angle—her denunciations fall on deaf ears. Everyone in the congregation leaves the church except a stranger named Hornsby—one of Riskin's cynical and greedy villains later to become a staple in Capra's films. A man with, in his own words, "no chains at all, no profession, no town, no particular belief, and no limit," Hornsby tries to exploit both Florence's despair and her eloquence. Counseling her to "get callous," Hornsby tells Florence that convictions only get people into trouble: "The answer is, don't have any. If you've got none, then you can assume any—the ones that happen to pay. . . . Religion is great if you can sell it, no good if you have to give it away." Promising her a way to get revenge on her father's congregation and other hypocrites like them, Hornsby convinces Florence to become a hypocritical faith healer herself.

Florence becomes an immediate sensation, successful both over the airwaves and in her own tabernacle, the "Temple of Happiness." Columbia was beginning to spend more than it had earlier on sets for Capra's films, and Capra made good use of sets and props: this stage has a huge curtain adorned in large letters with Florence's initials—FF—while Hornsby's office has signs reading "Heaven has no quota law" and "Love is the key to the pearly gates." All goes well until a blind songwriter, contemplating suicide, hears her give an uplifting (albeit hypocritical) speech on the radio in which she mentions the great poetry Milton wrote while blind. His faith restored, he puts suicide out of his mind. Later the blind man, John, meets Florence and gradually a romance develops. When Florence sees the effect she's had on John—the simple purity of his conviction—her conscience begins working (she's reminded of her earlier beliefs by a picture of her father she keeps on her desk, something that happens in later Capra films regularly to connect characters with traditional values). When Hornsby tells Florence that they need to leave town—their racket is on the verge of being discovered—Florence balks. Hornsby insists, and Florence is faced with a thorny dilemma. She attempts to resolve it by telling the truth about herself in her farewell sermon. When she does, Hornsby cuts off her microphone, as D. B. Norton would in *Meet John Doe,* and a fire accidentally begins. Stumbling over Florence in the smoke, John miraculously manages to get her out of the burning temple. In the final scene Florence, now a member of a Salvation Army band, reads a telegram from John saying his eyesight may be restored and proposing marriage. Hornsby, now managing a boxer, walks up to Florence and greets her. Then, as she marches away from the camera playing "The Battle Hymn of the Republic," he remarks: "And she gave up a million bucks for that. Poor sap."

Though the climactic fire and concluding scene are both somewhat strained, *The Miracle Woman* is notable largely because the conflicts it raises are those which would be repeated and refined in later Capra films. The film relates particularly closely to *Meet John Doe*—especially in Stanwyck's portrayal of a person who manufactures morality for financial gain, then regrets it. Capra's first encounter with Riskin, though a distant one, already revealed their compatibility.

Capra's next film starring Stanwyck and scripted by Swerling—*Forbidden*—was based on a story by Capra himself. It was released in the early 1930s, a period which Robert Sklar has called the "golden age of turbulence" in American film history, a time characterized by films which "called into question sexual propriety, social decorum and the institutions of law and order." *Forbidden*, which raises questions about genteel notions of sexuality and morality, is part of a cycle of films about "fallen women" which include *Susan Lenox, Safe in Hell* (both 1931), *Blonde Venus, Faithless,* and *Letty Lynton* (all 1932). (These pictures contributed to an outraged public's demand for increased censorship by the Hays Office).[8]

When viewed today, however, *Forbidden* seems less a challenge to genteel values than a 1930s version of *The Story of Adele H*: a study of how a woman's intense romanticism leads to personal self-sacrifice bordering on self-destruction. The story is of a spinster librarian, Lulu Smith, who falls in love with a married politician, Robert Conover (Adolphe Menjou), on a cruise to Havana. She has a child out of wedlock by Conover, then gives the child up when Conover's crippled wife decides to adopt it. To help prevent Conover from being exposed when he runs for governor, Lulu marries Al Holland (Ralph Bellamy), a news editor who has been out to get Conover for years. On election night, when Holland confronts Lulu with evidence that Conover's adopted child is really hers, Lulu kills her husband with a pistol. Immediately after, news of Conover's election is reported on the radio while Lulu burns the incriminating evidence. In the final scene, Lulu, pardoned by Conover, visits him in the governor's mansion. Deathly ill, Conover gives a paper willing half his estate to Lulu, "mother of my daughter, Roberta, in belated gratitude for a lifetime of devotion and sacrifice." After Conover dies in her arms, Lulu rips up the paper, tosses it, and exits, melting into a crowded street as the camera pulls back into a long shot.

As the plot description suggests, Capra can't be faulted by describing the film as "two hours of soggy, 99.44% pure soap opera" (NATT, 134). Except for the strikingly poetic opening shots of spring—Dovzhenko-like images of ground being plowed, an orchard, a blossoming fruit tree, a close-up of blossoms—the film is constructed in the functional style of classical Hollywood cinema, complete with commentative music in dramatic scenes, something Capra often avoided in his early talkies. The newspaper dimension of the story—Ralph Bellamy as cub reporter who works himself up to editor, giving Lulu a position as an advice-to-the-lovelorn columnist—may have been inspired by the success of *The Front Page* the previous year. Indeed, several details in the film—the politician who is nearly ruined by an illicit relationship, the snappy newspaper milieu, the burning of evidence in a fireplace at the end of the film—recur in *Citizen Kane* nearly a decade later. Yet the film's melodramatic tone—rarely lightened by comic touches—overburdens the viewer. And instead of empathizing with Lulu when she tells Conover, "Your honors have been my honors, your success, my success," and when she burns the will, one feels more anger and pity toward a woman who seems never to have confronted her own human needs and desires, living—like Truffaut's Adele H—in a pure yet self-destructive romanticism.

Looking back at Capra's early years at Columbia, one might make a few observations. First, Capra did learn his craft during these years, not only polishing his visual style and editing rhythms but also adapting to sound quite quickly. Second, he had not yet found the film form within which he could express his social vision (indeed he had probably not yet clarified his social vision). Instead, he was willing to experiment in various forms and to follow trends. Thus, he made detective films (*Donovan Affair*), comedies loosely structured like his Langdon features (*That Certain Thing*), male adventure films (the "*Wings* trilogy"), newspaper films, fallen women films, and so on. One feels that during most of the period Capra

Photos from *Forbidden*: (top) Capra instructs Barbara Stanwyck as co-star Adolphe Menjou looks on; (bottom) Menjou and Stanwyck—the self-destructive lover, Lulu Smith, in the arms of Bob Grover

was generally more involved in how he told his story than in what his story was about. His films were generally successful at the box office, and Capra gradually earned enough of a reputation to slow down the hectic pace he began with, moving from seven films in 1928 to two or three a year in the early 1930s. And in several films—*The Younger Generation, Dirigible, The Miracle Woman*—a careful viewer even finds thematic and formal premonitions of the contributions Frank Capra would make to American film in the 1930s and 1940s.

3

Making It (1931–35)

BY 1931, Frank Capra's name was just beginning to be known outside of Columbia's back lot. His work on films like *Dirigible* and *Miracle Woman* had won him some recognition as a director whose talents were at least a cut above the norm. Yet by early 1935—only six films later—he was one of the hottest directors around. At the Academy Awards ceremony that year his quickly shot masterpiece *It Happened One Night* had been showered with the five major Oscars: for best film, director, writer, actress, actor. Only *One Flew over the Cuckoo's Nest* (1975) and *Silence of the Lambs* (1991) have repeated such a sweep. Hence we find a curious paradox that Capra was climbing the ladder of success most swiftly during precisely those years when the American economy and the confidence of the American people in their country were at low ebb.

The two—Capra's rise and America's decline—are related. It's tempting to suggest that Capra's movies in the early 1930s were safety valves, providing audiences with psychic escapes from their pressing burdens. The better the safety valve, according to this position, the better the release. Yet this interpretation needs qualification. During these years Capra was searching for and gradually finding elements of his own distinctive narrative form and social vision, best embodied in films like *Mr. Smith Goes to Washington* (1939) or *It's a Wonderful Life* (1946). Yet because his democratic vision was so close to the majority of his audience and because he presented that vision in such attractive ways, the films became popular.

In making these films—*Platinum Blonde* (1931), *American Madness* (1932), *The Bitter Tea of General Yen* (1933), *Lady for a Day*

Photo (left) from Lady for a Day: *Apple Annie (May Robson), surrounded by her cohorts, thinks about her daughter*

(1933), *It Happened One Night* (1934), and *Broadway Bill* (1934)—
Capra gradually discovered his voice. This chapter tells the story
of that discovery.

Several important things besides his filmmaking that happened
to Capra between 1931 and 1935 deserve mention. In 1931 he
became a member of the Academy's board of governors, no small
tribute to a young director from a smaller studio like Columbia. On
February 1, 1932, he married Lucille Reyburn, to whom he is still
married and deeply devoted. Though Lucille had a miscarriage in
early 1933—another of the reverses of fortune Capra has found in
his life and career—the Capras' first child, Frank, Jr., was born a
year later. Besides gaining recognition in the industry and beginning
a family during these years, Capra also began his long and fruitful
relationship with screenwriter Robert Riskin.

Riskin was Capra's most constant collaborator. Born the same
year as Capra, Riskin's roots were in New York, where he attended
Columbia. After serving in the military during the First World War,
Riskin became a playwright. Some of his plays were produced on
Broadway, and at least three that he coauthored were turned into
films: *Illicit, Many a Ship,* and *The Miracle Woman.* Like Ben
Hecht and Herman Mankiewicz, Riskin was one of the generation
of playwrights and journalists to come to Hollywood to write screenplays after the introduction of talkies in the late 1920s and early
1930s.

After coauthoring the play upon which *The Miracle Woman* is
based, Riskin began to work quite regularly with Capra. He wrote
the dialogue for *Platinum Blonde* (Swerling is credited with the
adaptation), then received sole or major screenplay credit for eight
Capra films: *American Madness, Lady for a Day, It Happened One
Night, Broadway Bill, Mr. Deeds Goes to Town, Lost Horizon, You
Can't Take It With You,* and *Meet John Doe.* In addition, Riskin
played a smaller collaborative role in *Riding High, Pocketful of
Miracles* (both remakes of Riskin films), and *Here Comes the Groom*
(based on a story he coauthored).

It's undoubtedly true that Riskin contributed to the success of his
and Capra's films. In his autobiography and often in interviews,
Capra praises Riskin's talents and remembers with pleasure their
compatibility. They collaborated closely in writing the screenplays.
In an interview Capra admitted: "It's difficult to remember who
would and would not" write the first draft of a script. But he also

added: "Generally I would be a little ahead of him on material; then we'd talk it over and he'd put it together in words. So we'd have a rough draft. We'd go back, and I'd do the casting and all the rest, and he'd polish it up."[1]

What precisely did Riskin add to Capra's films? Of course, no one will be able to answer this for sure; even Capra cannot say exactly who contributed what. Just as in the Langdon-Capra relationship, no certain answers are possible. But a number of people have written on what Riskin provided Capra, and some guesses can be made.[2] First, Riskin probably did much to introduce the cynical urban types that appear in Capra films. People like Binjy in *Platinum Blonde*, Oscar Shapely in *It Happened One Night*, and Corny Cobb in *Mr. Deeds* have an urban vitality rarely present in earlier Capra films. Second, Riskin added vernacular and slang dialogue to the Capra films: the focus on Stew Smith's "puttering" or Peter Warne's "dunking" or Longfellow Deeds's "doodling" both amuse audiences and draw them closer to the characters. Finally, Riskin helped make the narratives tighter and more satisfying. Except for *Meet John Doe* and *Lost Horizon* the Riskin films are all more successfully constructed than a Swerling script like *Forbidden*. Riskin said himself that he tried to write in three acts, directing the story toward the first two "curtains" so that he could create enough suspense to "hold the audience throughout the picture."[3] (For example, Peter and Ellie's experiences at the tourist camp in *It Happened One Night* end the first act, while Ellie's discovery that Peter has left their room at the second tourist camp ends the second act.)

So Risken introduced Capra to urban cynics, while improving the dialogue and tightening the story construction of Capra's films. Evidence also suggests Riskin *reinforced* key thematic preoccupations in Capra's films, but Stephen Handzo claims too much when he suggests that Riskin added the subject of the little people to Capra's work (FC, 167). The Riskin scripts Handzo uses as examples were all written after he began his collaboration with Capra, and one can go back as far as *The Strong Man* for evidence of victimized yet resilient little people in Capra's movies. Riskin was an important sounding board for Capra; he did not create Capra's social vision.

Capra's first five collaborations with Riskin all had American settings, and all focused in part on some type of romance. It's instructive to look at these five films to see how Capra and Riskin gradually found a narrative structure that worked with audiences. In *Platinum*

Blonde the middle-class hero marries an upper-class woman, then leaves her for a middle-class woman at the end of the play. In *American Madness*, the romance is a subplot—it unites an assistant bank cashier and a secretary. *In Lady for a Day*, a lower-class girl becomes Cinderella, marrying into European aristocracy. *It Happened One Night* produces a key switch: the upper-class woman must "democratize" and lower herself to earn the middle-class hero, unifying the classes and—unlike the other films—denying class barriers and upper-class cultural control. It's a key to understanding Capra's work to note that this film was the most successful of the group. Finally, *Broadway Bill* finds a middle-class hero who has married into wealth, only to reject the upper class for fulfilling poverty at the racetrack. His wealthy sister-in-law and even her stuffy father follow his lead and drop out of the rat race. In finding his own voice, Capra was gradually coming to affirm certain middle-class American values. To see how it happened we need to look more closely at each of the films.

A scene in the first of these films—*Platinum Blonde*—shows us one of the lessons Capra was learning. Stew Smith (Robert Williams), a crack news reporter, is also writing a play. Encountering extreme difficulty, Stew keeps changing the setting of the opening scene: he tries—and discards—Siberia, the Middle East, Norway, and Madrid. Then Gallagher (Loretta Young), one of his newsroom "pals," suggests that he write from his own experience. Stew soon turns to an American setting and a character whose situation is close to his own. In a sense Stew's realizations were Capra's. Not only was Capra learning to use American settings that he was familiar with, but more importantly he was also searching for a hero who could embody some of his own values and attitudes. It's interesting to note that Capra's friendship with Myles Connolly was beginning in 1930 and 1931. Connolly, an Irish-Catholic newsman, served as a sort of moral prod to Capra, challenging him to make more ambitious and personal films when most people were simply congratulating Capra on the popularity of his movies (NATT, 120–22, 128–31).

Platinum Blonde begins the process, though it is only a beginning. Trying to capitalize on the economic success of *The Front Page*, Capra, Swerling, and Riskin adopted a story about a news reporter who tries, then rejects, the life-style of the leisure class. Capra doesn't write much about the film: he simply calls it an "out-and-out comedy" done to raise his stock after the failure of an "idea" film like *The Miracle Woman* (NATT, 134). Nevertheless, it does contain some skillful filmmaking and begins to develop what would become some constant Capra preoccupations.

Platinum Blonde opens in a hectic newsroom, reminiscent of *The Front Page*. Stew Smith, the newshound parallel to Hildy Johnson, hears about and vows to get a story on some mysterious goings on at the mansion of the fabulously wealthy Schuyler family. He gets the story—settlement of a breach-of-promise suit brought by Gloria Golden against Michael Schuyler—and also meets the vivacious Anne Schuyler (Jean Harlow). After a brief courtship, Stew and Anne marry, much to the surprise, consternation, and skepticism of Stew's fellow newsmen and the suspicions of the Schuyler family. But immediately problems develop. Anne won't live in Stew's apartment, while Stew feels like a "bird in a gilded cage" in the Schuyler mansion. When an old friend calls Stew a "gigolo," Stew responds with a strong right hook. A headline results: " 'I WEAR THE PANTS,' SAYS ANNE SCHUYLER'S HUSBAND." From here, things degenerate. Stew bounces around the spacious walls of the mansion for a time, then invites some old friends to a party. Dropping his formality, Stew reverts to his old lovable self, seeing fellow reporter Gallagher's romantic appeal for the first time. "I'm out of my own crowd," Stew concludes, then proceeds to tell off Anne and her mother, leaving the mansion for good. In the final scene, Stew rejects a payoff from a Schuyler emissary and professes his love for Gallagher. The play he's writing concludes, as does the film, with the poor but honest boy telling the poor but honest girl, "Darling, I'm sorry. I always loved you. I want you to marry me."

The narrative of *Platinum Blonde* is notable for a number of reasons. It posits two world views—middle class and upper class—suggests that they are irreconcilable, and upholds the middle-class perspective as superior. By celebrating the inherent virtue of middle-class informality over upper-class snobbism, *Platinum Blonde* is really the first Capra film to recognize, at least implicitly, that a Depression was on. The narrative is also significant in the creation of Stew Smith and Gallagher. Stew is the prototype for later Capra heroes, closely related to the commonsensical, brash, yet ultimately sentimental Peter Warne in *It Happened One Night*. When he's tagged as "The Cinderella Man" by newsmen, he also shares a distinction with Longfellow Deeds. Gallagher, on the other hand,

Photos from the two worlds of *Platinum Blonde*: (top) the *mise-en-scène* of the news-room and (bottom) the Schuyler mansion contrast the vital world with the effete world

is an early version of the worldly-wise yet humane working woman who supports the Capra hero in moments of crisis; her direct ancestors are Babe Bennett in *Mr. Deeds*, Saunders in *Mr. Smith*, and Anne Mitchell in *Meet John Doe*.

Capra tells the story engagingly. Setting and costume are skillfully used to contrast Stew's world with Anne's. The cluttered, frenzied newsroom is hectic and alive compared to the spacious opulence of the mansion. When Stew moves to the mansion, he's asked to wear new clothes, and he surely looks out of character when he dons such formal attire. Capra's high angle long shot of Stew pacing aimlessly on the first floor of the mansion creates an apt visual equivalent for the aimlessness and emptiness Stew feels in his new location. Likewise, when a caged bird is prominently evident in Stew's bedroom, we're reminded of Stew's own earlier fear of being "a bird in a gilded cage."

The comedy energizes the film. Mrs. Schuyler's snobbishness is frequently mocked by presenting in close-up her pained reactions to the casual vernacular manner of the newsmen. Stew's spontaneity and playfulness is captured in the scene when he and the butlers made "booping" noises, then hear the echoes off the high ceilings (a scene recurring in *Mr. Deeds*). Riskin's penchant for slang and vernacular dialogue also adds to the comedy. When Stew has to explain to the butlers what "puttering" is, he's playing with vernacular just like the Colonel and his "helots" in *Meet John Doe*. And instead of saying no amount of money could buy him off, Stew uses more vivid language. He tells Schuyler's lawyer that he couldn't be bought off by a "bucketful of shekels."

Platinum Blonde is pleasant to watch even today, though it's hard to accept Jean Harlow with her platinum hair, slinky dresses, and forced accent as the scion of an upper-crust family. What actually sold the film to the public was Harlow's outrageously bleached hair. "Platinum blondes" became the fashionable rage for a while. Yet the film remains significant in that it does represent Capra's early attempt to speak in his own voice to a Depression audience. Though the newspaper and upper-class worlds in *Platinum Blonde* were somewhat narrow, discrete, and separate from the experience of most of Capra's audience, he would involve his audience more directly and grapple even more explicitly with the problems of the Depression in his next film with Riskin: *American Madness*.

Forbidden, the Swerling-Capra collaboration that we looked at earlier, appeared between *Platinum Blonde* and *American Madness*. While the central character of *Forbidden* was a woman, *American Madness* focused on a most unlikely hero in 1932: a banker. It grappled with issues as central to the times as the causes of the economic depression and mob panic, and at least one critic believes it's "the first film in which Capra demonstrated his maturity as an artist."[4] The film itself does much to uphold that contention.

Tom Dickson (Walter Huston), the banker hero of *American Madness*, was loosely based on I. A. Giannini, an Italian-American who founded what later became the Bank of America. Like Tom Dickson, Capra has said, Giannini would "lend money on character" (FC, 29). In preparing the script, Riskin even visited Giannini.[5] The film places this resolute banker in the midst of the Depression; spurning "escapism," the film abounds with references to the economic situation. The cashier Matt (Pat O'Brien) can't marry Dickson's secretary Helen because their finances don't permit it. One cashier jokes with another, "See you in the breadlines." A woman comes into the bank, despairing that a check she received had bounced. Matt jokes with tellers that they are "six reasons why banks fail," and Dickson speaks to the board of directors about reasons for the decline. Indeed, the climactic action of the film— the attempts of a huge, panic-stricken mob to withdraw their money from the bank—was based upon one of the most frightening spectacles of the Depression. Between 1930 and FDR's inauguration in March 1933, over 5,000 banks closed their doors, leading thousands to lose their savings. A movie about bank runs could hardly have been more topical.

The story itself is both swift-moving and tightly structured. Between the order evident in the parallel opening and closing scenes, American madness is rampant. The first and last scenes both begin at the start of a banking day. A telephone operator answers the bank phone, Matt opens the vault for the other tellers, and Dickson enters the bank. On the way in Dickson greets the doorman, a teller named Carter, a guard, Matt, and Helen. From the start (and at the end), we're assured of Huston's personal style—he's friendly with and concerned about all his employees.

But madness abounds within this frame. Cluett, one of the bank employees, owes $50,000 in gambling debts to some gangsters. In payment he agrees to set the vault timer (which Matt usually handles) for midnight, so the vault will open for the gangsters to rob.

Photo: Tom Dixon (Walter Huston) attempts to quell a bank run in *American Madness*

He does, and they do, killing a guard in the process. As an alibi, Cluett spends the evening with Dickson's wife, Phyllis, whom Dickson has been ignoring. The next day rumors about the bank robbery spread, growing from the actual $100,000 theft to a story which alleges Dickson's personal embezzlement of $7 million. A bank run ensues. Dickson speaks to the mob, urging caution and attempting to preserve confidence. He's only partially successful, and his board of directors pressures him to accept a merger with a large trust that he has been resisting. Matt, who has been under police interrogation about the theft, is exonerated when Cluett turns in the gamblers. To protect himself, Cluett also tells police (and Dickson) that Phyllis was with him in his apartment when the crime took place. Though the crime is solved, Dickson loses his desire to save the bank when Phyllis confirms over the phone that Cluett's story is true. But Matt does not give up. He calls the small businessmen to whom Dickson lent money, and they come to his rescue in the nick of time. As the shocked mob looks on, the businessmen rush into the bank to deposit money, showing their confidence in the bank and their gratitude to Dickson. Reinvigorated by his wife's assurance that Cluett meant nothing to her and by the acts of his friends, Dickson shames the board of directors into depositing some of their funds and saves his bank. American madness is brought under control and order returns.

The story is engrossingly and skillfully told; Capra's hand is sure throughout the film. An early tracking shot follows Matt down the row of teller windows; it's leisurely, smooth, accompanied by typical voices and sounds of the start of the work day in a bank. Later, during the bank run, Dickson hurries down the same row to give hurried advice to his tellers. The tracking camera moves in fits and starts; its jerky, uneven movements, accompanied by Dickson's forceful words and the din of the mob in the background, create an opposite, precisely appropriate atmosphere. Another powerful scene presents the rumor. The telephone operator casually mentions the robbery over the phone to another operator, who calls to a friend with money in the bank, and the telephone lines begin to sizzle. After the initial calls, Capra includes a long series of close-ups (thirty-five, by my count) of people's faces as they all call their friends to remove their money from the bank. Most of the shots are accompanied by a few words of hurried advice; some are framed in oblique angles to reinforce the urgency and disorientation of the situation (over fifteen years before *The Third Man*). The pace of the film from this scene to the final one is frenzied, a point Capra discusses in his autobiography (NATT, 139–40). The accelerated rhythms are especially evident when Capra intercuts among three situations: the bank run in the outer lobby, the police interrogation of Matt in an office, and Dickson's backstage attempts to control the panic. Examples of Capra's skillful use of film language in *American Madness* could easily be multiplied; even today it's an absorbing film.

The thrust of the film might best be described by looking at three problems which confront Tom Dickson: one private, one public, and one philosophical. The private problem stems from Dickson's absorption in his work; it leads him to neglect his wife, Phyllis, which makes her vulnerable to the philanderer Cluett. The public problem pits Dickson's desire for his bank to remain independent against his board of directors' advice to merge with the New York Trust. Though such a merger would restrict Dickson's personable style, it begins to seem inevitable during the bank run. Finally, Dickson is faced with a philosophical problem: his ideological approach to the Depression is a curious mixture of New Deal Keynesianism and nineteenth-century individualism. Like Keynes, he believes the Depression has persisted because fearful people have hoarded money, keeping it out of circulation. That problem can only be overcome by encouraging spending. But Dickson's criteria for lending the money that would stimulate the economy come from the era of precorporate America. Referring to Alexander Hamilton, he says that security is measured not by a man's stocks but by his *character*. As a result, his loans have gone to small businessmen he knows he can trust. His stress on character extends even to the people he hires to work for him—though Matt is an ex-con, Dickson trusts him and expects him to be reliable.

When Dickson's three problems confront him at once, the film approaches its climax. In a scene that presages Babe Bennett's telephone conversation to Longfellow Deeds, Phyllis confirms she was in Cluett's apartment at the time of the robbery. Just before, the board of directors had refused to deposit enough money to stave off the bank run, pressing instead for the merger. And Dickson's faith in character is challenged: for a time he feels Matt betrayed his trust, then learns that both Phyllis and Cluett did. With all these problems converging, Dickson even considers suicide, which Capra

shows by following Dickson as he places his picture of Phyllis into
his desk drawer. The camera then dollies in to a close-up of a
handgun in it. When Phyllis rushes into the office, the camera
subjectively pans to find Dickson silhouetted despondently before
his window, a scene which recurs in *Mr. Deeds* and *Mr. Smith*.
Only Phyllis's explanations and the arrival of the dependable small
businessmen revive his faith and resolve, at least temporarily, the
three problems which face him.

American Madness presents with precision and power several
dilemmas quite common in American culture: the contrary pulls of
occupational and familial responsibility, the ideal claims and harsher
realities of the success ethic, and, as John Raeburn has elucidated
so well in his essay on the film, the danger that a society based on
the fullest freedom for people can lead, especially in times of crisis,
to mob action. In treating these cultural dilemmas, Capra was raising
issues he would deal with later, particularly in *It's a Wonderful Life*
and *State of the Union* (at times Tom Dickson seems very close to
George Bailey and Grant Matthews). Here in *American Madness*
we first perceive Capra's particularly skillful ability to deal with the
dilemmas of American culture. Arguing that the happy ending of
American Madness only "nominally" resolves the tension between
Tom Dickson's individualist values and the actions of the mob who
create the bank run, John Raeburn concludes that "it is the verve
and subtlety with which this tension is made palpable that gives the
film its significance as both a social document and an important
work of the imagination" (FC, 67). Capra's first full collaboration
with Riskin surely constituted an auspicious start.

But *American Madness* received no Oscar nominations and
Capra—concerned about "winning the grail"—turned to *The Bitter
Tea of General Yen*. His only film of the early 1930s not set in
America and the only one after 1932 not scripted by Riskin, *The
Bitter Tea* was produced by Walter Wanger and scripted by Edward
Paramore. Capra tells us part of the reason he agreed to do the
project was because it seemed to him an "arty" subject that would
appeal to Academy voters. Though it didn't—*Bitter Tea* received
no nominations—Capra still calls it "one of *my* pet pictures" (NATT,
140–42). And it certainly has a very different setting, subject, and
feel from all the other films treated in this chapter.

The film is set in China, at first in Shanghai, later in General
Yen's palace. In its Eastern setting and its *mise-en-scène, Bitter Tea*

resembles only *Lost Horizon* among the Capra films. Its visual texture seems to come from von Sternberg. The subject is the confrontation between two people of widely different cultural traditions: a New England missionary filled with Christian zeal and a Chinese warlord whose apparent mixture of brutality and poetic serenity both repulses and fascinates her. As the film progresses, the missionary gradually lifts the veil of her provincialism and begins to see the warlord not as a stereotype but as another human being. Though it is common in Capra films for one character first to spurn another and then gradually to convert to that person's perspective, in no other Capra films are the perspectives so culturally different than in *The Bitter Tea*.

The missionary, Megan Davis (Barbara Stanwyck), arrives in Shanghai at the beginning of the film. She's come to China to marry a childhood sweetheart, Dr. Robert Strike, and to rescue Chinese orphans amidst the civil disorder. She and her fellow missionaries are initially presented as extremely provincial in their total lack of sensitivity to Chinese cultural traditions. In her first confrontation with Yen, Megan sees a car run over the man pulling her rickshaw. When the military-clad Yen emerges from the car and seems little bothered by the accident, saying, "Human life is the cheapest thing in China," Megan is shocked. "He is fortunate," Yen adds. "Life at its best is hardly endurable." At her wedding, Megan asks about this curious incident, but a woman mouths the extreme missionary stereotype. All Chinese, she says, are "tricky, treacherous, and immoral. I can't tell one from another."

But the wedding is postponed while Megan and her fiancé attempt to rescue some orphans. Yen issues a false pass, scorning Strike's foolishness for putting off his marriage. In a frenzied crowd Megan is separated from Strike, barely saved by Yen, and taken to his palace, the setting for the remainder of the film. There the mixture of brutality and appreciation of beauty continues. While Megan is given breakfast and flowers in an opulent bedroom, the cracks of rifles indicate executions outdoors. When Yen apologizes for them, Megan—confused and afraid—calls her host a "yellow swine." From this point on Megan's stereotypes begin to break down.

A skillfully presented dream sequence—rare in Capra's work—conveys Megan's ambivalent attitude toward Yen. In it Megan is awakened by a stereotypic Chinese fiend with buck teeth and long fingernails. As he prepares to rape her, a masked man in Western garb enters and saves her. The man removes his mask to reveal the handsome features of Yen. The two embrace and kiss, ending the dream. Clearly Megan is attracted to Yen, yet refuses to admit that his cultural background has anything to do with his appeal.

While Megan becomes fascinated with the enigmatic Yen, he prizes her for her beauty. Living in a harsh, brutalized society, Yen has learned to prize beautiful objects and human beauty as one stay against the confusion of his world. As Megan struggles to shed some of her preconceptions, Yen compromises his own principles by granting Megan's request to let her be responsible for Mah-li, one of Yen's servants. But he believes that he will "convert a missionary." As Yen expected, Megan's do-goodism and ethic of forgiveness backfire: Mah-li passes along information that leads to Yen's financial ruin and eventual loss of power. But instead of seeking retribution, Yen is stoic. As Jones, Yen's financial advisor, says, Yen can "take it on the chin."

Resigned to death, Yen tells Megan he wants her love but only if she gives it wholeheartedly. In the climax of the film, Megan dresses in silken Chinese clothes (for the second time; the first time she quickly changed back) and goes to Yen's tea room. In the meantime Yen has poured poison into a glistening, brilliant teapot. In a restrained, nearly ritualistic fashion, Yen looks at the statue of an ancestor while Megan weeps at his feet. He drinks his tea, assured in his belief in immortality, and dies within seconds, a resolution unlike that in any of Capra's other films.

The final scene presents a coda. While Megan and Jones are sailing on a boat headed for Shanghai, a relaxing, light melody plays in the background. It's the same theme first played on a phonograph when Megan goes to see Yen after Mah-li's betrayal, and later during the suicide scene. Jones, half drunk—and like Connell in *Meet John Doe,* a half-doubting cynic—rambles on about Yen: "Yen was crazy. He said we never really die. We only change . . . . Maybe he's a cherry tree now . . . . Maybe he's the wind that's playing around your hair. Oh, it's all a lot of hooey. . . . Just the same I hope when I cool off, the guy that changes me sends me where Yen is. And I bet I'll find you there too." Capra ends this most curious of all his films with a close-up of Megan. Her radiant expression tempers the tragedy of Yen's death, for it reveals her love for him and her hopes that his transcendent faith was true. Leland Poague has suggested that Yen and Megan are typical Capra characters, finding fulfillment

Photos from *The Bitter Tea of General Yen*: (top) costume and culture separate Megan Davis (Barbara Stanwyck) from General Yen (Nils Asther) in a film notable for (bottom) its exotic *mise-en-scène*

in love freely given, but that the warring world of the film has no place for their "emotional honesty."[6] If we consider the relationships between Gallagher and Stew Smith, Peter Warne and Ellie Andrews, George Bailey and Mary Hatch, or a number of other Capra lovers, we can begin to see what Poague means.

The Bitter Tea received no Oscar nominations. Capra's next film, *Lady for a Day*, did: for best picture, actress, director, and writing. Scripted again by Riskin, *Lady for a Day* combined the contrast between rich and commoner in *Platinum Blonde* and the topical references to the Depression in *American Madness*, emerging with an irresistible fairy tale about human kindness and good will. Though the film won none of those Oscars, Capra liked the story enough to remake it in his last film, *A Pocketful of Miracles* (1961).

The story was perfectly tailored for movie audiences during the Depression. The main character, Apple Annie (May Robson), is a kindly, shrewd old woman who makes ends meet by selling apples and by "taxing" her employees: other down-and-outs who sell pencils or wave tin cups on the streets of New York. From the start of the film, the beggers stress how hard times really are. Surely one of the reasons for its success and the relative failure of *Pocketful of Miracles* stems from the story's topicality in 1933 and lack of it in 1961.

The story line is pure and simple. Apple Annie has a daughter, Louise, being educated in Spain. Louise believes her mother is a wealthy dowager, Mrs. E. Worthington Manville (Annie has a friend working in an elegant hotel pick up her mail). When Louise writes Annie of her engagement to the son of a Spanish nobleman, Count Romero, the problems begin, for before the wedding plans can be made the Count and his son must visit Annie in her New York home. Annie needs a savior—fast—and he appears in the person of Dave the Dude, a gangster who attributes his good fortune to Annie's good-luck apples. Marshaling all his forces, Dave finds Annie a tailor, a hairdresser, a penthouse, and a husband, "Judge" Blake (memorably played by Guy Kibbee). The guests arrive, and matters proceed smoothly until newsmen get suspicious and the Count requests a reception to meet friends of the family.

Dave the Dude finds solutions to both problems. He has the reporters locked up, planning to keep them out of the picture until the Count leaves. He also plans a reception to be peopled by his carefully trained and dressed friends and associates (the only thing separating the rich and the poor are elegant clothes and polished phrases). On the night of the reception, as the cagey Judge bilks the Count at the billiard tables, Dave is arrested, suspected of kidnapping reporters, and his trainees are kept from the reception. However, Dave pleads his case to the police chief, the mayor, and the governor; when they understand Dave's motives, they not only free Dave and his companions, but they even attend the reception themselves. The party is a great success, Annie is radiant, the Count, his son, and Louise return to Spain, and Mrs. E. Worthington Manville again becomes Apple Annie. Everyone, as in fairy tales, lives happily ever after.

Tightly structured, quickly moving, and entertaining, *Lady for a Day* is much more fluid than Capra's meandering wide-screen remake. (*Lady* runs only eighty-eight minutes, nearly fifty minutes shorter than *Pocketful.*) The performances—particularly those of Robson, Kibbee, and Walter Connolly (the Count)—are also strong. The film satisfied audiences: a *New York Times* reviewer called it "a merry tale with touches of sentiment, a picture which evoked laughter and tears." And Raymond Carney sees it as a key Capra film, in which "visionary dreaming and pragmatic scheming" (or transcendent yearnings versus social conflicts, concerns kept separate in earlier Capra films) are blended for the first time.[7] Instead of visionary films like *Forbidden* and *Bitter Tea* or social tension films like *The Miracle Woman* and *American Madness*, Carney argues, Capra began to blend the two in *Lady* and continued to do so in many later films.

Following *Lady for a Day*, Capra and Riskin set out to adapt "Night Bus," a long story of a romance that develops between an heiress and a worldly commoner on a trip from Miami to New York. It hardly looked like a promising subject—a couple of bus films had recently bombed at the box office, despite the increasing popularity of bus travel. Returning from MGM—he had been loaned there by Columbia—when Louie B. Mayer canceled *Soviet*, Capra convinced Cohn to let him go ahead with the project. After several actresses turned down the script, Capra and Riskin rewrote it, transforming Peter Warne from a Greenwich Village painter into a sharp-tongued reporter, a character much more sympathetic to audiences. When MGM assigned Clark Gable to Columbia for one film—he was in Mayer's doghouse—Capra had his Peter Warne. To play Ellie Andrews, the beautiful yet spoiled heiress, Capra recruited Claudette Colbert, but under her stipulation that shooting should or must be

Photo from *Lady for a Day*: Apple Annie as Mrs. E. Worthington Manville

completed two days before Christmas, hardly a month later. So, roughly between Thanksgiving and Christmas 1933, shooting on a modest budget which demanded a good deal of exterior footage, Capra, his crew, and his cast rollicked through *It Happened One Night* (NATT, 159–72). By February 23, 1934, the film was released to both critical and popular acclaim in New York, and at the 1935 Academy Awards ceremony the film—as Capra is fond of saying in discussions—"shook the Oscar tree."

The story of *It Happened One Night* is well known. After Ellie Andrews escapes from her father's yacht, she buys a bus ticket in Miami, hoping to travel incognito to New York to marry the wealthy King Westley. On the bus, the brash newsman Peter Warne discovers who she is, smells a story, and agrees to escort her to New York in exchange for a scoop. As they ride the bus, spend a night in a motel cabin separated by a blanket flung over a rope ("the Walls of Jericho"), do some hitchhiking, and stop at another cabin just outside New York, Ellie's pretensions break down, and Peter begins to see her inner warmth. But complications arise: Ellie mistakes Peter's evening trip to New York as a rejection, whereas Peter had gone to write a story on their impending marriage and to collect enough money for a honeymoon. Much to the chagrin of Alexander Andrews, Ellie's father, the day of her marriage to Westley arrives. But just before her vows, Ellie—who has learned from her father of Peter's love—reconsiders and flees from the altar to a waiting car. Andrews pays off Westley, and, in a remote motel cabin, the Walls of Jericho go tumbling down.

One of the most appealing aspects of *It Happened One Night* is its casual, almost improvisatory humor, conveyed convincingly by a wonderful cast and rendered skillfully by Capra's camera. Recall for a moment some of the humorous scenes: Ellie Andrews jumps from her yacht. She falls asleep aloof and apart from Peter, and wakes up with her head on his shoulder. Oscar B. Shapely annoys Ellie on the bus ("when a cool mama gets hot, she really sizzles, believe you me"). Before investigators in their cabin, Peter and Ellie feign an argument as husband and wife. While riding along, bus passengers sing "The Daring Young Man on the Flying Trapeze." An obnoxious singing driver ("Young people in love are very seldom hungry") serenades the lovers, then steals their suitcase. King Westley arrives on his wedding day in an autogyro. Nearly all the humor in the film either mocks the pretensions and impulsiveness of the rich, celebrates the warmth of common life, or basks in the behavior of a real "character" like Shapely.

The shift of Gable's character to a confident vernacular news reporter was a key one; it provided Capra with an ideal narrative situation. A middle-class representative hero, familiar with the ways of common life, manages to teach those ways to a snobbish woman. Ellie doesn't know how to dunk a doughnut. She misunderstands what a "piggyback" ride is, presumably because of her deprived upper-class roots. Though hungry, she won't at first consider eating raw carrots, and the notion of hitchhiking is completely new to her. But—and this is key—Ellie is willing to learn and to experience. A viewer may think for a time that she's merely slumming, but it gradually becomes clear that Ellie feels more alive away from the butlers, maids, yachts, mansions, champagne, and caviar of her normal effete surroundings. And as Ellie changes she begins to fit Peter's requirements for a lover: she's "real" and "alive." Though their differences are less distinct than Megan's and General Yen's, Ellie and Peter go through the same process of shedding pretensions and preconceptions on the path toward love.

It Happened One Night is one of the earliest and one of the purest "screwball comedies." Not accidentally, Peter tells Alexander Andrews after professing his love for Ellie, "Don't hold that against me. I'm a little screwy myself." Andrew Bergman has argued that the screwball comedy as a form served a distinct social function. At a time of cultural uncertainty, the screwball comedies "became a means of unifying what had been splintered or divided. Their 'whackiness' cemented social classes and broken marriages . . . . Screwball comedy was implosive: it worked to pull things together" (FC, 69). Because *It Happened One Night* rejects the desire to be politically topical—as *American Madness* was and most Capra films between 1936 and 1948 would be—Bergman's thesis works quite well. Alexander Edwards may be rich, but he's also benign, happy to welcome a sensible lad like Peter into the family. By the end of the film, Westley is happy—he's paid off. So is Ellie's father, for he would much rather have an energetic, sensible person like Peter marry Ellie than, in his own words, "a mug like Westley." The common people seem relaxed and secure in the film: the only hint of the Depression comes when Ellie gives her money to a woman and small boy on the bus who are faint from hunger. But generally the casual good humor and community spirit

Photos from the epochal *It Happened One Night*: (top) the democratic hero, Peter Warne (Clark Gable) eats raw carrots, but Ellie Andrews (Claudette Colbert) won't yet; (bottom) the famous "Walls of Jericho" separate the lovers temporarily, but lead to an Academy Award sweep

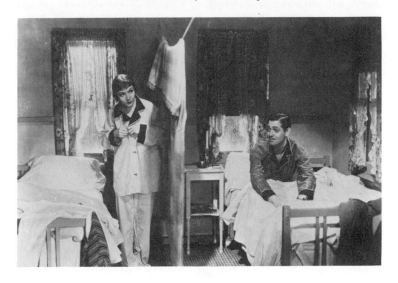

in the background of the film are best suggested by the scene where, as elsewhere in his films, Capra has characters sing. Though the songs don't further the narrative, they do help warm the audience to the characters. And—as I've suggested—they help to unify rather than divide. Finally, Ellie and Peter are reconciled at the end of the film, a fact made so much more satisfying because it seems so desirable and so unlikely during the last quarter of the film.

After searching for a successful story line which would satisfy audiences, the industry, and himself, Capra finally found it with *It Happened One Night*. In it, the hero is a middle-class representative American. With his "common sense" and understated moral charisma, he has the ability to convert or even redeem those who know him well—in this case, Ellie and (to some extent) her father. By making this figure both a romantic hero and a moral spokesman who converts the heroine to his perspective, Capra hit on a structural center that would animate many of his best films. Though Stew Smith was a romantic and moral character, he couldn't convert the rich. In both *American Madness* and *Lady for a Day*, the romance was relegated to subplot. *The Bitter Tea of General Yen* deviated from the American scene. Finally, with *It Happened One Night* Capra hit on a powerfully effective way to express his own moral inclinations within a feature film. With variations he would return to that same situation in most of his features until 1948.

Perhaps because *It Happened One Night* succeeded so completely, Capra's next film, *Broadway Bill*, has been neglected. Made and released between *It Happened One Night* and the 1935 Academy Awards ceremony, the film was another Riskin-Capra collaboration done before the pair was pressured to make another hit as huge as *It Happened One Night*. In his autobiography Capra only mentions it in passing—and then in reference to the remake, *Riding High*—which is unfortunate, since it's clearly another example of the Riskin-Capra team developing their storytelling skills.

The central conflict of the story is presented economically at the beginning. The opening shot is of a sign: "Welcome to Higginsville, population 20,339." We cut to a second sign: "Jeremiah Higgins: 1834–1897. Founder of Higginsville," after which the camera tilts up to reveal a statue of this august personage. Rapidly, Capra and editor Gene Havlick wipe to the Higgins National Bank (J. L. Higgins, President), the J. L. Higgins Iron Works, the J. L. Higgins Lamp Shade Company, and the J. L. Higgins Paper Box Company.

Each of J. L. Higgins's sons-in-law runs one of the businesses; we learn that Dan Brooks (Warner Baxter), president of the paper box company, is out training horses instead of working.

Thus from the opening images we see the conflict. Out at the training grounds, J. L.'s only unmarried daughter, Alice (Myrna Loy), tells Dan: "It doesn't make sense. Your heart and soul are in horses and you're making paper boxes . . . . You've been dying to get out of Higginsville ever since you got here." Later at dinner J. L. sits at the head of the table, husbands on the left, wives on the right, all in formal attire, visually representing the stifling atmosphere of the life-style. J. L. announces his purchase of the lumber company, telling Alice she should marry so he'll have someone to run it. Dan, who feels he's "dying a slow death" away from the tracks, challenges J. L.: "You're only interested in one thing—accumulating money, expanding the Higgins enterprises, and gobbling up the little fella." Though his wife, Margaret, is upset with Dan's outburst, Alice is pleased, and Dan decides to return to the life he really loves—the racing world.

From there, the story traces the difficulties encountered in getting Dan's horse, Broadway Bill, trained and registered for the big race. Alice comes to lend support, as do Dan's trainer, Whitey (Clarence Muse), Colonel Pettigrew (Raymond Walburn), and a host of others. After numerous snags, Broadway Bill finally wins the race but collapses after crossing the finish line, the victim, a vet announces, of a burst heart. After a sentimental funeral at the track—the racing commissioner calls Bill a "lesson in courage and loyalty," bringing tears even to crusty gamblers—Dan returns to the Higgins mansion and claims Alice—his "Princess in the dark castle." J. L., who's decided he's "a man, not a whale who gobbles up minnows," has sold his companies "back to the people that founded them," and tells his other sons-in-law to look for work. When he sees their dour responses, he heads out the door and follows Alice to Dan's car, all setting c 1t for the racing world.

However improbable the story, *Broadway Bill* is notable for a number of reasons. Dan Brooks is very similar to Stew Smith in *Platinum Blonde*; he's a middle-class American drawn into the world of wealth, only to feel that he's become a "social parasite," thereupon rejecting the way of life. Unlike Stew Smith, however, Dan Brooks even convinces his rich father-in-law that making money is not the measure of a man's worth or his peace of mind. Like the later Capra heroes, Dan Brooks can convert at least some doubters through his words and actions.

Broadway Bill also reveals a control of character, narrative, and tone which Otis Ferguson aptly described as an "incidental human worth and naturalness" (FC, 101–102). In comedy, Capra had moved beyond the gag humor of *The Strong Man* to build humor on character and situation. Probably the best example in *Broadway Bill* is when Dan and the Colonel dine at the Ritz Hotel. Both dress elegantly, both are broke, and both expect the other to pay. To extricate themselves, they engineer an "accident," getting a waiter to spill soup on them, gaining their free meal in the process. The human warmth of the film extends to other comic scenes, as well as to the romance. From the start Alice admires Dan, and like later Capra heroines supports Dan during his moments of self-doubt. Just as it takes Stew Smith a long time to recognize Gallagher's attractiveness, so Dan fails to realize his spiritual kinship to Alice until near the film's conclusion. When he does, he gratifies both Alice and the audience.

Capra's films from the early 1930s reveal at least two of his abilities as a director. The first is his ability to get strong performances from all his actors. Robert Williams was little known before *Platinum Blonde,* yet turned in a superior performance. May Robson in *Lady for a Day* played her first screen role and deserved her Oscar nomination. Gable and Colbert established an ideal for romantic comedy acting rarely matched in American screen comedy. Even Warner Baxter—just off "a sad succession of recent duds," according to Ferguson—is relaxed and convincing (FC, 102). Add to this Capra's ability to get star performances from even the bit players, and it's clear that this is one of several reasons for Capra's success with audiences in the 1930s.

Another reason stems from the tendency to celebrate the common life of Americans and to belittle the life of leisure. Rising from the common life himself, Capra knew and believed in its vitality. So the wealthy in Capra's films in the 1930s don't come off well unless they admit the virtues of the middle-class heroes. Though this criticism of wealth might seem radical to some viewers, it really isn't. In fact, it's a good example of a common phenomenon in American film during the 1930s and 1940s and present even today which, following *Citizen Kane,* we can call "the Rosebud syndrome."[8] The Rosebud syndrome admits the unequal distribution of wealth and

Photo from *Broadway Bill*: Dan Brooks (Warner Baxter) and "the Princess" (Myrna Loy) enjoy life at the racetrack

power in America but asserts that the wealthy are unhappy people and that real satisfaction can only be found in the common life-styles of most of us, the audience. Such a position, it seems to me, is much more therapeutic than radical: it makes us happy that we're poor and serene rather than rich and alienated. In times of depression or any severe economic decline, the Rosebud syndrome is particularly attractive because the chances for upward financial mobility are less likely than usual, and we need to be happy with what we have. In his early 1930s films Capra defended characters who were much more concerned with having fulfilling lives and close human ties than with accumulating wealth. And he did it with such skill, such humor, and such human warmth that it's easy to see that his film-making apprenticeship was over.

4

"The Ecumenical Church of Humanism" (1936–41)

THE FIRST few years after the Stock Market crash posed severe challenges to traditional American values and attitudes. The breakdown of the economy, characterized by a drastic decline in productivity and a rise in unemployment to well over a quarter of the work force, shook people's faith in free enterprise, competition, individualism, and hard work. With the economy at a virtual standstill, certitudes shattered for some like a light bulb dropped on the sidewalk. Though some intellectuals began to search for alternatives, often attributing the problem to industrialism or capitalism and proposing various solutions, by the time of Roosevelt's inauguration in 1933 the dominant cultural tone was one of anxiety and uncertainty.[1]

Yet, as the decade wore on, various events began to mend the torn fabric of the American cultural mythology. Successful implementation of various New Deal legislation—the Wagner Act, Social Security Act—and the establishment of such programs as the WPA, CCC, and Federal Theater Project served to restore the confidence of many Americans in their government. Likewise, the growing power and threat of fascism in Spain, Italy, and Nazi Germany became increasingly evident in the mid- and late-1930s. The Communist party's Popular Front policy (1935–39) of cooperation with any anti-Fascist forces led, in America, at least, to the existence of a large, relatively nonideological yet unified group of middle-of-the-road and leftist people working together to oppose fascism. As so

Photo (left): James Stewart as Jefferson Smith, one of Capra's mythic American heroes of the late 1930s

often happens, a group threatened from the outside began to pull together itself.[2]

As that Fascist threat began to seem more apparent and more severe, many Americans began to feel that the cultural uncertainty fostered by the Depression was dangerous. America, many felt, needed to define its fundamental and essential principles. Robert Sklar defines this impulse: "In politics, industry and the media there were men and women, as often of liberal as conservative persuasion, who saw the necessity, almost as a patriotic duty, to revitalize and refashion a cultural mythology."[3] This effort to revivify American myths was as strong in Hollywood as in any other area of American life in the late 1930s, and no Hollywood director so consciously and skillfully treated American myths then as did Frank Capra.

These were Capra's peak years as a prestigious and successful director in Hollywood. After sweeping the Academy Awards with *It Happened One Night*, Capra had solidified his creative autonomy to choose his projects and make them as he saw fit. He had earned the respect of the film industry generally: in 1935 he was elected president of the Motion Picture Academy and in 1938 he became president of the Screen Directors' Guild. He served in both posts through 1939. The industry also honored his films: his five films between 1936 and 1941 were nominated for thirty-one Oscars, winning six, including two for best director and one for best film. Outside the industry Capra was also known. His films were widely reviewed, usually favorably, and they all were strong at the box office, especially *Mr. Smith Goes to Washington*, which earned the second-largest domestic box-office gross in 1939. Only *Gone With the Wind* earned more. Even the popular press honored him; in 1938 his picture appeared on the cover of *Time* magazine, the ultimate legitimation of American celebrity in the 1930s.

Most of this recognition and attention was earned, for Capra's films during these years develop a remarkably consistent social vision and exhibit a firm mastery of film language. Capra had finally arrived: he knew what he wanted to say and how to say it. It is no surprise that much of the best criticism of Capra's work focuses wholly or largely on Capra's five films in this half-decade: *Mr. Deeds Goes to Town* (1936), *Lost Horizon* (1937), *You Can't Take It With You* (1938), *Mr. Smith Goes to Washington* (1939), and *Meet John Doe* (1941).[4]

One major reason for the unity and power of Capra's social vision in the late 1930s stems from Capra's own life. In 1935, after the tremendous success of *It Happened One Night* earned Capra the Oscar he had so desperately sought, he began to have self-doubts about his talents. Unsure of how to follow up on *It Happened One Night*, Capra first feigned sickness, then actually became seriously ill with some undiagnosed malady which led him to lose over thirty pounds and to suffer constantly from a high fever.

But then Capra experienced an incident that deeply affected his self-perception as a filmmaker and fundamentally shaped the feature films he would make through *Meet John Doe* (1941). As Capra describes it in his autobiography, one day during his illness, languishing in his home, he was visited by a nameless man. Accusing Capra of vanity and egotism, the man told Capra that he could exert a strong positive influence through his films and that he was an offense to God and humanity if he neglected to do so. Though the man quickly left, Capra was intensely moved, experiencing what should probably be called a conversion experience. The director who had earlier boasted that he could shoot a successful film with the phone book as a script became committed: "Beginning with *Mr. Deeds Goes to Town* my films had to *say* something. . . . No more would I accept scripts hurriedly written. . . . From then on my scripts would take from six months to a year to write and rewrite; to carefully—and subtly—integrate ideals and entertainment into a meaningful tale. And regardless of the origin of a film idea—I made it mine" (NATT, 185).

What was the substance of Capra's social vision? Though he had been called an advocate of nearly every political position imaginable—from communism to fascism, capitalism to socialism, and McCarthyism to New Dealism—none can adequately define the main thrust of Capra's social vision (even though many do describe some situations, characters, or dialogue in individual Capra films). In essence, Capra's films in the late 1930s and early 1940s are strongly shaped by both Christian and American values. To understand the influences of both helps to get to the center of Capra's vision.

Capra was raised a Roman Catholic, though he drifted from regular church ritual in his years of early manhood. In his autobiography he describes himself as having been a "Christmas Catholic" at the time he began directing *The Strong Man*. Later, he mentions attending a Christian Science church for a time in the mid-1930s and being influenced by its optimistic theology for much longer. Perhaps his most explicit statement of religious conviction comes later in the book, when he tells a group of scientists that he is a "Catholic in spirit; one who firmly believes that the anti-moral, the intellectual bigots, and the Mafias of ill will may destroy religion, but they will never conquer the cross" (NATT, 67, 179, 443).

Clearly Capra is not a systematic theologian. But he is a moralist, concerned about questions of good and evil, and rules of humane conduct. His understanding of how his religious convictions related to his films is indicated by a response to a student question which I heard him make in 1978. After a film showing, one student told Capra that John Doe was clearly a Christ figure and *Meet John Doe*, a Catholic film. Accordingly, the student believed that John Doe should have died at the end of the film (then be reborn symbolically through the John Doe clubs) to make the story consistent. Capra considered the question, then replied that he never believed in explicitly defending or expressing in his films the doctrines of any particular religious denomination. "We all," he concluded, "can worship in the ecumenical church called Humanism."[5]

This refusal to defend explicit religious doctrine extends to politics. Instead of defending Republican or Democratic or Socialist political positions, Capra's films in the 1930s, especially later in the decade, defended American nationalism. A man who had been rewarded with prestige and success within the American economic system, Capra was clearly thankful for it. After his fortieth birthday, he tells us in his autobiography, he made a vow to create "films about America and its people; films that would be my way of saying, 'Thanks, America'" (NATT, 240). Quite clearly, therefore, a Christian and American mythology animates Capra's films from the late 1930s on, though the films are not doctrinaire, instead expressing the values of what Capra accurately described as the "ecumenical church called humanism."

In some senses, then, Capra's films were "message" films in an industry which generally believed all messages should be left to Western Union. These message films succeeded for at least two reasons. The first is that Capra consistently retained comedy in his films. In an interview Capra explained that "I use comedy to . . . warm people to my subject. I don't say, 'Now I'm going to tell you a moral tale and you'd better like it.' No, first I entertain then I get them in a spirit of laughter and then, perhaps, they might be softened up to accept some kind of moral precept. But entertainment comes first."[6] By disarming his audiences with comedy, Capra made his moral thrust more palatable.

But the messages succeeded for another reason. Between 1936 and 1941, Capra's social vision projected a mythology to a culture that, for historical and cultural reasons outlined above, hungered for an affirmation of the very social values Capra believed in. Capra's case in the half-decade before Pearl Harbor provides a rare and fascinating example of a film director almost perfectly attuned to his audience. Though his vision was less palatable after World War II, for a time Capra created moral fables which created and resolved human conflict in a way that clearly responded to the psychic needs and desires of his audiences. Yet since the social vision of Capra's late 1930s films is important only insofar as it is embodied in them, it is to those films we must now turn. Capra's first effort after his conversion, *Mr. Deeds Goes to Town,* is in many ways the purest and cleanest example of Capra's new approach to filmmaking. In it he established a narrative pattern that he would return to, with minor variations, in all of his next four films save *Lost Horizon.*

That narrative pattern consists of four conventions. The first is a Capra hero, who combines several traits. He is an idealist who defends American political ideals and the Christian injunction to love thy neighbor. Though he holds these strong convictions, the Capra hero is often untested. He has a childlike innocence (related to Langdon's comic persona) that more worldly and experienced people scoff at and take advantage of when the Capra hero is placed, as he usually is, in a strange environment. Though challenges to his social vision lead the hero to moments of self-doubt, the Capra hero emerges, in Robert Sklar's apt phrase, as "a man of unusual will and imagination," able successfully to articulate and defend his values against the greedy, cynical, and spiritually decayed (FC, 130).

The second convention is the Capra heroine. After the Hays Code began to be more rigorously enforced in 1934, many working women—strong, competent, and energetic—began to appear on movie screens. Capra's heroines were such working women, usually reporters or secretaries played by either Jean Arthur or Barbara Stanwyck. The heroine generally responds cynically to the naive hero early in the film, takes advantage of him, then gradually converts to his idealistic vision of the world. This conversion is made more believable by having the heroine mention that her father was a humane, altruistic doctor or that her small-town background provided her with the same values as the hero (or both). By the end of the film the heroine supports the hero during his moments of self-doubt: her declaration of love at a crucial moment of the narrative gives him part of the strength he needs to carry on.

The third convention relates to plot rather than character: the ritual humiliation of the hero. Placed in a foreign environment, the hero is made to look foolish by the villain or villains, often with the cooperation of the media. The villains, who become increasingly powerful and threatening between 1936 and 1941, are spiritual descendants of Hornsby in *The Miracle Woman*, all characterized by a lust for power and wealth. The media, in contrast, are more nearly neutral. Their function is to make the private actions of the hero public. Challenged by the villain who uses the media for his advantage, the Capra hero is humiliated at some public forum—a courtroom, a Senate chamber, a ball park. Most often, the humiliation results in part from the betrayal of the hero by someone he trusts, usually the heroine.

The ritual humiliation prepares for the final convention—the ritual victory, in which the Capra hero takes forceful action to overcome his self-doubt, affirm the values in which he believes, and emerge with his social vision intact. Two important character types participate in the ritual victory. The first is a benevolent authority figure—a judge, the vice-president—who supports the hero in moments of crisis. In one sense this figure is a metaphorical God (or FDR), looking with approving eyes over the hero's shoulder. The second character type is multiple: a crowd of common people who publicly support the hero and, implicitly, his values. The crowd here functions in some ways as the representatives of us, the movie audience. With the support of the benevolent authority and the crowd, the Capra hero emerges at the end vindicated, assured that his values are infinitely superior to those of the people who sought to undermine him.

Though elements of this narrative pattern do vary in Capra's four American films between 1936 and 1941, they are present in the purest form in *Mr. Deeds Goes to Town*. The hero is Longfellow Deeds (Gary Cooper) from Mandrake Falls, Vermont, who inherits $20 million at the start of the film and goes to New York to manage the estate. Deeds's connections to Christian mythology are stressed by the fact that he is the son of Joseph and Mary Deeds (the names are changed from the story "Opera Hat," on which the film is based) and that he is the owner of a tallow works (providing light for the world). He is linked to American traditions when he visits Grant's Tomb, solemnly affirming American opportunity, and when he quotes Thoreau on the gap between American material and spiritual achievement. His innocence is stressed by his childish enthusiasm for fire trucks, his almost chivalric conception of love (as romantic as Harry in *Long Pants*, Deeds is waiting to save a "lady in distress"), and his utter inability to fathom the manners and attitudes of the city vultures with whom he comes into contact. One of those vultures, the shyster lawyer Cedar who seeks to bilk Deeds of his fortune, explicitly sums it up. "He's as naive," he gleefully tells his colleagues early in the film, "as a child."

Another of the vultures—at least for a time—is Babe Bennett (Jean Arthur), the Capra heroine. A Pulitzer prize winning reporter known for her relentless pursuit of a headline, Babe impersonates an unemployed secretary to win Deeds's confidence, then writes biased exclusive stories mocking him as the "Cinderella Man." But as she spends more time around him, Babe begins to reconsider her amoral cynicism. In a key scene, unable to write another story, Babe confides to her roommate: "That guy's either the dumbest, stupidest, most imbecilic idiot in the world or he's the grandest thing alive." Regretfully admitting she's "crucifying" Deeds, Babe goes on: "Here's a guy who's wholesome, fresh. To us he looks like a freak. He's got goodness, Mabel . . . but we're too busy being smart alecs" to notice. As time goes on, Babe becomes totally convinced of Deeds's goodness, marshaling the support of newsmen and the public when Deeds is accused of insanity for attempting to give away his fortune to unemployed farmers.

The ritual humiliation and victory are clear in *Mr. Deeds*. The humiliation takes place in three stages: first Babe betrays Deeds and humiliates him in her stories. When he learns of her betrayal and decides to return home, Deeds is humiliated by an unemployed farmer who breaks into his house and accuses Deeds of being a "money-grubbing hick," unconcerned about the suffering of those around him. (This scene, reminiscent of the nameless man who shamed Capra a year earlier, provides a good example of the "submerged autobiography" that works itself into a number of Capra's films between 1936 and 1948.) This leads Deeds to formulate a plan that would give 2,000 ten-acre, fully equipped farms to unemployed Depression farmers. But then comes the final and most devastating humiliation: Cedar has Deeds locked in the County Hospital, accused of insanity, and Deeds lapses into a battered, heart-torn silence.

That silence continues for the bulk of the insanity hearing. There Cedar has stacked a case against Deeds, eliciting damaging testimony from city cynics and snobs, an effete psychologist, and even two eccentric old women from Mandrake Falls (whose behavior added at least temporarily to the language the word "pixilated"). But, goaded by Babe Bennett's declaration of love, supported by H. B. Warner's kindly judge and the urgent pleas of the common people in the gallery, Deeds breaks his silence, explains his position articulately, and even manages to land a punch squarely on Cedar's nose. After deliberating, the Judge declares Deeds "not only sane, but the sanest man in the courtroom." The final shot, accompanied by the strains of "For He's a Jolly Good Fellow" and "Auld Lang Syne," both Capra favorites, shows Babe in Deeds's arms: the hero has won not only his freedom but also, presumably, a wife.

One reason for the success of *Mr. Deeds* is the engaging narrative pattern, but another reason, closely related, is the implicit value structure endorsed by the film through Deeds. We have already noted Capra's tendency to use topical issues in his films. In *Deeds,* the problem of unemployment during the Depression is powerfully raised by the man who bursts into Deeds's mansion and castigates him. Deeds's solution to what is essentially a political problem —a potentially explosive issue which could easily have alienated part of the audience—provides a good example of Capra's Christian/American humanism.

Deeds's solution is conservative in ideology, liberal in sentiment. The plan to give away 2,000 separate ten-acre farms to individual farmers is almost Jeffersonian: it would have created 2,000 yeoman farmers, each with a stake in society. Since Deeds's plan proposed voluntary (not governmentally imposed) redistribution of wealth, one can only conclude that it encouraged traditional American values of individualism, self-help (the farmers would be given the land if they worked it for three years), and voluntary philanthropy. On the other hand, Deeds's concern for the plight of the poor and unemployed, as well as his willingness to aid them, paralleled closely the humane concern which many of Capra's audience per-

Photos from *Mr. Deeds Goes to Town*: (top) Longfellow Deeds (Gary Cooper) in a romantic moment with Babe Bennett (Jean Arthur), and a hostile moment (bottom) with shyster lawyer Cedar (Douglas Dumbrille)

ceived in various New Deal programs that gave jobs or financial assistance to the ill-fed and ill-housed. Because Deeds's proposal is both liberal (in its concern for humans) and conservative (in its implicit acceptance of individualism and other traditional American values), the film at times seems to support and at other times to reject the New Deal, confusing both contemporary reviewers and later critics. But the position is at the core of Capra's humanism.[7]

Recalling his intentions in making *Mr. Deeds*, Capra wrote that he sought to show how "a simple honest man can, if he will, reach deep down into his God-given resources and come up with necessary handfuls of courage, wit, and love to triumph over his environment" (NATT, 186). By so clearly setting Deeds's generosity, innocence, and honesty against the greed, cynicism, and duplicity of the city dwellers, Capra succeeded in his intentions and delivered his first sermon in the ecumenical church of humanism.

Though Capra's next film, *Lost Horizon*, deviated from the narrative pattern and American setting so central to *Deeds*, it continued to develop his version of humanism. Based on James Hilton's best-selling novel, *Lost Horizon* is topical, though in a way different from most of Capra's other films. When nagging domestic problems persisted in America and foreign conflicts like the Spanish Civil War forecast worse conflicts to come, a story of an ideal society free of social discord and civil strife clearly had some appeal. Capra surely thought so, for immediately after reading the novel, he convinced Cohn to purchase rights to the novel and budget $2 million for the film, nearly half of Columbia's production budget that year (NATT, 190–91).

The structure of the completed film follows the British diplomat Robert Conway and four others as they escape a civil war in China and are taken to a lamasery in the Valley of the Blue Moon, a peaceful Utopia in a remote part of the Himalayas near Tibet. There Conway and the others learn amazing facts about the peaceful and harmonious society, and Conway is told he has been chosen to be its new leader. When his brother George convinces him the society is a hoax, Conway reluctantly leaves to return to civilization. Along the way, however, he realizes that Shangri-La is real, and, struggling nearly a year in the frigid weather, returns to the ideal society.

The center of the film is the character of Robert Conway and his response to Shangri-La (a name that Franklin D. Roosevelt appropriated for the presidential retreat in the Maryland mountains that

President Eisenhower would later less imaginatively rename Camp David after his only grandson). From the start of the film, when he calmly directs the evacuation of British citizens from Baskul, Conway is presented as a leader. Though he is known as a public hero and diplomat—his brother George says that he is likely to be named the British foreign secretary—Conway also seems to be an accomplished author of metaphysical treatises, a man able to see above mundane affairs and to grasp the universal hopes and ideals of mankind. When Conway is first granted a visit to the High Lama— a former Belgian priest who leads Shangri-La—the High Lama expresses admiration for a line from one of Conway's books: "There are moments in every man's life when he glimpses the eternal." Calm, contemplative, idealistic, Conway flourishes in Shangri-La and seems an ideal leader for it.

It's interesting to examine the society he has been chosen to lead and the values upon which it rests. Besides the High Lama, and the priests of the Lamasery, who live on a hill in an elaborate temple, Shangri-La consists of common people who live in the valley and work mostly, we presume, at agriculture activities. The society produces a sufficiency of all goods, so that there is no envy among people. In addition, the inhabitants live extremely long lives—the High Lama is well over 200 years old. This longevity, Chang tells Conway, is due to "the absence of struggle," a key characteristic of Shangri-La. In contrast to Western societies, which are living, the High Lama tells Conway, in an "orgy of greed and brutality," life in Shangri-La is "based on one single rule: be kind." Though feminists would not much like Shangri-La—Conway is told men don't argue over women because it is considered impolite for a man to possess a woman that another man desires—the society is portrayed as one of complete peace, cooperation, and harmony. Its mission is to preserve the values of brotherly love until the conflicts among nations lead to their self-destruction. "When the strong have devoured one another," the High Lama tells Conway, "the Christian ethic may at last be fulfilled and the meek shall inherit the earth." Though the American dimension of Capra's humanism is absent, the Christian dimension is strong in *Lost Horizon*.

Nevertheless, *Lost Horizon* is for me an unsatisfactory film. Capra reports having difficulties with the film: at the preview, audiences became restive and it looked as if Columbia's substantial investment would not bring returns. In his autobiography Capra tells an en-

Photos from *Lost Horizon*: (top) the funeral procession for the High Lama at Shangri-La; (bottom) attentive Robert Conway (Ronald Colman) learns of Shangri-La's social harmony from Chang (H.B. Warner)

gaging but dubious story about solving the problem by burning the first two reels of the film. McBride demonstrates that it's apocryphal, noting that Capra changed the film all through postproduction, but the story does point to the problem of the film: the structure is dramatically flat (McB, 361–64). Though Capra tries to build in some tension by having George completely reject Shangri-La and successfully tempt Robert into leaving, George is so obnoxious that it's difficult to believe that Robert would ever capitulate. From the start, Conway is presented as a confident, serene man. When placed into Shangri-La, he has no reason to leave. Though absence of conflict may create a wonderful society, it's no way to construct a film. Capra's best films are characterized by a problem confronting a hero who struggles to solve it. *Lost Horizon,* as a friend once told me, is all solution and no problem.

Some people, however, prefer *Lost Horizon* to any of Capra's other films. The British novel of the same title by James Hilton, on which the film is based, had also been a runaway best-seller, especially after being vigorously touted by Alexander Woollcott, America's self-appointed "Town Crier," on his influential radio program. Generally, its admirers are people who are uncomfortable with the blend of comedy and moralism in Capra's American masterpieces, preferring instead the exotic settings and *mise-en-scène* of *Lost Horizon* or *The Bitter Tea of General Yen.* Certainly the temple is one of the most elaborate sets in all of Capra's films. Though it sometimes seems an Eastern design too much tempered by a Frank Lloyd Wright functionalism, the temple is striking in long shots, especially in the procession marking the passing of the High Lama. Though I can understand the appeal of the film for some people, I'm happy that Capra returned to American settings in his next film and stayed there for the rest of his career.

You Can't Take It With You, that next film, was aptly dubbed by Otis Ferguson as "Shangri-La in a frame house."[8] Based on a successful Broadway play by George S. Kaufman and Moss Hart about a family of eccentric individualists who all get along by pursuing their individual interests, the play does seem at times an American *Lost Horizon.* Capra, in fact, saw the play when he was in New York for the preview of *Lost Horizon* and was so intrigued with the portrayal of a bunch of people pursuing their interests and still living in harmony with those around them that he talked Harry Cohn into paying $200,000 for the film rights.

Though Capra did not completely return to the narrative pattern he established in *Mr. Deeds*, elements of the pattern are evident in *You Can't Take It With You*. Grandpa Vanderhof is the spokesman for the Capra humanism, while the romantic dimension of the Capra hero is provided by Tony Kirby. Though the hero is not betrayed by the heroine, nor does she need to be converted by him (Alice Sycamore, Tony's prospective wife, is heir to her grandfather's humane values), one character is converted in the film: the villain, Tony's father. And, just as in *Mr. Deeds*, the moral struggle between hero and villain—absent in *Lost Horizon*—is central.

You Can't Take It With You succeeded both at the box office and within the industry. It was one of the top fifteen money makers in 1938–39 and won Oscars for best film and best director. Surely a good part of the film's success relates to the romance between Alice and Tony, as well as the comic zaniness of nearly everyone in the Vanderhof household—from ballerinas and xylophone players to the manufacturers of firecrackers—but for our purposes the conflict between Grandpa Vanderhof and the villain is central. Grandpa Vanderhof is an ex-businessman who succeeded at his work, then dropped out—went down the elevator, in one of the film's central visual metaphors—because he wasn't having any fun. As head of his household, he encourages everyone to do just what satisfies them. He keeps himself busy by collecting stamps (and appraising them, seemingly his only source of income), playing the harmonica, and attending graduation ceremonies of nearby educational institutions. He considers himself and the other members of his family "lilies of the field," and his trust that Providence will care for them is made explicit by the prayers he gives before meals. His patriotism is shown when he explains to Alice's mother, Penny, about what he calls "ismology": "Sure, you know, communism, fascism, voodooism. . . . When things go a little bad these days, you go out and get yourself an ism, and you're in business." Advising Penny to give the characters in the play she's writing Americanism, Grandpa runs off a long list of American historical heroes, then goes on: "When things got tough for those boys, they didn't go running around looking for isms. Lincoln said, 'With malice toward none, with charity for all': Nowadays they say, 'Think the way I do or I'll bomb the daylights out of you.' " The High Lama of the home, Grandpa invokes Lincoln to attack rigid adherence to ideology and support a value system of compassion and altruism toward other people.

Grandpa's antagonist is Anthony Kirby, Sr., played with sinister power by Edward Arnold, in the first of three consecutive roles as the Capra villain. He counters Grandpa's charity, rejection of materialism, and kindness with malice, a celebration of laissez-faire, and ruthless brutality. Capra and Riskin altered the play by making Kirby a magnate aggressively attempting to monopolize the munitions industry, hopeful of capitalizing on the conflicts brewing in Europe. Kirby's ruthlessness is portrayed most graphically in his attempts to drive a competitor, Ramsey, out of the munitions market. His spiritual malady is metaphorically suggested by a physical ailment: throughout the film he suffers from a bad stomach. All in all, Kirby is an excellent example of the type described by Chang in *Lost Horizon*: the aggressive man of Western culture who drives himself to an early grave.

Capra aptly described the conflict between Grandpa Vanderhof and Kirby as a clash of two philosophies: "Devour thy neighbor versus love thy neighbor" (NATT, 241). The contrast is made most clearly in the jail scene, which occurs after the Vanderhof family and the Kirbys, who are visiting in order to meet Alice's family, are arrested for disturbing the peace when some firecrackers explode. Kirby, of course, is enraged that he should be thrown into a cell with "commoners." When Kirby talks of worrying about his business deals, Grandpa inquires why he is so interested in "making more money than you can ever use. You can't take it with you. The only thing you can take with you is the love of your friends." Kirby resists, countering the ethic of friendship with the survival of the fittest. Grandpa calls him a "lion in the jungle," and Kirby retorts, "That's how I got where I am, on top, and scum like this [pointing to the other inmates] are still in the gutter." In his only angry moment in the film, Grandpa Vanderhof calls Kirby an "idiot" and a "dull-witted fool" for believing himself superior: "You may be a high mogul to yourself, Mr. Kirby, but to me you're a failure— failure as a man, failure as a human being, even failure as a father."

The scene develops a dimension of Capra's social vision that would return with much greater power in *It's a Wonderful Life*—the belief that abiding human friendship is a value above the struggle for wealth and power. The conflict is resolved in this film by the next scene. Taken into court, Kirby is defended by four of his personal lawyers and pleads innocent. Grandpa, defending himself, pleads guilty and is given a suspended sentence and a $100 fine. Though

Kirby offers to pay the fine (Grandpa had asked the judge to let Kirby off), Grandpa declines. Instead, his friends and neighbors, who have filled the courtroom after learning of the Vanderhof plight, pass a hat and collect the fine. The bemused judge—another of Capra's benevolent authorities—even tosses in a coin. Grandpa's vision has been vindicated.

This scene, along with the final one, do as much as any film in all of Capra's work to justify the critical claim that Capra is a blindly optimistic Pollyanna, a purveyor, in Richard Griffith's words, of a "fantasy of goodwill."[9] In that final scene Kirby visits the Vanderhof home. Smarting from two blows—his son's decision not to join his business and the sudden death of Ramsey following Kirby's brutal treatment of his competitor—Kirby has thought hard about Grandpa's denunciations in the jail. Anxious to reclaim the affections, or at least the respect, of his son, Kirby makes peace with Grandpa and even sits down to play a duet of "Polly Wolly Doodle" with him on the harmonica. Though Capra structures the narrative in such a way as to make Kirby's conversion understandable, though he uses all his knowledge of film language to try to bring the ending off, he doesn't manage to do so. We mentioned earlier that Capra knew both success and failure, and that in his best films he affirmed an optimistic vision of the world without slighting the power of the challenges to it. In You Can't Take It With You, the challenge is adequately presented through Kirby's perspective, but having the ruthless capitalist converted by the whimsical Grandpa Vanderhof simply strains our imaginations too much.

Yet the popular success of You Can't Take It With You stressed to Capra that the moral thrust in his comedy was acceptable to audiences. His growing recognition in 1938 and 1939 (picture on the cover of Time, another Oscar for best director) moved him to even more ambitious aims. Instead of simply pitting a good democratic hero against a greedy villain, Capra decided to become a more explicit engineer of cultural mythology, to make his hero the embodiment of American ideals. In Mr. Smith Goes to Washington (and his next film, Meet John Doe) Capra dedicated his filmmaking talents to instructing audiences in what he perceived as the essence of Americanism.

That Capra was the primary engineer of the social vision in his films is reinforced by details of script collaboration. For the first time since The Bitter Tea of General Yen (1933), Robert Riskin did

Photos from *You Can't Take It With You*: (top) a typical moment in the Vanderhof living room; (bottom) jailed, an embarrassed Anthony Kirby, Sr. (Edward Arnold) is scolded by Grandpa Vanderhof (Lionel Barrymore), while Tony, Jr. (James Stewart) looks on

not do the script for Capra. Instead, Sidney Buchman wrote the screenplay for *Mr. Smith*. Though Buchman's dialogue is less rooted in urban vernacular than Riskin's, the structure of *Mr. Smith* follows that of *Mr. Deeds* almost exactly, as a close comparison of the segments in each would reveal. Based on a little-known story, "The Gentlemen from Montana," *Mr. Smith Goes to Washington* clearly stems from Capra's aims as a committed filmmaker.

The story also returns to the narrative conventions established in *Deeds*. The idealistic and patriotic Jefferson Smith (James Stewart), leader of the Boy Rangers, is named to the United States Senate after a senator's sudden death. Scorned by his cynical secretary, Saunders (Jean Arthur again), and mocked by newsmen when he arrives in Washington, the wide-eyed Smith eagerly attempts to introduce a bill establishing a boys' camp in his state. When a powerful newspaper and industrial magnate, James Taylor, and the state's senior senator, Joseph Paine, learn that the proposed camp would be built on land which Taylor has quietly bought and planned to sell at a huge profit under the provisions of another pending bill, they attempt to buy off Smith, then to break him. Paine falsely accuses Smith of owning the land himself, then urges the Senate to oust him. Disillusioned, Smith almost leaves Washington, but with the aid of Saunders, who has become entranced by his simple idealism, decides to remain and fight. Gaining the Senate floor, Smith filibusters for twenty-four hours, hoping to bring news of Taylor's corruption to his home state. Though Taylor's newspapers carry only negative reports of Smith, Senator Paine cracks under the pressure and confesses his complicity in Taylor's scheme of corruption, which brings about the ritual victory and the vindication of Smith's idealism.

Released less than two months after World War II broke out in Europe, *Mr. Smith* argued, in essence, that though America did have its problems (most notably, a disproportionate amount of wealth and power, sometimes in the hands of evil men), it also had political traditions and ideals worth preserving. In discussing the film, it is probably best to consider its powerful rhetoric by examining more closely the narrative and Capra's use of film language, then to define as precisely as possible the ideology that Jefferson Smith defends.

Much more convincing than *You Can't Take It With You*, the narrative of *Mr. Smith Goes to Washington* creates greater tensions, more interesting characters, and a more satisfactory (though not as satisfying) resolution. Jefferson Smith, whose name combines a founding father of democracy with the most common of American surnames, is portrayed as a childlike innocent who grows to manhood through the film, doubting yet ultimately retaining his patriotic idealism. Smith is called "Don Quixote," "Daniel Boone," "Old Honest Abe," and "Daniel in the Lion's Den," by various characters in the film; the names stress his intense idealism, his connection to American frontier and democratic traditions, and his vulnerability as an innocent in the world of experience. When Senator Paine tells Taylor later in the film that he doesn't want to play a part in "crucifying" Smith, the Capra hero is again, as he so often is, compared to Christ. These allusions and Jimmy Stewart's exceptional performance combine to make Jefferson Smith the archetypal Capra hero during these committed years.

The conversion of characters in *Mr. Smith* is much more convincing than in *You Can't Take It With You*. James Taylor, the villain of wealth and power, remains unconverted at the end, making Smith's victory a tentative and limited one at best. The two important characters who do convert are Saunders and Senator Paine, and their conversions are clearly prepared for in the narrative. Saunders, who complains about "carrying bibs for an infant with little flags in his fists" early in the film, later reveals nostalgically that her father was a doctor "who thought more about ethics than collections." Her memory of his altruism and her observation of Jeff's vulnerability in Washington combine to make her conversion more understandable. Paine, we learn in dialogue, once knew Jeff's father, a newspaper editor who was murdered for printing exposés of a corrupt mining company. Thirty years earlier, Paine recalls, he and Jeff's father had been "twin champions of lost causes." During the film's climax, Jeff, looking at the "Taylor-made" telegrams from his state, reminds Paine of his father's memory and of Paine's former fights for the lost causes. With Jeff 's words prodding his conscience, Paine's attempted suicide and confession are understandable, thoroughly prepared for in the narrative.

Capra's mastery of the film medium also contributes to the power of *Mr. Smith*. Stephen Handzo has accurately pointed out that though critics may have disparaged Capra as a spinner of fantasies, audiences remember Capra as a *realistic* director (FC, 170). The Senate chamber in *Mr. Smith* was meticulously copied on Columbia's

sound stage, right down to the gash on Daniel Webster's desk, a
feat in set design as impressive as Gordon Jenkins's recreation of
the *Washington Post* offices in *All the President's Men*. The use of
the Lincoln Memorial, Union Station, the Capitol Dome, and all
of the Americana during Slavko Vorkapich's patriotic montage also
contribute to the realistic *mise-en-scène*.

Dimitri Tiomkin's score also adds to the power of the film. During
the montage, familiar American tunes abound: the National An-
them, "Yankee Doodle," "My Country 'Tis of Thee," "When Johnny
Comes Marching Home," and "Red River Valley." At Smith's send-
off banquet "Auld Lang Syne" is played, just as at Deeds's departure
from Mandrake Falls. At least twice "I Dream of Jeannie" softly
accompanies Smith's romantic scenes with Saunders, while "Bury
Me Not on the Lone Prairie" quietly plays when Paine wistfully
recalls Jeff's father and his earlier idealism. *Lost Horizon* used as
much commentative music as *Mr. Smith*, but the effect is much
more powerful in *Smith*, in part because of its appropriate place-
ment.

Lighting and editing pace are also effectively used. Joseph
Walker's careful lighting of Saunders in a soft focus close-up, as she
begins to respond to Smith's idealism, creates a perfect—and appropriate—aura of radiance. Jeff's deepest moment of self-doubt at
the steps of the Lincoln Memorial is lit in low-key, indirect, back
lighting, making Jeff visible only in silhouette and reinforcing the
tone of the narrative at that point. The editing creates a brisk pace
through most of the film: straight cuts dominate within segments;
wipes connect them. At the end of the film, when Jeff reminds
Paine of lost causes, Capra focuses the camera on Jeff for thirty-five
seconds in two shots, broken only by a two-second reaction shot of
Paine. This stresses the acting, characterization, and thematic importance of the dialogue. But when Smith collapses (part of another
twenty-five-second take), leading to Paine's confession and the ritual
victory, the editing pace becomes frenzied: in the last hundred
seconds of the film, Capra cuts twenty-five times. Excluding two
relatively long takes for Paine's confession, there are twenty-three
shots in eighty seconds.

Finally, compositions are skillfully done and reaction shots help
draw the audience into active participation in the film. When Paine
tells Jeff, "This is a man's world, a brutal world. . . and you've got
to check your ideals at the door," a picture of James Taylor is

composed directly above Paine's head, a visual metaphor of Taylor's control over Paine. The reaction shots are especially important—as in the cut to Saunders's sneer after a senator's sarcastic comment—for they do much to guide the reaction of the audience to events in the film. The reaction shots dominate in the Senate scenes, when cuts to Saunders, the press corps, the gallery, the pages, and the sympathetically smiling vice-president—yet another benevolent authority figure—direct audience response and intensify the drama of the filibuster. The brief expressions on faces of familiar characters do much to stimulate audience absorption and to make the film's ideology seductively appealing. Capra had never before used the film medium so effectively to develop the narrative, and only once—in *It's a Wonderful Life*—would he surpass the stylistic achievements of this film.

What of Jefferson Smith's ideology? In essence, it is another example of the American/Christian humanism that Capra began with *Mr. Deeds*, modified by a greater stress on patriotism and adherence to the ideal of human liberty. The image of the Capitol Dome is particularly affecting to Smith; it reminds him of the American commitment to liberty. The connection between Smith and Lincoln—author of the Emancipation Proclamation and advocate of government of, by, and for the people—is surely key, as is Paine's allusion to the Christ-like crucifixion of Smith. During the filibuster, Smith reads from the Declaration of Independence and from I Corinthians 13 ("the greatest of these is charity")—combining American independence and Christian love. Made at a time when many Americans were searching for the essence of America, due largely to the threat of Nazi aggression and tyranny, this tribute to Christian love and American liberty as something worth fighting for, if necessary, was a powerful one. Although its production costs kept its profit margin down, *Mr. Smith* was both popular and more critically acclaimed than any other Capra film before it.

The engineering of cultural mythology worked, and Capra's next film, *Meet John Doe*, attempted an even more ambitious exploration of Americanism. Working on an independent production with Riskin after both had left Columbia (it was released by Warner Brothers), Capra set out to make a film that would show even the critics that he could treat serious themes with skill and imagination. He and Riskin, Capra wrote later, "would astonish the critics with contemporary realities; the ugly face of hate; the power of uniformed bigots

Photo from *Mr. Smith Goes to Washington*: Jefferson Smith (James Stewart) is inspired by the Lincoln Memorial

Photo from *Mr. Smith Goes to Washington*: Jefferson Smith (James Stewart) is challenged by Senator Paine (Claude Rains) in Columbia's faithful reproduction of the Senate chamber

in red, white, and blue shirts; the agony of disillusionment; and the wild dark passions of mobs" (NATT, 297). The resulting film is a fascinating failure, filled with submerged autobiography, a movie that tempered Capra's ambition to be a maker of cultural mythology and enabled him to make his masterpiece, *It's a Wonderful Life*.

Meet John Doe is about a domestic fascist who desires to manufacture American idealism through the media and to use that idealism as a way to dominate and control others: it's Capra's most distressing, darkest film. The theme was surely fresh for films, though the threat of home-grown fascists was treated in fiction much earlier; both Nathaniel West's *A Cool Million* (1934) and Sinclair Lewis's *It Can't Happen Here* (1935) had dealt with it. But with Nazi Germany occupying France and bombing England, a film about fascism in any form automatically generated interest.

From the first shots following the titles, Capra's ambitious aims show: a jackhammer destroys a sign on a wall which says, "The Bulletin: A Free Press Means a Free People." Next, workmen put up a new sign with more modern design and lettering. It reads, "The New Bulletin: A Streamlined Newspaper for a Streamlined Era." Tradition and freedom are out; publicity-conscious modernity is in.

The film concerns a newswoman, Ann Mitchell (Barbara Stanwyck), who devises a publicity stunt to help sell papers (and save her job). She writes a letter by an imaginary John Doe, in which Doe threatens to jump off the roof of City Hall in protest against the disastrous state of civilization. Hiring a drifter to play John Doe, she publicizes him through newspapers and radio, and a national movement of John Doe clubs springs up. A national John Doe convention is planned, and the owner of Anne's newspaper, D. B. Norton, orders John Doe to give a speech endorsing Norton as the John Doe third party candidate for president. Doe refuses, Norton reveals Doe's true identity, and the people turn against him. But Doe, who has come to believe in the John Doe philosophy, climbs to the top of the City Hall on Christmas Eve. Only an appeal by Ann, who has fallen in love with him, and the pleas of several John Doe club members persuade John not to jump and instead to lead a reborn John Doe movement.

A look at the central characters gives a better idea of the film's complex thrust than does this bare plot outline. The man who agrees to play John Doe is Long John Willoughby (Gary Cooper), an ex-baseball player with a bad arm who agrees to the plan mostly because the money he earns will allow him to have arm surgery. Like Jeff Smith, John speaks nervously at first but gains confidence as a spokesman of values as the film progresses. Unlike Deeds or Smith, however, Doe is not an idealist, a settled spokesman of values, early in the film; rather, he must become *converted* as the film progresses, a key point we will return to later. It's enough now to note that Doe, with his name, former profession, and penchant for apple pie, is the embodiment of the common American.

Accompanying Long John is the Colonel, another drifter (Walter Brennan). The Colonel is a cynic, certain that "the world's been shaved by a drunken barber" and upset that Long John gets drawn into the John Doe scheme. Though he leaves Long John in disgust when John agrees to go on a lecture tour, the Colonel is the only person to stand by John when the conventioneers turn against him. He also appears at City Hall to prevent John from jumping. The fact that only a cynic "loves his neighbor" at a huge gathering of people who profess to live that philosophy throws a dark shadow over the whole film.

Ann Mitchell develops in a more complex, ambiguous way than the cynicism-conversion-faith pattern of Babe Bennett or Saunders. Like Babe and Saunders, she is converted to idealism and falls in love with the hero, but she's converted by her deceased father, not by the hero. Like Saunders's father, Ann's was an altruistic doctor, and Ann's speeches are culled from her father's diary. These speeches, along with John's mistaken belief in Ann's sincerity, which convert John, who in turns helps to convert Ann. Yet throughout the film—at least to the convention scene—Ann's motive for writing the speeches is financial: she's engaged in a publicity stunt which she conceived as such, and Norton pays her well in salary and gifts for it. Only in this film does the Capra heroine conspire so closely with the villain.

Finally, Edward Arnold portrays the sinister D. B. Norton. Whereas Kirby wanted to control an industry and Taylor, a state, Norton wants to control the nation with, in his own words, "an iron hand." A wealthy industrialist who buys the *Bulletin* to further his aims, Norton has his own private uniformed stormtroopers, the D. B. Norton Motor Corps. On Norton's office desk a statute of Napoleon is prominently displayed, signifying his ruthless lust for power. The extreme close-up of Norton's calculating reaction when his servants respond enthusiastically to a John Doe radio broadcast is one of the most frightening in all of Capra's work. It tells all about the man. Significantly, except for a butler, Norton is home alone on Christmas Eve. A man of wealth and power, Norton has no family or friends.

As these characters interact, the film raises a problem for which there is no solution. (If *Lost Horizon* is all solution, *Meet John Doe* is all problem and no solution.) Sounds, images, and rhetoric of Christianity and Americanism abound in the film. The crux of the John Doe philosophy is embedded in John's conclusion to the first radio speech: "The meek can inherit the earth when the John Does start loving their neighbors." Clubs spring up to foster the neighborliness that will allow the members to remain "free people." Yet at the convention—powerfully shot with low-key lighting and pelting rain—the John Does quickly and savagely turn on Long John. An image in the montage immediately following the convention scene—a crumpled poster of John Doe being washed into a storm sewer—would almost serve as a logical conclusion to the film.

After the stadium scene, Capra had nowhere to go. He and Riskin had, as he wrote in his autobiography, "written ourselves into a corner" (NATT, 303). They tried to get out by considering a number of different endings. In his production history of *Meet John Doe*, Charles Wolfe has studied existing records to detail at least some of the various endings Capra and Riskin considered.[10] In both the original June 27, 1940, shooting script and a revision on January 2, 1941, Ann, coming to the City Hall roof, successfully pleads for John not to jump while Norton appears to be converted, as Kirby had in *You Can't Take It with You*. Connell and the Colonel, absent in the first version, appear in the second. No John Doe club members appear in either scene. Capra told me about another considered option—one that would have been more logical and extremely powerful—in which John does jump. In this ending, Capra would have focused on the Colonel standing outside City Hall. He sees John fall, walks over to the body, kneels down, and, in medium close-up, cradles John's head in his arms, whispering the final words of the film: "Long John, you poor fool, you poor sucker." Though potentially devastating, this ending was attuned neither to Capra's sensibility nor to the temper of the times. Wolfe, in fact, uncovered no records of this ending and has noted that as early as February 1940 Capra changed the film's working title from *The Life and Death of John Doe* to *The Life of John Doe.*

Photo from *Meet John Doe*: John Doe (Gary Cooper) helplessly pleads for understanding during the stadium scene

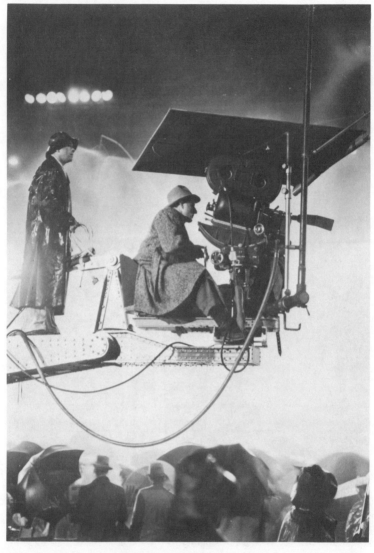

Photo from *Meet John Doe*: Capra and cameraman George Barnes prepare crane shot
during the stadium scene

Thus, it appears unlikely that the suicide scene, however potentially intense, ever reached the shooting stage.[10]

The film premiered on March 12, 1941, with the second ending featuring Ann's plea and Norton's conversion. Two days later, however, Capra pulled the film because of negative audience response and revised it again. In the present ending—suggested, says Capra, by an anonymous John Doe who saw the premiere and wrote him (NATT, 305)—Capra deletes Norton's conversion and brings six John Doe club members to the roof to help dissuade John from jumping. As in the premiere version, Ann pleads that "the first John Doe" had already died for the cause 2,000 years earlier, while Norton and five of his yes men stand impotently at the side. Although Connell boasts to Norton about the power of the people as Beethoven's "Ode to Joy" resounds in the background, this ending too remains singularly vexing. I'd like to suggest why.

One reason, as Capra himself notes, is simply that Long John Willoughby is not the idealistic Capra hero at the start of the film— he's simply a bum willing to play along with the publicity scheme in return for money. This makes his willingness to jump off a building for principle highly unlikely (NATT, 303). In fact one cannot imagine Deeds or Smith committing suicide for their principles— their optimistic faith in the sanctity of human life wouldn't permit it. How much less likely that Long John would do so, since his experience at the convention contradicts his newly accepted faith, and his only friend in the crisis, the Colonel, would shoot himself before dying for a principle.

A more important reason for the failure of the ending and the film generally lies in the film's subtext and is related to what I'd call submerged autobiography.[11] Whether consciously or unconsciously, Capra projected his own experience—and his own doubts about his vocation as a committed filmmaker—into the characters of Ann Mitchell and Long John. Like Ann, Capra created an imaginary character, John Doe, to represent or embody certain idealistic principles; indeed, since his conversion in 1935, that had been his new mission as a filmmaker. When Ann tells her mother, "I created someone who's giving up his life for a principle. . . . Unless he says something sensational—well, it's just no good," she could have been Capra. Capra himself created such a character, and he too sought in *Meet John Doe* to say something sensational. He even tried—in this film and the four previous—to follow Ann's mother's advice: to reject "doom and despair" and to say instead "something simple and real, something with hope" in his films.

Yet Capra seems to have had misgivings, seems to have wondered if he might be a huckster like John Doe. Doe's picture appears on the cover of *Time*, just as Capra's had in 1938. Both were getting recognition, and both wondered if they deserved it. When Doe tells Ann in the airport waiting room that he's beginning to see the true meaning of the platitudes he had heard for years and been spouting for weeks, one senses that Capra is also speaking. Yet Capra, like Doe, seems to be torn: who is he (the Sicilian immigrant, the ex-ballplayer) to be a national spokesman of values, communicating to millions through the media? Capra's doubt about his role as a maker of cultural mythology resides, consciously or not, at the center of *Meet John Doe*. His ambitious desire to be a cultural mythmaker and his doubts about whether he deserved to be one—and indeed, his doubts about the validity of his own Christian/American humanism—helped to make the demands of *Meet John Doe* absolutely irreconcilable. *Meet John Doe* is Capra's *Connecticut Yankee*—a work that just wouldn't coalesce because of its creator's doubts—and it is no surprise that Capra's next feature, *Arsenic and Old Lace*, abandoned cultural mythmaking entirely and that the feature following, *It's a Wonderful Life*, expressed his vision in a much more intimate, personal form. In a sense, *Meet John Doe* brings the circle back to where it started—to *Mr. Deeds Goes to Town*.

Before concluding our examination of this fascinating period—when Capra's vision so closely coincided with the needs, desires, and predilections of his audience—we need to say a few words about the social and political significance of the Capra films between 1936 and 1941. I began the chapter by discussing the breakdown of American cultural values in the early 1930s and the gradual mending of that breakdown into a cultural consensus in the late 1930s and after. According to John Highman, that reconsolidation of American culture constituted an "ideological revival" characterized by "a reassertion of democratic ideals, an upsurge of nationalism, and a return to religion."[12] How could one describe the thrust of Capra's Christian/American humanism more precisely?

Though I would be foolish to argue that Capra's films caused that revival—social scientists tell us that people's attitudes rarely change by the experience of viewing a single film—I am convinced that Capra's late 1930s films, by presenting the ideology Highman describes in such an emotionally satisfying narrative form, significantly contributed to that revival of cultural values. Compared to the values of the genteel tradition—the dominant American cultural value system up to the 1920s (and the one obliquely defended in Capra's *The Strong Man*)—this new cultural consensus did not stress genteel respectability so much. Instead, it was more vernacular: its hero was not the upwardly mobile Horatio Alger, animated by the Protestant ethic and "character," but rather John Doe, the common yet neighborly and good man that made America work and that made America worth fighting for. The political thrust of these Capra films is thus not essentially Republican or Democrat—though they were partly both—they were, as we noted above, nationalistic. They helped to prepare the country for war by portraying the best of American values as worth fighting for, but they also helped to create an image of America as the ideal free society which led to such cultural complacency—and at times, tyranny—during the Cold War. Though in his best films Capra never neglected the threats to his values—the Kirbys, the Taylors, the Nortons—it was easy, given the times, for Americans to remember only the Deeds, the Smiths, and the Does and to believe they represented the only reality in America. But I guess we can hardly blame Capra for that.

5

Capra and World War II
(1941–45)

IN ONE of the most memorable scenes in *Meet John Doe* the tough, worldly-wise editor Connell, half-drunk, takes Long John Willoughby into a bar and warns him about the speech Norton wants him to make. Surprisingly, this man, so harsh on the surface, turns out to be a soft-hearted patriot, a veteran of World War I. He tells John he's a "sucker" for the flag and "The Star-Spangled Banner." Appalled by Norton's opportunism, he praises the examples set by Washington, Jefferson, and Lincoln. All three, he tells John, are "lighthouses in a foggy world." Two years later, the army released to the public the first of the "Why We Fight" series, *Prelude to War*. One of the early sequences of that film presents a series of religious and political leaders throughout world history; all of them, intones narrator Walter Huston, are "lighthouses lighting up a foggy world."

Frank Capra directed both of these films. He directed the first as Frank Capra, major Hollywood filmmaker. He directed the second as Major Frank Capra, Commanding Officer of the 834th Signal Corps Photographic Detachment, on special assignment to the army's Special Services Division. As with many other workers in the Hollywood feature film industry, Capra devoted his talents and energies toward serving his country during World War II. This chapter will examine how Capra became involved in making orientation films (and what he did during the war) and then look briefly at the approach, achievements, and effects of the "Why We Fight" series.

Photo (left): Major Frank Capra at the War Department in Washington, 1942

credit: National Audiovisual Center

After the traumas involved with the ending of *Meet John Doe,*
Capra was becoming more and more aware of the Fascist threat.
In mid-1941 he took a trip to Washington, volunteered to head a
photographic unit, and was offered a major's commission in the
Army Signal Corps. Capra consented and was told to go home and
wait for a call (NATT, 309).

Capra returned to California and, while waiting, decided, in his
own words, to "make a cheap film for a fast buck to keep my family
going" (NATT, 309). The occasion for his scheme was a hit Broadway
play, Joseph Kesselring's *Arsenic and Old Lace.* Discussion of this
film belongs in this chapter on Capra and World War II for a couple
of reasons. First, the film wasn't publicly released until 1944 (troops
overseas saw it a year earlier): in purchasing screen rights for the
play, Warner Brothers had to agree not to release the film until the
play closed. More importantly, however, *Arsenic and Old Lace*
deviates widely from the method of filmmaking Capra had developed. Instead of working for several months with Robert Riskin on
adapting the source (the significant changes in *You Can't Take It
With You* are a good example), Capra shot a fairly imitative script
of the play done by Julius and Philip Epstein, better known for
their collaboration on *Casablanca.* And the film had almost none
of the topical social and political interest evident in most of Capra's
1930s films. Perhaps exhausted by the strain of making *Meet John
Doe,* Capra seemed quite willing to make "an anything goes, rip-
roaring comedy about murder" (NATT, 309–11).

And a very funny film it is. The humor derives from a number
of characters and situations. The hero is Mortimer Brewster (Cary
Grant), a drama critic and confirmed bachelor, author of such vol-
umes as *The Bachelor's Bible* and *Marriage: A Fraud and a Failure.*
Mortimer lives in an old Brooklyn house with his aunts, Abbie and
Martha, though he has decided to break his principles and marry
Elaine Harper, the daughter of a neighboring minister. The events
of the film take place on the day immediately following Mortimer
and Elaine's wedding when Mortimer discovers to his astonishment
that his aunts have been poisoning lonely old men. Their method
is to add a teaspoon of arsenic, a half-teaspoon of strychnine, and
a "pinch of cyanide" to their elderberry wine and then serve it to
their guests. Eleven or twelve bodies are buried in the cellar, with
Mr. Hoskins ("a Methodist") awaiting burial in the cubicle beneath
the window seat.

Photo: Cary Grant, Edward Everett Horton and Peter Lorre with the homicidal sisters, Josephine Hull and Jean Adair in *Arsenic and Old Lace*, Capra's "anything goes, rip roaring comedy about murder"

The movement of the film traces Mortimer's attempts to convince his aunts that their actions are morally wrong and to find a safe place where they will not harm others. With an uncle who believes he's Teddy Roosevelt (his sword-brandishing charges up the "San Juan Hill" stairs are unforgettable), a criminal brother, Jonathan, and now two murdering aunts, Mortimer begins to doubt his sanity. The return of Jonathan (Raymond Massey) along with his accomplice, Dr. Einstein (Peter Lorre), complicates matters, but Mortimer finally is able to put things in order: Jonathan is returned to the Indiana asylum from which he escaped; Teddy, Abby, and Martha are committed; and Mortimer learns that he's not a true member of the family. His mother was the Brewster cook. Relieved, Mortimer is able to embrace Elaine and finally enjoy his marriage. Both funny (a policeman tells Mortimer he's working on a play: "I got good ideas but I can't spell 'em") and frightening (the medium close-up of Jonathan entering through the window is as scary and as skillfully conveyed as almost anything in Hitchcock), *Arsenic and Old Lace* again reveals Capra's compatibility with actors, his comic sense, and his mastery of the medium.

The shooting schedule for *Arsenic and Old Lace* was just four weeks long, and, with only a week left in the shooting, Pearl Harbor was bombed. A day later, Capra was sworn into the army by two Signal Corps officers. He asked for and received six weeks' leave of absence to finish shooting and editing the film. By February 14, 1942, Major Frank Capra was on active duty in Washington, D.C. (NATT, 317).

The story of the "Why We Fight" series and Capra's participation in the making of it has been treated in a variety of sources.[1] The story begins with Capra's reassignment from the Signal Corps to the Morale Branch (later renamed Special Services) immediately after arriving in Washington. The Morale Branch had been established on March 14, 1941, primarily to deal with the building of both civilian and military morale in the United States. The branch was commanded by Brigadier General F. W. Osborn. Capra was perplexed and disturbed at first with his reassignment, for the Signal Corps had long been in charge of whatever filmmaking needs arose in the army. Little did he know that his reassignment had been ordered by Army Chief of Staff General George C. Marshall.

Marshall had been concerned about troop morale long before Capra arrived in Washington. Isolationist feeling still persisted

among some Americans, and Marshall attempted to challenge such
attitudes among soldiers by calling a conference on November 18,
1941, to initiate an army-wide orientation program which would
explain to soldiers the reasons for American involvement. The Bu-
reau of Public Relations did manage to write a series of lectures on
the topic, but they were not successful. "To soldiers bone-tired
from their initial encounter with basic training," writes George
Thompson, the lectures "proved baffling, bewildering, or just plain
boring."[2]

With the orientation lectures not working, Marshall turned to
films instead. The reason for Capra's transfer to the Morale Branch
was partly to extricate Capra from the red tape and cumbersome
chain of command in the Signal Corps. Shortly after arriving in
Washington, Capra met with Marshall. According to Capra's account
of the meeting (NATT, 324–28), Marshall told Capra that in spite
of the Nazis' power, American soldiers could fight bravely if they
were convinced that what they were fighting for was worth dying
for. When Capra protested that he'd never made documentary films,
Marshall replied that he'd never been Chief of Staff before nor had
many young men been soldiers before. Wounded, Capra replied:
"I'm sorry sir. I'll make the best damn documentary films ever
made" (NATT, 327).

Not long after talking with Marshall, Capra saw Leni Riefenstahl's
Triumph of the Will, the orchestrated paean to Hitler, Nazism, and
the "Master Race." Awestruck by the spectacle, Capra was also
horrified by the film's use of symbols and geometric masses of humanity to vivify the Nazi ideology. Watching the film gave him a
sense of how formidable the Nazi threat was; it also gave him the
idea to use enemy propaganda films as some of the visual material
for the orientation series he was ordered to make.

In his first weeks Capra became embroiled in a jurisdictional
dispute about who would actually put his films together—the Morale
Branch or the Signal Corps. Colonel Schlosberg of the Signal Corps
assumed that Capra would merely write the scripts, get them approved, then send them to the Signal Corps, where they would be
filmed in their film facilities in Astoria, Long Island. Capra, however, was determined to oversee the making of the films himself.
Though he initially had no facilities, he believed the typical army
"how-to" film style would be inappropriate for a film which tried
to explain the reasons for the war. The struggle between the Morale

Branch and the Signal Corps was resolved—at least officially—on May 2, 1942. On that date a letter announced the establishment of the 834th Signal Service Photograph Detachment. Its commanding officer was Frank Capra, who would be responsible to Brigadier General Osborn, the Chief of Special Services (the Morale Branch had been renamed Special Services in early 1942). The Signal Corps would be involved only upon request (NATT, 334–35).

Capra's unit began to grow, eventually reaching forty-three men. At first the unit worked in a section of the North Department of the Interior Building called "The Cooling Tower," the first two floors of which housed some 16mm and 35mm film equipment. Successfully negotiating for some Japanese and German newsreels, Capra and his crew went to work. About half of his group were civil service personnel; the other half were professionals, many of them Hollywood writers, directors, and editors who had enlisted. The unit was divided into three working groups. One group translated German and Japanese dialogue into English. A second group methodically catalogued and cross-filed the contents and sources of individual shots (shot-by-shot breakdowns of most of the "Why We Fight" series are available at the National Archives). The third group worked on research and scripts. Since time was a pressing factor, smaller groups of men worked together on each of the films planned for the series.

Very quickly, conditions in the Cooling Tower became too cramped, and Capra received permission to move his unit to California. Darryl Zanuck let Capra use some abandoned Twentieth-Century Studio facilities on Western Avenue to house the unit, and there most of the "Why We Fight" series was made. The series drew an impressive array of talent, both in and out of uniform. Among the people involved at one time or another in making films for the 834th were Anatole Litvak, Stuart Heisler, John Huston, George Stevens, William Wyler, Eric Knight, James Hilton, Walter Huston, Robert Stevenson, Robert Flaherty, and Alfred Newman. Capra's usual collaborator from his feature films—Dimitri Tiomkin— did a number of scores for the series, and two of the unit—editor William Hornbeck and cameraman Joseph Biroc—continued with Capra on his postwar masterpiece, *It's a Wonderful Life*.

The first of the "Why We Fight" series—*Prelude to War*—was screened for General Marshall in October 1942. By 1945 it had been shown to 9 million soldiers; in addition, 150 prints were made

available without rental to commercial theaters across the country
in 1943, the first of several "Why We Fight" films to receive theatrical distribution.[3] During the next year the rest of the "Why We
Fight" series were completed. They were (2) *The Nazis Strike;* (3)
Divide and Conquer; (4) *The Battle of Britain;* (5) *The Battle of
Russia;* (6) *The Battle of China;* (7) *War Comes to America.* Besides
this series, the Capra unit was involved in making a number of
other films: the "Know Your Enemy" and "Know Your Ally" films,
The Negro Soldier (directed by Stuart Heisler),[4] and a newsreel for
troops called the *Army-Navy Screen Magazine.*

As the "Why We Fight" series neared completion, the army
filmmaking units were reorganized. On September 1, 1943, the
834th was reassigned from Special Services to the Signal Corps and
was made a part of the Signal Corps' Army Pictorial Service (APS).
In the resulting reorganization Capra was temporarily assigned to
the Public Relations Staff of General Alexander Surles (and Anatole
Litvak was named to head the Western Avenue filmmaking activities). For General Surles, Capra headed a Special Coverage Section
that organized photographic coverage on those fronts approved by
commanding generals. One of the projects resulting from his work
for Surles was the joint British-American film *Tunisian Victory,*
released in 1944.

One of Capra's last projects during his three years in the army
was his help in making *Two Down and One to Go!* As the tide of
the war in Europe began to turn in favor of the Allies, General
Marshall became concerned. He feared that after Germany's defeat
"an uninformed and unreasoning clamor to 'bring the boys back
home' might play havoc with discipline and morale and greatly delay
the defeat of Japan." Capra participated in a secret meeting in early
1944 and suggested that a film be made to help prevent the potential
problem. Shot in great secrecy in the summer of 1944, the film was
given its official title—*Two Down and One to Go!*—on September
8, 1944. Over 1,300 prints of the film were made. On May 10,
1945—three days after the German surrender—civilian and military
audiences were shown the film. Sources have estimated that in the
next two weeks over 97 percent of all troops had seen the film, as
well as audiences in about 800 first-run theaters.[5] Again Capra's
belief in the power of film bore fruit.

So much for Capra's activities during the war. What of the "Why
We Fight" series? What are the films like? What do they say? How
do they say it?

Essentially, the films of the "Why We fight" series are compilation films made up almost completely of footage taken from other films or from stock shots stored in film libraries. Except for some footage shot by people like Robert Flaherty included in *War Comes to America* and a good number of animations made specifically for the series by the Disney studios, the series is nearly all compilation. Because the footage garnered for compilation films is unpredictable and because "Why We Fight" had to explain the reasons for fighting, it's understandable that the narration is very important in commenting on the image and leading the viewer toward a clearly defined interpretation of the events seen on the screen. In addition, musical scores were added to the films to help make the images more satisfying (in presenting the Allies) or more horrifying (in picturing the Axis powers). To give a better idea of the sources for sounds and images in the series, let's look specifically at two of the best films of the series—*The Battle of Russia* and *War Comes to America*.

The Battle of Russia, the longest film of the series—eighty minutes as opposed to about fifty for the others—was released in two parts. The first half gives a history of Russian conflicts with the German people and a description of the land and its diverse people; it ends with December 1941, about six months after the Nazi invasion. Part Two traces the war on the eastern front through early 1943, stressing especially the Russian defense of Leningrad and Stalingrad. Overall, the film draws footage from 105 different films. Much of the footage in the series came from films handled by Artkino, an American distributor of Russian films.[6] Artkino provided footage from both newsreels and such features as *Alexander Nevsky*, *The Conquests of Peter the Great*, and *Peter the First*. Besides Artkino, the following sources were used: Canadian National Film Board, newsreels from Fox, RKO, Paramount, MGM, Hearst, Pathé, Universal and the March of Time, captured enemy footage, the Museum of Modern Art, Disney animations, and a German UFA production, *Sieg im Western*. Much of the feature film footage was used in the history section early in the film.

Appropriately, Dimitri Tiomkin's score drew heavily from the work of Russian composers (some of the music was simply taken from the sound tracks of features whose images were used in the film). Tchaikovsky was the most heavily represented composer. His Symphonies Four, Five, and Six were used, as well as "Romeo and Juliet," "1812 Overture," "Waltz of the Flowers," and "Piano Concerto in B Flat Major." Parts of Stravinsky's "Rite of Spring," "Firebird Suite," and "Dance Infernal" accompanied images. Finally, pieces by Prokofiev, Shostakovich, Rachmaninoff, and Rimsky-Korsakov were also used. Unsurprisingly, the film—shown at Stalin's order—was popular with Russian audiences.

If *The Battle of Russia* celebrated the Russian courage in warding off the Nazi blitzkrieg, *War Comes to America* celebrated American traditions and the life-style of modern Americans, going on to explain the process by which the public gradually moved from isolationism to support of the war effort from the early 1930s to Pearl Harbor. Footage from the film came from four major kinds of sources: newsreels, documentaries, feature films, and production footage shot in California specifically for the film. Much of the newsreel footage came from March of Time and Pathé. The titles of documentaries used in the film read like a list of the major documentaries of the 1930s. They include *Triumph of the Will*, Lorentz's *The River* and *The Plow that Broke the Plains*, Flaherty's *The Land*, Van Dyke and Steiner's *The City*, Joris Iven's *The Power and the Land*, *The Spanish Earth*, and *The Four Hundred Million*, and Leo Hurwitz's *Native Land*. Among the features drawn from were Warner Brothers' *The Roaring Twenties* and *Confessions of a Nazi Spy*, and Paramount's *Wake Island* and *Union Pacific*. Robert Flaherty and others shot much of the production footage of Americans living their daily lives.

Tiomkin's score reveled in Americana; he used even more identifiably American music than he did in *Mr. Smith Goes to Washington*. Folksongs and patriotic music predominated: "Oh, Susannah," "America," "Yankee Doodle," "Hail, Columbia," "America the Beautiful", "Red River Valley," "Bury Me Not," "Camptown Races," "Coming 'Round the Mountain," and "Old Kentucky Home." Some more recent compositions appeared: Jerome Kern's "Old Man River," Gershwin's "Rhapsody in Blue," Duke Ellington's "Don't Get Around Much Anymore," and a part of Grofé's "Grand Canyon Suite." Two advertising themes—the "Rinso White Theme" and "Pepsodent Theme Song"—play on a radio, and some of Alfred Newman's original work for *Prelude to War* is borrowed. Finally, at various moments, often in describing the Nazis, an unidentified German march and Wagner's "Niebelungen March" are played. Generally, the music in both *The Battle of Russia* and *War Comes to America* was designed to help celebrate national traditions through music.

If the "Why We Fight" series as a whole has any unifying idea, it is that the Axis Powers, the "Slave World," must be conquered because they threaten to subjugate and overwhelm the Allies, the "Free World." Each of the films opens with a title: "The purpose of these films is to give factual information as to the causes, the events leading up to our entry into the war and the principles for which we are fighting." Next, Secretary of War Henry Stimson is quoted: "We are determined that before the sun sets on this bitter struggle our flag will be recognized throughout the world as a symbol of freedom on the one hand . . . and of *overwhelming* power on the other." Each film closes by quoting General Marshall: "The victory of the democracies can only be complete with the utter defeat of the war machines of Germany and Japan."

With this major theme organizing the films, three different preoccupations follow. The first is to dispel the notion that America is safe and can avoid participating in the war. This theme comes out most strongly in *Prelude to War* and *War Comes to America*. A second preoccupation is to present graphically the perverse brutality and totalitarianism of the Axis Powers, a primary concern of *Prelude to War*, *The Nazis Strike*, *Divide and Conquer*, and, to some extent, *The Battle of China*. Finally, the series praises the fighting strength and courage of American Allies, the key concern of *The Battle of Britain*, *The Battle of Russia*, and *The Battle of China*.

The films use a number of strategies to convey their ideology: one is a clear, forceful, and direct narration which gives a simple and cogent direction to the images. When documentary footage of the bombing of Rotterdam is shown in *Divide and Conquer*, the narrator calls it "one of the most ruthless exhibitions of savagery the world has ever seen." In that same film the narrator uses repetition. Each time a European country is overtaken, the narrator ominously concludes, "The Dutch [or whomever] will not forget." Allies are praised; even after night bombings of London begin, "British spirit was higher than ever. . . . In their hearts was a grim determination that this enemy must be destroyed." Conversely, enemies are condemned: "The German mind has never understood why free people fight on against overwhelming odds." They are also stereotyped; the Germans have always displayed a "love of regimentation and harsh discipline."

The films also let leaders speak for themselves. *Prelude to War* superimposes a passage from *Mein Kempf* over a poster of Hitler, his answer to these Germans who favored freedom: "Only the application of brute force used continuously and ruthlessly can bring about the decision in favor of the side it supports." *The Nazis Strike* quotes from a Hitler interview in 1933: "I am willing to sign anything. I will do anything to facilitate the success of my policy." If enemy leaders condemn themselves, Allied leaders voice their common aims. In *The Nazis Strike* Churchill is quoted: "Nothing is more certain than that every trace of Hitler's footsteps, every stain of his infected and corroding fingers will be sponged and purged and if need be blasted from the surface of the earth."

Emotionally charged images also characterize the films. One particularly symbolic shot occurs in *Prelude to War*. As the narrator talks about repression of religious freedom in Germany, a shot of a stained-glass church window appears. Suddenly, a rock flies through, shattering the glass. The resulting jagged hole reveals a poster of Hitler's glaring face in the background. Certain sequences of footage stand out: the Russian defense of the besieged Leningrad in *The Battle of Russia*, the building of the Burmese road in *The Battle of China*, and footage of the German bombing of London in *The Battle of Britain*.

Some of the most powerful rhetorical images came from Disney animations. In one shot in *Prelude to War*, a globe of the world separates into two: one light (the Western Hemisphere), the other dark. A superimposed title quotes Henry Wallace: "This is a fight between a free world and a slave world." Later in the same film the narrator talks of Japanese propaganda. Concentric circles radiate outward from an animated radio tower: each circle has the word "Lies" printed along its circumference. In *The Battle of Britain* an animated map of Europe begins white, but gradually black spreads over all of it to convey the German occupation. The effect is both graphic and powerful, as in many of the animations.

Most of the rhetorical power of the "Why We Fight" series, however, stems from editing—the skillful juxtaposition of images and sounds. A few examples will suffice. In *Prelude to War*, a shot presents in close-up pictures of Tojo, Hitler, and Mussolini. Accompanying is the somber voice of the narrator: "Take a look at this trio. Remember these faces. Remember them well. If you ever meet them—don't hesitate." One of the most powerful sequences in the whole series, from *Prelude to War*, presents images of Nazis marching; the sound track contains no dialogue, only a synchronized, insistent drumbeat. The combined effect is hypnotic and ominous. Later in the film American children play on a playground, accompanied by playful music. The film cuts to German children playing on tanks, to Italian and Japanese children training for war, then back to American children outside a school contributing to a Japanese Earthquake Relief Fund. Both *Battle of Russia* and *War Comes to America* contain skillfully edited sequences summarizing the historic traditions of each country. In *The Battle of China,* editing creates meaning: we see a shot of a working man looking up, followed by an aerial shot of a city burning, then a shot of him looking back down at his work. The cumulative effect is to show how America's Chinese allies go on in spite of adversity. A final example comes from *War Comes to America.* The narrator asks what kind of people Americans are, and a long sequence on the American self-image appears. As the narrator says what kind of people Americans are—working, inventive, vacationing, sports-loving, eating, joining, worshiping, and so on—a series of images appears for each. For example, the "sports-loving" section includes shots of people playing or watching football, baseball, racing, track, rodeo, basketball, golf, bowling, marbles, skiing, swimming, boating, and boxing. The skillful editing in the series seeks to instill in the audience an anger against the enemy, a sympathy for and confidence in the Allies, and a feeling for the goodness of American society.

While making use of all these filmic devices, how effective was the "Why We Fight" series? Audience response is, of course, a very difficult matter to measure. Concerning the "Why We Fight" series, however, we are fortunate to have the findings of an experiment designed by social scientists to measure the effects of the series on soldiers who saw the films.[7] Their experiment involved testing two groups of soldiers (2,100 total) at two different army camps during February and April of 1943, then again nine weeks later. Though the test could not measure if seeing the films made the soldiers more effective and enthusiastic fighters, it did measure knowledge and opinions. The researchers found that the films had "marked effects" on soldiers' knowledge of factual events which led up to the war. It also had "some marked effects" on opinions specifically related to *interpretations* treated in the film. (For example, *Prelude to War* suggested that Hitler would close all churches if he conquered America; 11 percent more soldiers agreed that this would happen after seeing the film.) Finally, the study made up some overt questions designed to measure soldiers' motivations to fight (e.g., "If you had a choice, would you choose duty in an overseas outfit or in an outfit in the U.S.?"). The films showed no effects on these questions.[8]

At first glance, the evidence seems to suggest that while the series helped soldiers understand the war better, it did not make them more enthusiastic about fighting. Looked at more carefully, however, the films do seem to have had some important effects. Since the experience of a single film rarely changes fundamental beliefs and attitudes, it is unsurprising that the experience of viewing the films failed to make soldiers more enthusiastic about fighting: by early 1943, the culture had been immersed in the war so long that minds were made up. But this does lead to what I believe to be the greatest effect of the "Why We Fight" series: to reinforce and solidify attitudes of soldiers toward the Allies and the Axis Powers that had been dominant in America at least since Pearl Harbor. Though we don't know whether "Why We Fight" made better soldiers of those who viewed the films, it does seem clear that they reinforced an already dominant orientation toward American involvement and provided soldiers with facts to justify it.

So much for effects. To what extent is Capra's involvement revealed in the series? Especially in the American sequences of *Prelude to War* and *War Comes to America,* one senses a "Capraesque" sensibility at work: both reveal a feeling for common American life and a pride in American traditions ("lighthouses in a foggy world") which we've seen in Capra's feature films. Likewise, the stress on freedom and liberty as prized American values—evident at least implicitly in all of the series—seems close to Capra's social vision.

Yet before looking too closely for traces of Capra's imprint on the "Why We Fight" series, we must make two distinctions. The first is that all the films had to be approved by Capra's superiors before they could be released. They were important documents in conveying American military policy and positions to soldiers and at times even to the public. If we do discover some of Capra's social vision in the series, it is probably because his vision coincided with and followed American policy and not vice versa.

Second, the "Why We Fight" series was a collaborative effort and cannot be attributed to the vision and work of any single person. At times Capra seems to take more credit for some films—like *The Negro Soldier* or *The Navy-Army Screen Magazine*—than he deserves. It is important to note that though he received producer credit on all the "Why We Fight" series, he received sole director's credit on only one, and codirector credit on four others. On compilation films like this one, the role of producer and director is a lot less clear than on a fictional feature film (and even then it can be problematic). It's probably best to stress the importance of Capra's list of the many collaborators on the "Why We Fight" series (NATT, 340) and to say that Capra's biggest contribution was his feisty ability to keep the series rolling amidst the difficulties he encountered within the military chain of command. Surely Capra's struggles with Harry Cohn and —when he was president of the Screen Directors' Guild—with other producers helped him survive the military red tape and complete the job General Marshall had ordered him to do.

Certainly General Marshall thought so. On June 14, 1945, a month after the surrender of Germany and a day before Capra's release from the army, Marshall pinned the Distinguished Service Medal on Capra's uniform. The Oscar-winning director had now won the highest noncombat award the army could give, and with a mixture of excitement, pride, and trepidation he turned his eyes back toward civilian life and the art form he loved so much.

6

It's a Wonderful Life: The Masterpiece (1945–46)

IF FRANK CAPRA had to be remembered for only one work, that film would have to be *It's a Wonderful Life* (1946), his first feature film after World War II. Though it received as many negative as positive reviews when it was released—Bosley Crowther called it "a figment of simple Pollyanna platitudes"—the critical consensus in the last two decades has recognized the film's remarkable achievement (NATT, 382). For Stephen Handzo, *It's a Wonderful Life* "is one of the most personal visions ever realized in commercial cinema" (FC, 175). Andrew Sarris calls *Wonderful Life* "an all-time masterpiece," Jeanine Basinger terms it "one of the most beloved films in the history of movies," and Robin Wood judges it one of "the greatest American films."[1]

It's a Wonderful Life is clearly a culminating work. By that term I mean one of those rare works of narrative art in which an artist at last finds a form to express precisely the preoccupations he or she has been dealing with in a number of earlier works. In this respect *Wonderful Life* resembles *The Adventures of Huckleberry Finn*, the work in which Mark Twain finally managed to reconcile his personal ambivalence about the genteel and vernacular traditions by speaking through a young vernacular narrator. Or it's like *The Great Gatsby*, in which F. Scott Fitzgerald built on short stories like "The Rich Boy" and "Winter Dreams" to express in an almost perfectly wrought form his complex, ambivalent attitude toward wealth and the American Dream. Culminating works are rare; they are also extremely rewarding to study carefully. The rest of this

Photo (left) from It's a Wonderful Life: *James Stewart as George Bailey weighs his options in Bedford Falls*

chapter will first discuss the backgrounds and origins of *It's a Wonderful Life*, then examine the film closely as the culmination of Frank Capra's filmmaking career.

When Capra returned to Hollywood in mid-1945 after winning the Distinguished Service Medal, he had lost his place as one of the preeminent Hollywood directors. The war years were boom years for the movie industry; it seemed to get along quite well without Capra, Ford, Huston, Wyler, and the many other talents who spent the war in uniform. Capra himself remembers his own uncertainty about his vocation after spending time in the army.[2] After seeing women and children huddled in the halls of buildings or in subways while German bombers strafed London, Capra wondered whether filmmaking was simply a frivolous activity, whether he should spend his time and energy involved in such a pursuit. Indeed, he even wondered if he still had the ability, talents, and inner strength necessary to make a feature film in this new moment of history. We noted earlier the rises and declines in Capra's career and the self-doubts he often felt when on the way down. This was another moment of doubt in Capra's career; he felt, in his own words, "a loneliness that was laced with a fear of failure" as he faced his next project (NATT, 378).

Part of the anxiety was probably due to the fact that Capra had formed an independent production company, Liberty Films, with his friend Sam Briskin and two fellow directors, William Wyler and George Stevens. It was part of a larger movement in Hollywood right after the war years in which directors (and sometimes actors) broke away from the major studios to produce their own films, then distribute them through a major studio. Capra himself perceived in 1946 what he called a "pattern of sameness" in Hollywood. He believed that independent productions would add the creativity and individuality necessary to break (or at least supplement) that pattern.[3] With a large financial risk, however, Capra had to make a successful first film to keep Liberty Films viable.

After considering and discarding various sources for his next film Capra bought the rights to a story that had just been published as a Christmas card pamphlet by Philip Van Doren Stern: "The Greatest Gift." Because the story provides the starting point for *It's a Wonderful Life*, we must say a few words about Stern, the story, and its history.

Philip Van Doren Stern is a writer known more for his biographies (of Poe, Thoreau, and John Wilkes Booth) and his histories (various works on the Civil War) than for his fiction. He first conceived of the story in 1938 and immediately sat down and wrote an outline. In the next half-decade he rewrote it several times, finally completing a satisfactory version in 1943. After several magazines turned it down, Stern published the story as a pamphlet at his own expense and sent out about 200 copies as a Christmas card, including one to his Hollywood agent. After receiving Stern's go-ahead, the agent sold the rights to Hollywood. In 1945 Capra bought those rights, and as the film neared its release date in December 1946 the story was adapted to radio and broadcast on the "Lux Radio Show" and on CBS. Since the film's release, the story has been published in several editions, one a Portuguese Brazilian edition, most recently in a volume of short stories edited by Stern, *The Other Side of the Clock*. The resilience of the story's main idea is further stressed by Marlo Thomas's television remake of the film—*It Happened One Christmas*—in late 1977.[4] In that version Mary Bailey, played by Thomas, contemplates suicide and experiences what the world would be like had she not lived.

Yet a vast difference separates the story from the narrative of the film. It has frequently been suggested that the greatest works of film art come from original screenplays or adaptations of run-of-the-mill literary materials. Think of *Potemkin, Citizen Kane, Rules of the Game, The Bicycle Thief, Stagecoach,* or *Rashomon*. All are original screenplays or adaptations that vastly transcend their literary sources. *Wonderful Life* also clearly belongs to this category.

Its source, "The Greatest Gift," contains one notion central to the film: a despairing man is given a chance to see what the world would be like had he not lived. In addition, several other details are borrowed from the story, though presented differently in the film. The main couple are named George and Mary in both (though it's George Pratt, not Bailey, in the story). In both, the central character contemplates suicide at a bridge because he is frustrated with his job and feels he has never really lived. Both make use of Christmas Eve as a setting. The film takes two incidental details from the fantasy section of the story: George sees a tree without a gash that should have been there and discovers his brother has died. And in both, snowflakes signal to George that he has returned to life.

But the story is sketchy, providing none of the detailed richness and tightly woven narrative complexity of *Wonderful Life*. The reader knows little about George Pratt's reasons for suicide, while the first two-thirds of *Wonderful Life* builds up George Bailey's frustrations at constantly curbing his dreams of achievement. During the fantasy in the story George notices only a few changed details from his life. The film's fantasy sequence piles up many—all presented in a powerfully effective film style. The story is set in the present; the film goes into an extended flashback of George's life between 1919 and 1945 before going into the fantasy sequence. The story ends with George Pratt's discovery of a blue brush he encountered in the fantasy; the film ends in Capra's deepest and most effective affirmation of human life and social solidarity. Capra's transformation of "The Greatest Gift" is like an archaeologist's discovery of a few decaying bones. From those few bones, Capra added many more, assembled them into a whole, fleshed them out, and in the end had constructed an enduring human artifact.

More people worked on the screenplay for *It's a Wonderful Life* than for any other Capra film, yet it remains his most personal film. This apparent paradox might be explained by commenting that Capra was deeply and personally involved in the process and that he accepted and discarded those contributions from his screenwriters insofar as they contributed to his image of what he wanted the film to be. Though the story of how the script evolved would be a fascinating one—and I hope someone will be able to discover the various versions and tell that story at some point—it can't be told on the basis of what evidence we have today. We can, however, give a sketch of the collaborators involved.

Before Capra purchased rights to the story, RKO had already commissioned three different writers to adapt the screenplay. Dalton Trumbo, dramatist Clifford Odets, and Marc Connolley had all turned in complete scripts, though none, according to Capra, did justice to the story. After reading all three, Capra saved a few of Odets's early scenes, then—with both Robert Riskin and Sidney Buchman involved with other projects—Capra hired the husband-wife team of Francis Goodrich and Albert Hackett (*The Thin Man, Ah Wilderness!, Seven Brides for Seven Brothers*) to work on the story. After they wrote some scenes, Capra added some more which they wove into the story. Finally, Capra was pleased. Though he did talk with his old collaborator Jo Swerling about the script, Swerling left after learning he couldn't do a complete rewrite. So the script finally used appears to be the Goodrich-Hackett-Capra version supplemented by Odets's earlier version and Swerling's advice. The titles credit Goodrich, Hackett, and Capra as screenwriters, with Swerling credited as providing "additional scenes" (NATT, 376–78).

Casting was next, and Capra assembled an exceptional group. Jimmy Stewart—also nervous after his return from the armed forces—was chosen to play George Bailey. It's his favorite role, and Stephen Handzo is right when he calls George Bailey "less a character than a container into which James Stewart pours every nuance of his being" (FC, 173). To play the corrupt banker Potter, Capra chose Lionel Barrymore—a complete switch from his role as the benign Grandpa Vanderhof in *You Can't Take It With You*. Besides some newcomers—Donna Reed as George's wife, Mary Hatch Bailey, and Todd Kearns as his brother Harry—most of the actors were from the "company" Capra and John Ford shared: Thomas Mitchell (Uncle Billy), Beulah Bondi and Samuel S. Hinds (George's mother and father), H. B. Warner (the druggist, Gower), Ward Bond (Bert the Cop), and Frank Faylen (Ernie the cab driver). Gloria Grahame (Violet, Mary's rival) and Henry Travers (Clarence, George's guardian angel) rounded out the cast.

Capra chose other collaborators from his film crew in the army. Dimitri Tiomkin did the score, providing both despair (the fantasy) and exhilaration (the conclusion) with music. William Hornbeck received editing credit. And though Capra's old collaborator Joseph Walker and Joseph Biroc received dual camera credit, Biroc did nearly all of the photography. After Capra had to fire an uncooperative cameraman just as shooting began, Walker took over as a favor and supervised some early scenes until Biroc—whom Walker and Capra approved of—could get approved for head cameraman status.[5] Shooting began on April 8, 1946, continuing at the pace of a "four-month, non-stop orgasm" (NATT, 382). Released by Christmas, *Wonderful Life* lost out to Wyler's *The Best Years of Our Lives* in all the major awards for which it was nominated: best picture, best director, and best actor. Nevertheless, Capra had made what he considered "the greatest film *anybody* had ever made" and it still remains his favorite (NATT, 383).

"In the face of human anguish, doubt, unrest, and the struggle just to manage daily life," François Truffaut has written, "Capra was a kind of healer."[6] Surely this comment applies to *Wonderful Life* as much as any other Capra film. So does Capra's theory of comedy as he describes it in his autobiography: "Comedy is fulfillment, accomplishment, overcoming. It is victory over the odds, a triumph of good over evil. . . . The gospels are comedies: a triumph of spirit over matter. The Resurrection . . . is a divine comedy" (NATT, 453). This notion of comedy as affirmation and victory is a far cry from the gag writing Capra began with at the Hal Roach studios in the 1920s; it is a much deeper, weightier, one might almost say transcendent, conception of comedy. In *Wonderful Life* Capra realizes this theory of comedy as in no other film.

Wonderful Life differs from the late-1930s comedies in at least two ways that contribute to its success. First, in contrast to Deeds and Smith, who leave their homes to carry out their struggles in a foreign environment, George Bailey lives and works entirely within his home town of Bedford Falls. Not only does this give the viewer a good sense of George's place in the community, it also relieves George of the necessity to convert cynics who mock and misunderstand him in the foreign environment. In addition to the shift in setting, *It's a Wonderful Life* has a tightly woven narrative structure which traces George's life for more than a quarter century, much of it in an extended flashback. Capra's typical films covered weeks or months of a person's life; only *Forbidden* seems to have covered more than a decade of real time. Despite the fact that *Wonderful Life* covers so much time, however, the selection and presentation of details in the narrative are both dense and highly appropriate.

That narrative can be segmented into ten major parts, each one treating a particular time in George's life. Parts one, eight, and ten are in the present—Christmas Eve 1945, from 9:45 on. (It is impossible to fix precisely when the flashback ends. I have assumed that people are praying for George—part one—about the time George arrives at Potter's office—start of part eight.) Parts two through seven constitute an extended flashback lasting more than half of the film. Part eight returns us to the present, and the ninth part is the fantasy sequence, in which George sees what the world would be like had he not lived. Within each major part of the film, two or more scenes occur; they are distinguished either by an action, a changed location, a changed time, or a combination of the three. A breakdown of the film would look like this:

1. The present—Christmas Eve 1945, 9:45 P.M.
   People in Bedford Falls pray for George/in the heavens, Peter,
   Joseph, and Clarence discuss George's plight.
                          FLASHBACK
2. 1919
   Winter: George saves brother Harry, loses hearing in one ear.
   Spring: George notices Gower's mistake, saves him from disaster
   by not delivering poisoned pills.
3. 1928
   Graduation day: George prepares for trip in downtown Bedford
   Falls/Home: talks with father/School gymnasium: graduation
   dance/320 Sycamore: talks with Mary Hatch.
   Three months later: at board meeting, George asked to replace
   father.
4. 1932
   Harry returns from college with wife/George visits Mary/George
   and Mary's wedding day: Church steps/cab/bank run at Building
   and Loan/Dinner at 320 Sycamore.
5. 1935
   Martinis prepare to move into their home at Bailey Park: Leave
   rented home in Potter's field/Potter's office: agent warns Potter
   about growth of Bailey Park/Martinis new home: George and Mary
   welcome Martinis/Speak to Sam Wainwright/Potter's office: Potter tries to buy off George/Bedroom at 320 Sycamore: George
   learns of Mary's pregnancy.
6. 1935–45: montage (Voiceover narration from heaven)
   Images of George and Mary's family and 320 Sycamore, of the
   activities of the characters during World War II, and of church
   services on V-E and V-J Days.
7. Dec. 24, 1945—10:00 A.M.–9:45 P.M.
   Intercut between main street of Bedford Falls, the bank, the
   Bldg. and Loan, and later Uncle Billy's home, as Bedford Falls
   prepares for celebration in war-hero Harry's honor and Uncle
   Billy loses money and searches for it with George/320 Sycamore:
   George alternately despondent and angry with family.
                          PRESENT
8. Dec. 24, 1945—c. 9:45 P.M.
   Potter's office, George pleads for money/Martini's Bar: George
   slugged by irate Mr. Welch/George moves toward bridge: crashes
   car into tree, nearly run over by truck, contemplates suicide.

FANTASY SEQUENCE

9. Out of time

Bridge: Clarence jumps into water, George saves him/ Warming house by bridge: George and Clarence talk, George wishes he was never born.

The world without George: Nick's Bar/Downtown Pottersville/320 Sycamore/Ma Bailey's Boarding House/Cemetery/Mary in downtown Pottersville/Run to bridge.

PRESENT

10. Dec. 24, 1945—10:45 P.M.

George is returned to life/Runs through streets of Bedford Falls/Arrives home: members of community come with money to save George from ruin.

Wonderful Life is Capra's culminating work in part because it draws from earlier Capra films in theme, character, and incident, bringing together a number of his preoccupations and presenting them in a unified whole. One of the central motifs of the film—the notion that wealth is better measured by one's friends than one's bank account—comes directly from *You Can't Take It With You.* George Bailey himself is closely related to the idealists Deeds and Smith, both of whom are respected members of their communities. The run on the Bailey Brothers Building and Loan during the Depression recalls a similar scene in *American Madness,* just as George Bailey's willingness to loan money to people on the basis of character echoes Tom Dickson's philosophy. Like *Meet John Doe,* *Wonderful Life* concludes on Christmas Eve, and like D. B. Norton, Henry F. Potter has a statue of Napoleon in his office. Such similarities between *Wonderful Life* and earlier Capra films could be multiplied; these are just some of the most important.

Another reason *Wonderful Life* constitutes a culminating work is that it virtually sums up the cultural history of this American small town between 1919 and 1946. Capra was careful to fill his flashback sequences with visual and aural hints about the date of particular sequences, summing up, in a sense, the times that many of the adults in his audience had experienced. The year 1919 is suggested by the fact that Mr. Gower's son died of influenza—another victim of the terrible epidemic of that year—and also, for a careful viewer, by the picture of Woodrow Wilson on the wall of Peter Bailey's office. When George approaches Ernie and Bert on

Photo: Henry F. Potter (Lionel Barrymore), with a bust of Napoleon in the background, tries to tempt George with money

the streets of Bedford Falls, the headline on Bert's newspaper dates the scene: "Smith Wins Nomination" (1928). Appropriately, people do the Charleston at the graduation dance that night. In 1932, the bank run suggests the time; so does the picture of Herbert Hoover in George's office. Finally, the montage of how the central characters spent World War II—Mary as USO head, Harry as a fighter pilot, George as rationing director, Potter (appropriately) as chairman of the draft board—centrally locates the characters within the experience of Capra's audience. All of George Bailey's experiences take place within this background of the American cultural experience from the end of the First World War to the end of the Second.

At the core of the whole narrative of *Wonderful Life* is George Bailey, Capra's most fully realized hero. The central tensions and thrust of *Wonderful Life* can be best treated by examining the two main conflicts confronting George: one is external, between George and Potter, the other internal, within George himself. Though a number of earlier Capra heroes were involved in clearly external conflicts—Deeds versus the city cynics, Smith versus Paine and Taylor—no other hero, not even Long John Willoughby, was as deeply divided internally as George Bailey is in *Wonderful Life*. If Deeds or Smith doubt, it's because external forces cause the doubt. George Bailey is split within, never as content with his morality as Deeds or Smith. Let's look at George's external conflict first.

The external conflict pits George's way of dealing with other human beings against Potter's; it might be summarized as George's humanitarianism, kindness, altruism, and selflessness as opposed to Potter's materialism, ruthlessness, narcissism, and selfishness. It's clear from an early scene that the conflict is originally between Peter Bailey and Potter. When George goes to see his father in 1919, Peter Bailey is involved in a dispute with Potter, who calls Peter a "miserable failure" for running the Building and Loan like a charity ward instead of a business. George stoutly defends his father, and it's stressed throughout the film that George has inherited his father's values. He keeps a picture of his father in both his office and the living room of 320 Sycamore, and beneath the office picture is a sign that encapsulates Peter Bailey's philosophy: "All you can take with you is that which you've given away." (Significantly, the sign is presented most prominently just before George goes out of his office to control the bank run and use his honeymoon money to do so.)

This external conflict between George's benevolent capitalism and Potter's malevolent capitalism is poised most explicitly in the scene at the Building and Loan shortly after Peter Bailey's death. After the chairman of the board praises Peter Bailey for his "faith and devotion," Potter says he was a man "of high ideals . . . so called," adding: "But ideals without common sense can ruin this town." Peter's willingness to loan to people without collateral only creates a "discontented lazy rabble," Potter charges, then urges the dissolution of the Building and Loan. George, a black mourning band on his right arm, becomes irate and defends his father as a man who "never once thought of himself." Framed in medium shot with his father's picture to his right, George says, "People were human beings to him." Moving forward and left in the frame, George covers his father's picture, visually taking up his father's torch: "But to you—a warped frustrated old man—they're cattle. Well, in my book, he died a much richer man than you'll ever be." George's optimistic view of human beings as basically good and trustworthy is challenged twice during the film. The first is during the bank run, where George's friends threaten to behave as a panicked mob, but George's altruism and leadership prevent mob action. The second time is after losing the money. Though Potter—true to his philosophy—says that the town's "riff-raff" would "run him out of town on a rail" if he asked them for money, George's friends and neighbors do come to his aid with money when they learn of his plight.

Taken alone, the resolution of this conflict might seem like a "fantasy of goodwill," yet the resolution is made more complex by the fact that George himself is split, never entirely comfortable in his role as the town's Good Samaritan. In fact, vagaries of circumstance in some senses force him into the role, one which conflicts with another orientation and set of attitudes equally strong in his psyche.

George's internal conflict is between his sense of moral responsibility, inherited from his father, and his personal desires for adventure, achievement, and success. We have already outlined George's sense of commitment to family and community; his other side is equally evident in the film. In 1919, young George Bailey enters the drugstore with the words, "Wish I had a million dollars." He tells young Mary Hatch that he's a member of the National Geographic Society, knows about exotic places like Tahiti and the

Fiji Islands, and will someday travel around the world. In 1928 he's preparing to take that trip and then to go to college. The scene with Mary Hatch in front of the mansion at 320 Sycamore perfectly embodies George's desires, as well as the forces that thwart them.

Standing in front of the old mansion, George makes a wish, then breaks a window. When Mary asks what his wish was, George replies: "I'm going to shake the dust from this crummy little town and see the world." After traveling, he'll go to college, then spend a career building bridges, air fields, and skyscrapers. This wish reiterates his comments to his father earlier in the evening, indicating both his dreams and his desire not to be "cooped up the rest of my life in a shabby little office." Though George's aspirations are strong here, they immediately become more remote. Mary also throws her stone, wishing (though it's not stated until later) to marry George and move into 320 Sycamore, the building which becomes, as Lauren Rabinovitz has pointed out, a central visual motif in the film. George's adventuresome and success-oriented side sees it as a threat (a "drafty old barn"); his altruistic side sees it as a symbol of his close family and community ties.[7]

Much of the rest of the film until the fantasy sequence traces the frustration of George's desires for adventure and achievement and his only half-willing acceptance of Peter Bailey's sense of moral responsibility to others. When his father dies from a stroke, he must defer college and take over the Building and Loan until Harry returns from college. But Harry marries, is offered a lucrative job as a researcher, and George's dreams of college are shattered. The night he learns of Harry's marriage, George looks at some travel brochures as he stands alone outside his mother's house. When a train whistle reminds him of what he wants but will never have, he abruptly throws them down. Going indirectly to Mary's house, George hears a record of "Buffalo Gals" and sees a needlepoint caricature of George in a cowboy outfit lassoing the moon; both allude to the wishing scene at 320 Sycamore, while the picture suggests both George's aspirations and his desire to provide for her. In the longest take of the film—over ninety seconds—George's ambivalence about marrying Mary is stressed. He both hates Mary, for marriage will surely destroy his dreams of achievement, and loves her, for she offers the love and human compassion his other side desires. In a medium close-up of both listening to Sam Wainwright's financial schemes, George's anger at Mary instantly shifts to a yearning desire: his decision to marry her signals his repression of his adventurous side. This is further stressed later when Mary offers and George agrees to use their honeymoon money to save the Building and Loan during the bank run.

So George Bailey becomes the Good Samaritan of the town. He never realizes how important he is in town, or how much he is appreciated, and he never entirely shakes the nagging feeling that his life has been something of a failure. When Sam Wainwright stops by to say hello, wearing a rich man's clothes, riding in a chauffeured limousine, George can only compare unfavorably his plain, worn clothing and his balky Model T. When Potter—a skull on his desk, his own picture on his office wall—offers to buy off George with a salary of $20,000 a year, ten times George's earnings, George is clearly tempted. Though he rejects the offer, George returns to the bedroom of his house and hears the offer again in voiceover when he enters his bedroom, followed by a voiceover of the dreams he declared to Mary during the wish scene. But his personal self-doubt is quickly overridden when Mary awakes to tell him she's pregnant, offering him the rewards of family.

Both George's internal and external conflicts come to a head in two scenes after Uncle Billy loses the money. In the first—for me one of the most excruciating scenes in American film—a distraught George is angry and short tempered with his family, then goes to the corner of the room where a bridge and skyscraper made of blocks rest on a table. Frustrated, George swipes at the blocks, scattering those objects which symbolize his unrealized dreams. Leaving the house, George goes to Potter's office to ask for money to bail him out. Understanding George better than George understands himself, Potter calls him a "warped, frustrated young man." Though George, in contrast to Potter, has repressed the selfish desires of his ego, he is just as frustrated in his own way as the atomistic and greedy Potter and remains so until he realizes the positive and lasting contribution he has made to his family and community. Only the fantasy sequence, in which George sees what life would be like had he not lived, and the final sequence, when the community repays George for his altruism, resolve George's internal and external conflicts.

William Pechter has written that *Wonderful Life* "is one of the funniest and one of the bleakest, as well as being one of the most technically adroit, films ever made" (FC, 182). I agree with him.

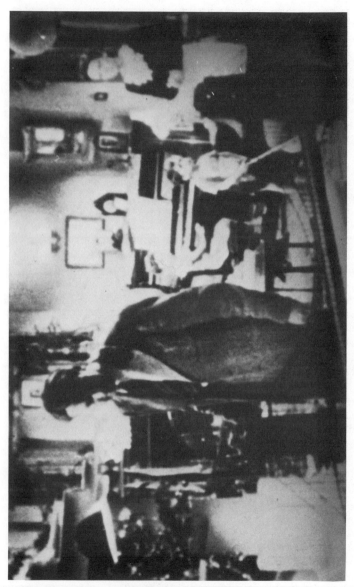

Photo: in a key scene, George contemplates the bridge and skyscraper that remind him of his unfulfilled dream before angrily smashing them to the floor

Surely *Wonderful Life* is filled with visual and verbal comedy. A list of funny situations and characters is a lot longer than one might first expect. In an homage to Chaplin's *The Rink* Capra has George and Mary unknowingly dance several times to the edge of the swimming pool, then finally tumble in. When Mary accidentally loses her robe, George first looks under it as it lies on the sidewalk, then gloats ("this is a very interesting situation"). The horrified reactions of Mary's mother to her daughter's romance and the astonished reaction of the man in the warming room to the angel Clarence both provide comedy through reaction shots. Uncle Billy provides comedy by his forgetfulness—in spite of the strings on his fingers—and by his penchant for a few drinks (at one point he knocks over an off-screen garbage can while singing "My Wild Irish Rose"). Clarence provides comic relief in the fantasy sequence, which otherwise would be too intense.

But perhaps the most amusing single scene is when George enters the rundown house at 320 Sycamore on his wedding night. First, Ernie, standing at the door to show George in, leans his head back toward the fully opened door and puts out his left hand for a tip. The back rim of his top hat hits the door, raising the front, as if he's tipping his hat. George, by this time coming through the door, looks down toward Ernie's hand, and water from his rain-soaked hat brim splashes into the center of Ernie's palm. Neither Keaton nor W. C. Fields could have improved the timing. As George moves by Ernie, he sees the inviting wedding bed and does a comic double take. Then he looks into the dining room; there a phonograph both plays a record and—aided by an improvised pulley and belt system—turns a spit roasting chicken over the fireplace. The scene ends with George and Mary embracing, while Bert and Ernie sing "I Love You Truly" outside. Finishing the song, Ernie lifts Bert's cop hat and plants a kiss on his forehead. Bert responds by reaching toward Ernie's top hat in the same manner, then smashing it almost flat.

So *Wonderful Life* is filled with funny moments. But I'd argue that the ending is the most exhilarating, indeed, the happiest moment of the film. Pechter calls *Wonderful Life* both funny and bleak—a strange combination—yet many viewers I've talked to have commented on the extreme range and power of the emotional journey they take in watching *Wonderful Life*, moving from utter despair in the fantasy sequence to transcendent joy in the conclusion.

After viewing the film countless times and thinking about the narrative, I think I am beginning to understand how it achieves much of its power. In trying to account for that power, I'd like to discuss two reasons: one stylistic, one cultural.

When Pechter calls the film "technically adroit," he points to one of the keys of the film's effectiveness. The combination of tight narrative structure and use of film style goes a long way toward explaining the film's power on audiences. I'd like to concentrate on the taut narrative and film style of the last two sequences—George's fantasy and his miraculous salvation through the support of his family and community—to demonstrate how the film rhetoric moves many viewers.

The fantasy sequence works in part because of the strangeness of the situation—a person seeing what his world would be like had he not lived. But what really makes the section effective is the wealth of detail. By my count, George notices over twenty changes from his Bedford Falls existence when he enters the fantasy world: (1) he hears from his deaf ear, (2) his lip has stopped bleeding, (3) snow stops, (4) his clothes immediately dry, (5) his car is gone, (6) the tree is undamaged, (7) Bedford Falls is now Pottersville, (8) Martini's is now Nick's, (9) Gower is a drunkard and ex-con, (10) George has no identification or wallet, (11) the rose petals in his watch pocket are gone, (12) Main Street is transformed, (13) Violet is a prostitute, (14) Ernie doesn't know him, (15) 320 Sycamore is abandoned and rundown, (16) Bert doesn't know him, (17) Ma Bailey, running a boarding house, doesn't know him, (18) Uncle Billy is in an asylum, (19) Bailey Park is a cemetery, (20) Harry's tomb indicates his death in 1919, (21) all men in the transport died because Harry couldn't save them, (22) Mary is a spinster librarian. Some of these even include more changed details: for example, Ernie's wife has left him and he lives alone in a shack in Potter's Field. But the point is that the entire transformation of Bedford Falls—both its physical layout and the people themselves—completely horrifies George and the viewer. When George again asks for life and notices his bad ear, his bleeding lip, and his wrecked car, he is ecstatic.

The way Capra uses film style in the last two sequences to present these changes also adds to the effectiveness of the scenes. Robin Wood has suggested that the central tension of *Wonderful Life* is produced by the "disturbing influx of *film noir* into the world of small-town domestic comedy."[8] Developing this notion, we might

Photos: (top) pharmacist Gower (H. B. Warner) discovers early in the film that George (Bobby Anderson) is right—the pills contain poison, and he avoids a tragic mistake; (bottom) in the fantasy sequence George discovers that Gower didn't catch the mistake and has become an ex-con and drunken bum

say that Capra uses two entirely different generic styles to shoot the final two sequences. The fantasy sequence draws from the tawdry, dark atmosphere of the urban *film noir* melodramas, while the conclusion reflects the affirmative, optimistic aura of small-town comedy. It's almost as if Philip Marlowe met Andy Hardy.

Though an exhaustive analysis of the contrasting film styles of the two sequences is impossible, a contrast of how various aspects of film rhetoric are used can give an idea of how Capra used his mastery of the medium to help achieve his aims.

Lighting: Generally the fantasy sequence is lit in low-key lighting or high-contrast lighting, while the ending uses high-key lighting. We move from darkness and shadows to no shadows at all. When George watches Violet being thrown into a paddy wagon, an off-screen neon light blinks on and off, adding to George's disorientation. Later, when George searches 320 Sycamore, only the glare of Bert's flashlight fights against the darkness. In contrast, the house is extremely bright in the ending, clearly illuminating George, his family, and those who come to his aid.

Sets: Here we contrast George's familiar Bedford Falls with the seedy, tawdry world of dance halls and one-night cheap hotels. The store fronts of Bedford Falls are completely redone in the fantasy: only bars, dance halls, and girlie shows line the streets. Of course, 320 Sycamore is dilapidated, and George's mother's home has become the unkempt "Ma Bailey's Boarding House." Bailey Park is a cemetery. On his return, George again runs down Main Street, this time through the familiar Bedford Falls: even Leo McCarey's *The Bells of St. Mary's* plays at the movie theater. When George arrives home, he grabs the loose newel as he runs up the stairs to embrace his children. Though it angered him earlier in the film, it now reminds him of how much he loves the warmth and security of his home.

Acting and composition: Stewart's acting is superb. He moves from expressions of bewilderment and fear to those of utter joy. Two close-ups of his wide-eyed astonishment and horror after leaving his mother's house underline his response to Pottersville. That response derives in part from the brusque treatment he receives from those he thinks should know him. Stewart is often composed alone in the frame in the fantasy. After he returns to his house and embraces his children at the top of the stairs, George is never alone in the frame during the sequence. His jubilant expression, and the warm smiles of all the people who crowd into his living room—nearly everyone George has befriended or helped in the film—help suggest George's "victory."

Camera movement: Though the camera movement in the final section is unobtrusive and only follows a character who is moving, a moving camera is subtly used to create disorientation in George's run down the Pottersville main street. In the twelve consecutive moving shots from George's start down Main Street until he sees Violet being pulled into the paddy wagon, four are left-to-right, high angle, long-shot pans or dollies of George. The other eight are moving shots from George's point of view. He looks on both sides of the street, and the moving camera reveals this by making five of the shots left-to-right dollies, three of them right-to-left dollies. The effect is to add subtly but certainly to the audience's sense of disorientation.

Music: Music is both realistic and commentative in both sections. Jazz on the piano in Nick's and emanating from dance halls in Pottersville adds to the town's aura of decadence. At other points, eerie commentative music reinforces George's feelings of uncertainty and fear. Only occasional bars of Clarence's theme—"Twinkle, Twinkle Little Star"—lighten the tone. In the final sequence, celebratory commentative music accompanies George down the main street of Bedford Falls. At the Bailey home, Janey plays the Christmas hymn "Hark, the Herald Angels Sing" (which she practiced earlier), and after Harry gives a toast to George, "the richest man in town," everyone sings a Capra favorite: "Auld Lang Syne." Eerie decadence changes to the apex of human warmth.

Sound effects: The fantasy sequence contains the sounds of *film noir*. At certain points we hear sirens. When George is at the cemetery a harsh cold wind whistles. After George punches Bert and runs for the bridge, several gunshots ring out. But when George arrives home, the key sounds are a constant din of undistinguishable comments by excited people and a bell ringing in the film's second to the last shot, indicating that another angel—presumably Clarence—has won his wings.

Editing Strategy: Reaction shots had long been a key Capra device designed to bring his audience into the film, to increase their absorption in the story. In both the fantasy and the final sequences the editing strategy stresses George Bailey's reaction to his environment, though the effect, of course, is very different. In the fantasy sequence, George's reactions are of bewilderment, while the cutaways to the changed faces of Gower, of Ernie, of Ma Bailey, and of Mary all stress to the viewer how different the world of Pottersville is. After George and Mary have been reunited in the final sequence, the general editing strategy alternates among medium shots of George with Zuzu in his arms, reaction medium shots of Mary, and long shots over George's shoulder of George's friends piling into the living room to support him.

Though this only sketches the contrast between the film styles of parts nine and ten of *It's a Wonderful Life*, it does suggest how that contrast of style contributes to the film's effectiveness. But style and narrative tautness alone cannot explain the powerful effect *Wonderful Life* has on audiences. Another factor stems from the cultural values expressed by the film.

The way human lives are generally structured in any society produces widespread cultural conflicts shared by many people in that society. Consciously or unconsciously, filmmakers often embody those conflicts in their movies. Exceptionally powerful movies like *It's a Wonderful Life* often derive much of their power by clearly presenting those cultural conflicts, then resolving them in a way satisfying to the audience. The resolution of the cultural conflict is what a Marxist critic would call the "ideological project" of the film: the film's tendency to reaffirm the society's dominant cultural values.

Elsewhere I have written that Capra's films raise and resolve a cultural conflict deeply embedded in the American tradition as far back as the New England Puritans. In capsule form, that conflict is the desire to do good versus the desire to succeed and acquire. In an influential book on American national character, psychologist Karen Horney described that tension as it appeared in the 1930s: "The first contradiction to be mentioned is that between competition and success on the one hand and brotherly love and humility on the other. On the one hand everything is done to spur us toward success, which means that we must not only be assertive but aggressive . . . . On the other we are deeply imbued with Christian ideals which declare that it is selfish to want anything for ourselves, that we should be humble, turn the other cheek, be yielding."[9] In Capra's films of the late 1930s that conflict was embodied in two characters—an aggressive and acquisitive villain and a humble, selfless hero.

But as we have seen, in *Wonderful Life* that tension is embodied both externally—in the struggle between Peter Bailey (and later George) and Potter—and internally—within George himself. The conflict between George's desires for adventure, travel, and achievement on the one hand and for altruism toward family and community on the other presents this American dilemma as accurately and forcefully as any American movie I've seen. And though the resolution doesn't erase the conflict—Potter is still unregenerate and George still hasn't realized his dreams of achievement—the ending is marvelously convincing, affirming the notion that, in Clarence's words, "no man is a failure who has friends," as well as the sanctity and wonder of human life itself.

This cultural reason for the power of *Wonderful Life* might be framed in a slightly different way. Though slogans of the French Revolution defined democracy as a combination of liberty, equality, and fraternity, in America the ideals of liberty and, to some extent, equality of opportunity have crowded out the importance of fraternity in the dominant culture. *It's a Wonderful Life* counters that bias in a couple of ways. In its portrayal of Potter—the freest but also the most isolated person of Bedford Falls—it implicitly tempers any absolute stress on liberty. And the conclusion is as affecting a presentation of human fraternity and warmth as anyone could hope to see. Though that conclusion succeeds in part because of film style, also important is that resolution of the cultural conflict between aggressiveness and human community.

Yet before concluding this discussion of Capra's masterpiece, we need to mention one more reason for the power of *It's a Wonderful Life*. No film so deeply felt could exist without the presence of an involved creator; by looking at the autobiographical details of Capra's life which parallel George Bailey's, one can see that Capra's involvement in the film is central. George becomes executive secretary of the Building and Loan in 1928, the same year Capra began at Columbia. George marries Mary in 1932, the same year that Capra married Lucille Reyburn. Except for the death of his son in 1938, the Capra family would, like the Baileys, have had a family of four children. And more important, as Stephen Handzo has observed, "one can find the same wild oscillations of euphoria and despair of Capra's films in his own life" (FC, 173). Capra and George Bailey both had dreams, both had moments of discouragement and self-doubt, and both were able to transcend that self-doubt by affirming the values of family and community. Here we find the link between Capra's autobiography and American culture—so central to Capra's work—most effectively portrayed. One can only agree with Robin Wood's assessment that *It's a Wonderful Life*—a film "fed by the fears and aspirations" of American culture—"at once transcends its director and would be inconceivable without him."[10]

7

Declining Fortunes
(1947–Present)

IT'S A WONDERFUL LIFE did not do nearly as well at the box office as Capra hoped it would. A little more than a year after the film was released, *Variety* listed its domestic rentals as $3.3 million. This was twenty-seventh on the list of films released in late 1946 and 1947, far behind the $11.5 million accumulated by William Wyler's *Best Years of Our Lives*. Since Wyler directed the film not for Liberty Films but for Samuel Goldwyn, to whom Wyler owed one more film, and since Capra had spent around $3 million in making *It's a Wonderful Life*, Liberty Films was in deep economic difficulties.[1] Less than two years after the release of *It's a Wonderful Life*, Capra's dreams of independent production had been shattered: Liberty Films was sold to Paramount Studios, and Capra's career began a steady decline.

A combination of forces contributed to that decline. Capra himself attributes it to his own failure of nerve in urging his partners to sell Liberty Films to Paramount. The sale, in Capra's eyes largely a result of his fear and uncertainty, began his slide: "Once I had lost (or sold) control of the content of my films and of the artistic liberty to express myself in my own way—it was the beginning of my end as a social force in films" (NATT, 402).

Though this personal reason undoubtedly contributed to the failure of Liberty Films and the decline of Capra's career, so did the state of the film industry after 1946. Due to a number of intertwined factors—increased competition for the recreational dollar, legal defeats in government antitrust action (the *Paramount* case), political

Photo (left) from A Pocketful of Miracles: *Apple Annie (Bette Davis) checks for mail in Capra's last film*

uneasiness after the Hollywood Ten trials of 1947, and the growing popularity of television after 1948—the movie industry began to lose audiences in droves after the peak year of 1946. In that year an estimated 90 million movie tickets were sold each week. By 1950 the number had dropped to 60 million, and by 1960, to 40 million.[2] Within this structure, it was difficult for any filmmaker to come up with consistently popular films unless he or she was especially attuned to the changing tastes of audiences and willing to follow the trends. Capra, who functioned best when working independently and developing his distinct social vision, was not one to chase the popular fads.

Finally, the climate of opinion in post–World War II American culture was much less responsive to Capra's brand of filmmaking than the late 1930s had been. In the late 1930s Capra's portrayal of the moral, democratic common man struggling to maintain his idealism when challenged by corrupted men of power and wealth struck a vital cultural nerve: a fragmented culture was beginning to unify, and Capra's optimistic faith in human potentiality helped to foster that unification. After World War II, however, that unification had solidified, hardening into an agreed-upon view of America that Geoffrey Hodgson has called "the Ideology of Liberal Consensus." Characterizing this cultural paradigm, Hodgson has written: "Confident to the verge of complacency about the perfectability of American society, anxious to the point of paranoia about the threat of communism—these were the two faces of the consensus mood."[3]

As a result of this growing consensus about America's essential soundness, Capra's formula from the late 1930s was doubly unacceptable. His pointed portrayal of corrupt Americans like Anthony Kirby or D. B. Norton—so central to the Popular Front "progressive" vision of America—seemed "un-American" in an era of HUAC, McCarthyism, and the increasingly frigid Cold War. On the other hand, the optimistic resolutions of his films—all presupposing the essential goodness of the common man—seemed naive and softheaded in an America which had gone through a brutal world war, learned of the concentration camp atrocities, and feared what it perceived as Soviet dreams of world domination. In fact, one of the dominant trends in America liberal thought in the 1940s, personified in the work of Reinhold Niebuhr, was a return to the notion of original sin: the belief that human beings inevitably tend toward evil, selfish behavior. Given such a shift, Capra's social vision was surely out of step with the times.

Clearly Capra's social vision of the late 1930s was inimical to these changed times; in fact, that vision was subtly but surely influenced by these changing circumstances, if we can draw his social vision from his autobiography and his films after *State of the Union* (1948). A look at Capra's diary during his visit as a United States representative to the 1952 International Film Festival in India gives an idea of how strong an anti-Communist Capra had become by 1952 (NATT, 429–40). (To be fair, I should note that just before the festival Capra had been denied security clearance by the Defense Department and asked to answer some charges about his past. The profound suspicion of Communism expressed in the diary may be partly a case of Capra's overcompensation. The patriotic immigrant would never want to be considered an ungrateful subversive.)

But Capra's films after *It's a Wonderful Life* also suggest that the energy and intensity of the social vision he developed in the late 1930s and perfected in *It's a Wonderful Life* were beginning to mellow. Leland Poague has called the post–World War II years Capra's "retrospection period,"[4] and it does seem clear that Capra often seems to be looking back over his career. Two of his films during this time—*Riding High* (1950) and *Pocketful of Miracles* (1961)—were remakes of *Broadway Bill* and *Lady for a Day*, respectively. The others—*State of the Union* (1948), *Here Comes the Groom* (1951), and *A Hole in the Head* (1959)—generally share a number of qualities. The heroes are more mature and older than most previous Capra heroes. Usually they are married and have families or at least are responsible for children (in *Here Comes the Groom*, Bing Crosby adopts two French orphans, while in *A Hole in the Head* Frank Sinatra is raising his son alone). Music becomes more important in these later films, though this is probably more due to the presence of Crosby and Sinatra than because Capra found this attractive. Finally, the narratives of these films contain much less intensity and dramatic conflict than a film like *It's a Wonderful Life*; they are much more mellow and relaxed. Throughout this period, especially after *State of the Union*, Capra's hand is clearly less dominant than it was in his features of the preceding years. Though they all are interesting in one way or another, Capra had already made his most important films.

Capra himself calls *State of the Union* "my last Frank Capra film, my last burst of autumn colors before the winter of artistic slavery to. . .Paramount Pictures" (NATT, 397–98). In the tradition of political films like *Gabriel over the White House, Mr. Smith, Advise and Consent, The Candidate,* and *All the President's Men, State of the Union* centers specifically on the difficulties an idealist encounters when trying to run for public office for the first time. If we define a Frank Capra film by the hero of the story, the aspiring politician Grant Matthews is the last typical Capra hero in a long line that began with Stew Smith and Tom Dickson.

Most of the details about Grant Matthews's background were added to the play from which the film was adapted. These details bring Grant Matthews closer to earlier Capra heroes and also to Capra's own life. Though Capra did not choose the name, it fits conveniently into Capra's American/Christian mythology: Grant alludes to Ulysses S. Grant (remember Deeds's visit to Grant's Tomb), Matthews to one of Christ's apostles. Early in the film we learn of Grant's past. Born in Nevada, he is a self-made man who sold newspapers as a kid and worked his way through school. He has a good war record; for his contributions as a fighter pilot in World War I he was decorated. Starting a small "two-by-four" airplane company, Grant built it up into the huge Matthews Aircraft. Besides being the first industrialist to introduce labor-management plant administration, Grant owns part of a baseball team. Shortly before the action of the film begins, Grant appears on the cover of *Time* along with the slogan, "Our planes have wings but not our ideas," and with a small picture of Rodin's *The Thinker* bound by chains.

Like Grant, Capra hawked newspapers, worked through school, served in World War I (and was decorated for his work in the Second World War), was instrumental in building a small company (Columbia) into a large one, and appeared on the cover of *Time*. The submerged autobiography at work in *Meet John Doe* seems also to be functioning in *State of the Union*: Grant's failure to retain the purity of his ideals and his decision to make deals with special interest groups resemble Capra's own dilemma about retaining Liberty Films or selling it (and some of his artistic control) to a major studio. Capra resolves the film by having Grant affirm his original idealism, much like Deeds, Smith, John Doe, and George Bailey defend their principles and receive support from the common people because of it. Besides resembling these heroes, Grant quite often recalls Tom Dickson, another businessman who is as much concerned about other human beings as about keeping his business running smoothly.

The core of the film revolves around two structural choices. The first is between realism or idealism in one's social orientation; the second is between professionalism or amateurism in politics. A chart indicating how characters embody the positions would look like this:

REALISM (Kay Thorndyke)——IDEALISM (Grant and Mary Matthews)
PROFESSIONALISM (Jim Conover)——AMATEURISM (Grant Matthews)

Kay Thorndyke, editor of the Thorndyke Press, inherits her realism directly from her father. In the opening scene, the ailing Sam Thorndyke calls his daughter to his bed and advises her: "Men are weak, vain, idealistic. . . . Women are the only realists, until they get sentimental. Don't you ever get sentimental, Kay." After giving Kay his cane and telling her to "make those heads roll," Sam orders her out and commits suicide. In a reversal of Capra's tendency to suggest the continuity of a moral tradition by having his good characters recall their parents, Kay has a bust of her father in her office. Played as a conniving seductress by Angela Lansbury, Kay also inherits her father's motto: "Life is war; don't count the casualties."

Balanced against Kay's realism are both Grant Matthews, who believes Americans need to become more cooperative and idealistic, and his wife, Mary, played, appropriately, by Katharine Hepburn. Mary's idealism is best suggested when we see her organizing CARE packages to be sent to Europe and when she tells Conover, "If you get him to compromise, he'll no longer be Grant Matthews." After Grant decides to run, Mary constantly urges him to retain his original vision and also seeks to deflate his ambition and growing sense of self-importance.

Jim Conover (Adolphe Menjou) is the professional politician who helps Kay persuade Grant to run for the Republican presidential nomination. Conover has just returned to public life; we learn he was associated with the Harding Teapot Dome scandal in the early 1920s. Like Potter in *Wonderful Life*, he has his own picture on his office wall. As soon as Grant decides to run, Jim begins urging him to forget his original notions about what the country needs and to start making secret deals with leaders who will guarantee agriculture, labor, and ethnic votes in exchange for preferential treatment.

The film begins with these two structural poles—realism/idealism and professionalism/amateurism—neatly balanced. But Kay and Jim notice two things about Grant: he has "the sincerity and drive the common herd will go for" (they share Potter's contempt for people); and he "sees ideals out of one eye and ambition in the other." Together they exploit Grant's ambition, and the structural balance of the film tips: Grant begins to compromise and make deals, winning convention votes but losing the confidence of the common people that he earned in his early speeches. The climax of the film restores the balance. At a nationwide television broadcast originating at the Matthews home, Grant sees Mary compromise her idealism for the first time by giving a short speech she hasn't written and doesn't believe, largely to demonstrate her love for Grant. Shocked into the realization of how far his ambition has taken him from his original reasons for running, Grant grabs the microphone, confesses his dishonesty, drops out of the race, and vows to go to both conventions and challenge every political candidate who compromises. The structural balance is restored.

A number of details remind us of the Capra films of the late 1930s. We've already noted the resemblance of Grant and Conover to earlier Capra heroes and villains. The conclusion of the film is similar to the ritual victories of Deeds and Smith. As in earlier films, newspaper headlines make the hero's actions public ("Hardy Hails Matthews as Friend of Labor: Leader Demands Industrialist as GOP Candidate"). Even the minor characters in comic roles, like the Matthewses' butler who puts the "double whammy" on Kay, bear similarities to characters in earlier Capra films.

Although the film successfully presents a dilemma central to the American political process—the fact that the qualities necessary to get elected often have little to do with one's ability to govern well—the film itself does not entirely succeed. A large part of the problem stems from the relatively static pace of the film. Much less kinetic than a film like *Mr. Smith, State of the Union* is much talkier. Grant's long speech at the end of the film is much more like Chaplin's problematic conclusion to *The Great Dictator* than Jeff Smith's ritual victory. Capra has to rely more on words than on events to conclude the story, and it weakens the film.

State of the Union did much less well than *Mr. Smith Goes to*

Washington, his earlier film primarily about national politics. It was much less widely reviewed than *Mr. Smith*, and most of the reviews were mixed or worse. In addition, *State of the Union* brought in $3.5 million in domestic rentals. Using the typical ticket prices in 1939 and 1948, I've calculated that nearly three times as many people paid to see *Mr. Smith* than saw *State of the Union*: 22 to 8 million. Why was this so? One reason is that the slowed pace of *State of the Union* does not absorb audiences as well as *Mr. Smith*, but another reason—this one cultural—also is important.

State of the Union was released in 1948, the year of the presidential race among Truman, Dewey, and Progressive party candidate Henry Wallace. Though Jeff Smith's brand of political idealism was perfectly appropriate in the Popular Front atmosphere of the late 1930s, the political atmosphere of the late 1940s—one of fear, distrust, and anxiety—was one which stressed a hardheaded realism in dealing with Russians and with domestic leftists. With his beliefs in idealism, cooperation with Russia, and the eventual necessity for a world government—expressed in his early speeches—Grant resembles Henry Wallace much more than Truman or Dewey. And Wallace's fate helps explain the fate of *State of the Union*: Wallace received slightly more than a million votes, less than 3 percent of the total votes cast, fewer even than Dixiecrat candidate Strom Thurmond.

Clearly, Capra's vision was unacceptable to Americans in the early years of the Cold War; he seemed too naive and fuzzy-headed. Thus, the sale of Liberty Films to Paramount is symbolic: it can be taken as Capra's admission that he was out of touch with his audience and was unwilling to travel farther down the risky road of independent filmmaking. From here to the end of his career, Capra's control over his productions was more limited by studio policy or the desires of an actor than in any of his films after *Submarine*.

After moving to Paramount, Capra tried to get various projects off the ground—Jessamyn West's *Friendly Persuasion, Roman Holiday* (both later directed by William Wyler), and a couple of others—hoping to fulfill his three-film contract with Paramount as quickly as possible. Encountering difficulties with all of them, Capra finally persuaded Paramount to bargain with Columbia for the remake rights to *Broadway Bill*, along with its negative. So Capra's next film—*Riding High*—was also his first remake.

Structurally, *Riding High* follows *Broadway Bill* almost exactly.

Photos: (top) from *State of the Union*, the last true Capra hero, Grant Matthews (Spencer Tracy), succumbs to ambition and makes a deal with Joe Conover (Adolphe Menjou) while Kay Thorndike (Angela Lansbury) looks on approvingly [credit: Museum of Modern Art Film Stills Archive]; (bottom) from *Riding High*, Joe (Dub Taylor), Happy (William Demerest), Colonel Pettigrew (Raymond Walburn), and the Princess (Colleen Gray) plead with Don Brooks (Bing Crosby)

Thematically, it asserts, as did the original, the superiority of everyday life at the race track over the stifling atmosphere of J. L. Higgins's business empire. But *Riding High* does differ in a few ways. Largely because of Bing Crosby's presence, it has more music—six songs in all. One plot problem from the original is settled: Dan Brooks is not yet married to Margaret Higgins in *Riding High*. Instead, he's her fiancé. This makes his decision to rescue Alice from the Higgins mansion at the end of the film, presumably to marry her, more acceptable. Finally, Clarence Muse, who plays Dan Brooks's friend and Broadway Bill's trainer in both films, plays a less stereotyped "happy darky" role in *Riding High*. *Broadway Bill* is a bit embarrassing to watch today for that reason, while Muse's acting and singing are two strong points in the remake.

The tone of *Riding High*, due in large part to Bing Crosby as Dan Brooks, is less pointed, less sharply critical of J. L. Higgins's world than *Broadway Bill*. For example, when a gambler comes to bail out Dan from jail on the day of the race, Dan says, "I'd invite you in, but the door's locked," then tells them that at least jail keeps him out of the pool halls. This casual banter is surely typical of Crosby's persona, but hardly appropriate for a character who loves the racing life so much and who so desperately needs his horse to win the race that very day. By softening the edge of the narrative, Crosby takes away much of its appeal.

In his reminiscence of *Riding High* Capra recalls a couple of details that deserve mention. First, he talks about recording songs directly while shooting the action rather than the typical method of prerecording the songs, then playing them back while the actors perform before the cameras. Capra used the method because he felt it was both faster and more natural for the actors (NATT, 408–409). While it is true that the songs seem much less staged than in, for example, *Here Comes the Groom*, the method had its problems. The "We Ought to Bake a Sunshine Cake" number, which Capra remembers as having "wonderful charm," is really weak in spots, due largely to Colleen Gray's poor singing. A little postrecording might have helped save the number. In discussing the film Capra also recalls shooting "ten minutes of film time (three days' work) in two hours" (NATT,415). This scene—the racetrack burial of Broadway Bill—was shot so hurriedly in the late afternoon because the day was very windy, and Capra was afraid it would be hard to match the long shadows and strong winds on another day.

Though the whipping wind does add an effective touch to the *mise-en-scène*, Capra exaggerated how much footage was actually used in the film. Instead of ten minutes, the scene of the burial and Dan's talk with Alice and J. L. takes almost exactly three minutes. That's still a lot of usable footage to be shot in two hours, but it's considerably less than Capra's claim. All in all, *Riding High* lacks the energy and democratic appeal of the original.

Here Comes the Groom, Capra's next film, resembles *Riding High* in several ways. Bing Crosby again plays the lead role. The film contains several production numbers, the most famous of which is the Oscar-winning "In the Cool, Cool, Cool of the Evening," by Hoagy Carmichael and Johnny Mercer. Perhaps because of the presence of Crosby, the tone is also relaxed and genial. In fact, the film is almost devoid of dramatic conflict compared to a film like *Mr. Smith* or *Meet John Doe*.

Unlike *Riding High, Here Comes the Groom* is not a remake but rather an adaptation of a story by Robert Riskin and Liam O'Brien. The film's central character is Peter Garvey (Crosby), a news reporter we first encounter in Paris, where he's writing articles on war orphans in hopes that they will find adoptive parents. Pete's writing, his relaxed kindness toward the orphans, and his active support of the United Nations all suggest his humanitarianism. Pete is in love with Emmadelle Jones (Jane Wyman), a secretary who impatiently awaits his return to the states. Her letter to Pete reflects her good 1950s self-concept of womanhood: "I was born to be a mother, not a poised pencil." Peter agrees to return but not before getting permission to take two orphans, Bobbie and Suzi, back with him to adopt when he marries Emmadelle. This takes two months; by this time Emma—impatient and unaware of Peter's intentions—has become engaged. A headline results: "Fisherman's Daughter to Marry $40,000,000: Emmadelle Jones–Wilbur Stanley Betrothal Announced." The rest of the film revolves around Emmadelle's decision as to whom she will marry, made all the more pressing by the fact that Peter must marry in five days or lose Bobbie and Suzi.

The film deviates from the iconography of the late-1930s Capra films in that the wealthy Wilbur Stanley (Franchot Tone) is genial, accomplished, and attractive, a stark contrast to the grasping men of wealth like Kirby, Taylor, and Norton. To Jonesy, Emma's vernacular fisherman father, Wilbur's a "mummy" and the Stanleys a "family of fossils," and it is true that the Stanleys' behavior is much more formal and restrained than Peter's outgoing spontaneity. Instead of having a clearcut choice, like Ellie Andrews, between the arrogant King Westley and the engaging Peter Warne, Emma has to choose between Wilbur's gracious charm (plus a half-million dollars) or Peter's relaxed humanitarianism. It's a much more difficult choice.

Capra helps resolve the dilemma through the character of Winifred (Alexis Smith), Wilbur's "fourth-cousin, twice removed." Like all the Stanleys, Win is overly stiff and formal; but she loves Wilbur. Only after Pete teaches Winifred how to loosen up and become alluring, however, does Wilbur take notice—at the wedding rehearsal. On the wedding day—in a scene reminiscent of *It Happened One Night*—Wilbur gives up Emma at the altar and, like a Shakespearean romantic comedy, all the proper lovers are united: Emma and Peter, Wilbur and Winifred. In the last shot of the film Emma (already a mother), Pete, Bobbie, and Suzi ride in the car, singing "In the Cool, Cool, Cool of the Evening."

Despite the similarities to *It Happened One Night* and—in the reaction of Emma's family to the Stanley wealth—to *The Younger Generation, Here Comes the Groom* has two annoying features. First are the musical numbers. Instead of using music as an interlude to draw characters closer to the audience—as when Deeds and Babe Bennett sing in the park—the songs in *Here Comes the Groom* are too obviously "production numbers." The worst is on the plane back to the United States where Peter sings "Christopher Columbo," while several Paramount contract players—Frank Faylen, Dorothy Lamour, and Louis Armstrong—all make cameo appearances, an inconceivable interruption had Capra controlled the film.

The second problem is the lack of dramatic conflict in the film. Perhaps because screenwriters and Capra himself were afraid of portraying a wealthy man negatively for fear of being branded Communist—the film was being made in the midst of the Korean War and during Joseph McCarthy's heyday—Wilbur Stanley is extremely attractive and engaging. During one scene I expected Capra's old formula to be unraveling. In it, Wilbur is accused of leasing the same house to Peter and another party. I expected Peter to write a scathing exposé of Wilbur's corruption but instead, Wilbur shows up, assures everyone that the dual lease was all a mistake, and promises to iron out all the difficulties. He does, and when he even offers to adopt Bobbie and Suzi, it's hard for a viewer to believe that Emma will choose Peter over Wilbur, especially since Peter retains his commitment to his work. All in all, the positive portrayal of Wilbur drains the film of dramatic content, much as the conflict in *Riding High* seemed muted. Audiences in 1951 were much more willing to watch the spectacle *David and Bathsheba,* the musicals *Showboat* and *American in Paris,* and *A Streetcar Named Desire* than *Here Comes the Groom,* which finished nineteenth (2.5 million) on *Variety's* list of top box-office grossing films for that year. Capra, getting credit for two films by both directing and producing *Here Comes the Groom,* decided to withdraw from an incongenial Hollywood.

After involving himself with several United States government activities in 1951 and early 1952—including serving as a member of the United States delegation to the Indian International Film Festival—Capra became involved in a project that would keep him busy for the next five years. Asked by American Telephone and Telegraph to do a series of four entertaining television programs sponsored by Bell Telephone on scientific subjects, Capra plunged headlong into the project. "The years 1952–56 were as productive and as packed with achievement as the war years of 1941–45," Capra remembers. "But this time I was not revealing the ugly facts of war but the awe and wonder and fascination of nature to youngsters from eight to eighty" (NATT, 443).

The four films were premiered at four-month intervals between late 1956 and early 1958. Their titles: (1) *Our Mr. Sun* (1956)—an examination of the sun as an energy source; (2) *Hemo the Magnificent* (1957)—blood and the circulatory system; (3) *The Strange Case of Cosmic Rays* (1957)—problematic makeup of cosmic rays; (4) *The Unchained Goddess* (1958)—weather patterns and prediction.

Because Bell Telephone wanted the informative programs to be presented in an entertaining fashion, they were wise to choose Capra. He begins *Our Mr. Sun* by having a live character, Mr. Fiction (Eddie Albert), stumped about how to find a gimmick to present the material. Suddenly, he decides to use imagination via a "magic screen." On it, an animated Father Time appears and talks about various religions that have deified the sun. As this happens, a bold, genial, round-faced man—Dr. Research (Frank Baxter)—enters and begins to discuss facts about the sun. The remainder of the program alternates between images—both photographic and animated—on the magic screen and discussions between Mr. Fiction and Dr. Research. As with all the other films in the series, *Our Mr. Sun* ends with a religious allusion, implicitly suggesting the compatibility of religion and science. The comment is from St. Francis of Assisi: "Be praised, my Lord, in what you have created; above all else be praised in our brother, Master Sun."

All the other films except *The Strange Case of Cosmic Rays* use this same Mr. Fiction–Dr. Research–magic screen format. The exception structures the program almost like a mystery story. Three puppets (Baird Marionettes), representing Poe, Dickens, and Dostoevsky, are judging a mystery story contest. The story of how scientists tried to solve the puzzling makeup of cosmic rays is one of the submissions. Of course, that story wins the award, and Dickens concludes, "The more we know of creation, the closer we get to the Creator."

The series does succeed in its aim of presenting scientific facts in an amusing way. Viewed today, however, certain details date parts of the series: in *The Unchained Goddess*, for example, Dr. Research blithely suggests that plans are under consideration to steer hurricanes by creating oil slicks on the ocean, then starting them on fire! In spite of such details which have been treated harshly by time, the series is skillfully done and is for some people, especially school children, their first introduction to the films of Frank Capra.

In 1957 Capra made a deal that would return him to Hollywood, agreeing to work with Frank Sinatra to make a film version of Arnold Schulman's play *A Hole in the Head*. Though he didn't have creative control of the film—Sinatra and Capra had equal votes on mutual decisions with an acceptable third party (William Morris agent Abe Lastfogel) deciding disputes—he was back to Hollywood. Sixty years old, Capra had two feature films left, this one and *A Pocketful of Miracles*. His only two color feature films and his only films shot in wide screen, they continued the more relaxed pace evident in *Here Comes the Groom*, in part because the wide screen demanded fewer cuts than the 1.33 screen standard before the 1950s.

A Hole in the Head is not one of Capra's more important films. It concerns the relationship between Tony Manetta (Sinatra), an impractical owner of a two-bit hotel in Miami Beach, and his son Allie (Eddie Hodges), in many ways more mature than his father. A subplot brings together Tony, who is a widower, and widow Eloise Rogers. Though Eloise says she needs someone, Tony refuses for most of the film to be that person, primarily because he wants to retain his highly unlikely dream of someday buying some beach property and building a park to rival Disneyland. The tension in the plot develops when Tony's brother Mario (Edward G. Robinson) and sister-in-law Sophie (Thelma Ritter) threaten to take Allie away from Tony: the disciplined, industrious, thrifty (and dull) Mario is appalled at Tony's casual, disorganized life. But the conflict is resolved when Tony realizes that he needs both Allie and Eloise. In the final shot of the film Tony, Allie, Eloise, Sophie, and even Mario—who has decided to take a vacation—walk along the beach during a brilliant sunset with all problems resolved.

Occasionally *A Hole in the Head* recalls earlier Capra films. The negative portrayal of Jerry Marks (Keenan Wynn), whose wealth prevents him from having time for old friends like Tony, recalls friendless Capra villains of earlier films. A gag from *The Strong Man,* in which a man backs up some stairs and then a small stepladder at the top, finally tumbling off, reappears here. When an inebriated tenant rushes up the stairs yelling, "Geronimo," a viewer might be reminded of "Teddy Roosevelt" in *Arsenic and Old Lace.* But generally this humor is strained, much less successful than in many of Capra's earlier films.

What probably attracted Capra to the material was the notion that humans need other humans for a satisfying life. Eloise explicitly tells this to Tony, but Tony initially resists. When he reluctantly admits that Allie might be better off with Mario and Sophie, Allie says, "They don't need me; *you* need me." Though Tony replies, "I need you like I need a hole in the head," Allie is right. Tony needs his dreams—his "High Hopes," as the key song in the film expresses it—for it's part of his makeup. But he also needs Allie— the close human relationship that makes life in the Capra universe worth living. The film's final shot—of Tony, Allie, Eloise and even Mario walking along the beach at sunset—underlines the need for close human ties.

A Hole in the Head did relatively well at the box office, doubling the $2 million production costs in domestic rentals. This relative success enabled Capra to get another project, this one a remake of his *Lady for a Day.* The deal he made for the remake, entitled *A Pocketful of Miracles,* indicates Capra's loss of clout in Hollywood. United Artists agreed to finance and distribute the film, while Capra entered an agreement with Glenn Ford similar to the one he had

Photo: from *A Hole in the Head*: Tony Marietta (Frank Sinatra) protects his son Allie (Eddie Hodges) from the stares of Tony's brother Mario (Edward G. Robinson)

with Sinatra in *A Hole in the Head*: both had equal voice on important production decisions, with Lastfogel again casting the deciding vote on any disputes. Working with such restrictions surely was difficult for the advocate of the "one man, one film" theory of film-making.

Compared to *Lady for a Day*, *A Pocketful of Miracles* is much more sprawling: at 136 minutes it's more than 50 percent longer than the original version. Surely a tighter film could easily have been made by paring down the Dave-Darcy dispute and some of the screen time alloted to Louise, Apple Annie's daughter, and her fiancé. In addition, the remake loses the topical appeal of *Lady for a Day*, which was made during the Depression and which it in part concerns.

Nevertheless, looked at as an accomplished filmmaker's final statement, *A Pocketful of Miracles* is a worthwhile film. In this respect, it bears much the same place in Capra's work as *Limelight* does in Chaplin's. Both films are nostalgic, the products of artists who are looking back at their preoccupations, summarizing and affirming those values they believe worth preserving. Though *A Pocketful of Miracles* lacks the intensity of dramatic conflict and the insistant pacing of Capra's best films, it does stand as Capra's final cinematic affirmation of kindness, altruism, and community over the desires for wealth and personal gratification.

Two plots intertwine to develop the thesis. The first is the rocky romance between Queenie (Hope Lange) and Dave the Dude (Glenn Ford). Queenie has dreams of marrying Dave and settling down in New Jersey as Mrs. Elizabeth Conway. (In Capra's postwar films, the heroines generally hope only for marriage, both reflecting the culture's stress on marriage and family and making those heroines generally less interesting than a Babe Bennett or a Saunders.) Like George Bailey, Dave wants "to be somebody" and hence initially resists Queenie. His gradual change stems from the second plot, in which Apple Annie (Bette Davis) is temporarily transformed from hag to duchess. Just as in *Lady for a Day*, Annie gets a visit from her daughter and the family of her aristocratic Spanish fiancé. Dave agrees to set up Annie in a penthouse apartment but threatens to pull out when the Count wants a reception to meet Annie's friends. Queenie is upset: "Oh, boy, and just when you were starting to act like a human. . . . Good people help, Dude. . . . We're a bunch of grabbers." But the Dude comes around, as is evidenced when he tells his cohorts they will be working for nothing at the reception: "Couldn't we just do something nice for somebody?" Dude's question recalls one of Deeds's comments to Saunders, as well as the simple philosophy of Shangri-La in *Lost Horizon*. To use Queenie's terms, *A Pocketful of Miracles* traces the transformation of "grabbers" into "helpers."

Of course the film is, as Dave's aide Joy Boy (Peter Falk) says, "a mother goose story," but it surely has its pleasing moments. Joy Boy himself is wonderful, a cynical descendant of the Colonel in *Meet John Doe*. His doubt about Dave's do-goodism helps balance the film, and his comic acting is superb. Two other veteran character actors also add to the nostalgic quality of the film and turn in wonderful comic performances: Thomas Mitchell (Diz in *Mr. Smith*) as the pool-shark "Judge" Blake and Edward Everett Horton (Lovett in *Lost Horizon*) as the butler. The film also has some good vernacular dialogue (someone says Annie's transformation is like "a cockroach what turned into a butterfly"), as well as some effective visual gags, as when Dave drops some darts on a thug's foot, then catches in mid-air the gun which the hood drops.

Ultimately, the film affirms Capra's long-standing defense of the emotional warmth which accompanies selflessness and altruism. On the evening of the reception, Judge Blake paraphrases, to no one in particular, one of Capra's favorite quotations (from Pascal): "The heart hath its reasons that reason itself knows nothing about." After the reception, everyone feels rejuvenated by their participation, from the beggars to the Governor. The film concludes with two musical allusions which tie up as well as any two songs could the bright side of Capra's vision: the beggars play "Polly Wolly Doodle" in the car on the way to the ship, the same song that Anthony Kirby plays with Grandpa Vanderhof in *You Can't Take It With You*, Kirby's admission that family love transcends money. The final song, "Auld Lang Syne," plays at the docks as the ship departs. That song figures often in Capra's films but most prominently at the end of *It's a Wonderful Life*, while George reads a note from Clarence saying that no man—or in this case no woman—is a failure who has friends.

After his parting film, Capra's life continued the rising and falling path it had followed since he came to America. He talked with Gore Vidal about *The Best Man*, later directed by Franklin Shaffner, then withdrew. He worked six months in Madrid trying to get *Circus* together, then dropped out; Henry Hathaway took over for him. Between 1964 and 1967 he tried to get a deal for a space film called *Marooned*; when he failed to do so, John Sturges eventually directed the film. With that, Capra—who had been suffering from intense "cluster" headaches since shortly before shooting began on *A Pocketful of Miracles*—finally decided to throw in the towel. It was a sad way for the proud Sicilian to end his accomplished career.

But Capra's wheel of fortune once again ascended in the 1970s. Between 1967 and 1971 he worked on his autobiography. Published in 1971, *Name above the Title* was selected as a Book-of-the-Month Club alternate. One of the liveliest autobiographies by an American director, the book reveals Capra as a witty, energetic man both aware of and articulate about what he tried to do in his films. Although Joseph McBride's recent biography notes a number of inaccuracies and apocryphal stories in the autobiography, the book remains valuable for Capra's observations about his aspirations in the films and for the portrait of the director as auteur that Capra wished to depict after his long filmmaking career was complete.

Certainly the autobiography helped to resurrect his public image. During the 1970s Capra was a popular speaker at film festivals held in his honor at colleges and universities and in other settings all over the United States. Honors and awards began to accumulate. In 1977 he traveled to Italy for an eightieth birthday celebration. In 1981 Wesleyan University presented him with an honorary doctorate degree. The following year he received the American Film Institute's Life Achievement Award, joining previous recipients like John Ford, Orson Welles, and Alfred Hitchcock, and in 1986 he was one of nine artists to receive a National Medal of the Arts from President Ronald Reagan. Capra's health declined after the death of his wife Lu in 1984, and on September 3, 1991, the Sicilian immigrant who became one of the premiere directors of the Hollywood studio era died of heart failure at the age of ninety-four. Yet if no man is a failure who has friends, Capra, through his films, his appearances in the last two decades of his life, and his honors, succeeded as few others have.

8

Conclusion: In the American Grain

AFTER SURVEYING Capra's films from *Fultah Fisher's Boarding House* to *A Pocketful of Miracles*, what can we say in conclusion about his significance and achievements? We can surely note that he has admirers within the film industry: when Victor Scherle and William Turner Levy asked for comments on Capra from film directors, they received tributes not only from Hollywood veterans like Henry King, Allan Dwan, Raoul Walsh, and William Wyler, but also from such younger directors like Blake Edwards (who calls Capra "a true genius"), Stanley Kubrick ("one of the world's most accomplished directors"), Arthur Penn, and even Sam Peckinpah ("a filmmaker of the first rank"). Some of the respondents, including William Friedkin and Martin Ritt, also said they have been influenced by his work; if we examine the kinetic editing in Friedkin's *Sorcerer* or the optimistic humanism of Ritt's *Sounder* and *Norma Rae*, we surely can see traces of Capra's influence. Besides these respondents, we also know that John Ford was long an admirer of Capra's work and that Akira Kurosawa has been influenced by Capra. It's clear that the energetic Sicilian has left an imprint on those professionals involved in making feature films.[1]

Once we note Capra's impact on his peers and professional colleagues, however, any further judgment or analysis depends on the critic's own understanding of what film criticism involves. When the American cinema was essentially rediscovered—in France during the 1950s, in America during the 1960s—the critical perspective fueling that rediscovery was the auteur "theory." Basically auteur-

Photo (left): Capra at 79, responding to a student comment at Lake Forest College, March, 1978

ism posited that the director was (or should be) the creative driving force in filmmaking and thus that a critic should examine the output of a particular director, noting the recurring stylistic and thematic patterns in his or her work. A strict adherent of auteurism as it was then practiced would conclude with a list of the central narrative, stylistic, and thematic patterns in Capra's work.

Yet it has become increasingly apparent since the late 1960s that popular feature films are distinctly related to the dominant cultural values and attitudes of their society. Influenced by the events of May 1968 in France, the editors of *Cahiers du cinéma*—the spawning ground, ironically, of the auteur policy in the 1950s—argued in 1969 that "*Every film is political,* inasmuch as it is determined by the ideology which produced it (or within which it is produced, which stems from the same thing)." For them, the film critic should explain how the ideology functions in particular films, to "demystify" and ultimately to "help change the ideology which conditions them."[2] Subsequent work in British and American cultural studies has extended this ideological approach to film studies, elaborating on the ways that movies not only reinforce widely shared cultural values but also, by presenting and developing narrative conflicts, depict tensions and conflicts that are widely shared by members of the culture in which the films are made.

Although the auteur policy and this ideological approach arose in different historical situations and began with very different assumptions, both have provided valuable insights about American movies. As a student of American culture, I always thought the auteur approach, as it arose in the 1960s, failed to appreciate how films are linked to their time and place of production and how filmmakers are shaped by the historical and industrial situations in which they work. Ideological criticism compensates for that blind spot by helping us think about the relationship between films, creators, and their societies. From the 1970s on, it also encouraged auteur critics to engage in the politics of film, deepening and broadening the work of auteur critics like Andrew Sarris and Robin Wood.[3] Fundamentally, I agree with Wood that a good critic should try to synthesize the valuable insights of different critical approaches rather than adhere rigidly to any one school. Thus, in concluding this examination of Capra's work, I'd like to draw on the ideological and auteur approaches, as well as the formalist approach that encourages close attention to a film's narrative and stylistic features, to sum up Capra's achievements as a filmmaker.

Such a "synthetic" film criticism must concern itself both with film form and with the attitudes and values that emerge from it. Let's begin with Capra's film form. Generally, Capra must be considered an acknowledged master of what historians of film form have called the " classical Hollywood cinema. " This style, which developed between 1910 and 1935 and which is still common in many American feature films today, stemmed from the desire of filmmakers to tell a story on film as clearly, crisply, and engagingly as possible; the central goal of the classical Hollywood style is to absorb the attentions of the audience as fully as possible, to draw their imaginations completely into the "world" of the film. Surely Capra shared this notion. He begins his autobiography by saying that dullness is the worst sin in filmmaking, and he frequently has said that he judged whether one of his films was successful by how well it worked on audiences. To make those films as successful with audiences as possible, he used "preview tapes," which recorded audience response at previews. If audiences laughed at inappropriate times, missed comic lines because of laughter from a previous gag, or made noises indicating their boredom during certain sections of the film, Capra would reedit the film before its general release (NATT, 278). For Capra, as for classical Hollywood cinema generally, the audience is always right.

With this general assumption, the classical Hollywood style developed a characteristic narrative form which focused on individuals as causal agents in a story; it assumed that single human beings could change and affect society and that the actions of significant characters should provide the focus of the film (contrast this notion to the masses as the heroes of the early Eisenstein films or the twenty-four central characters in Altman's *Nashville*). The classical narrative form is also characterized by the "closed ending." That is, all conflicts arising from the central character's actions are resolved and all loose ends securely tied. Here again Capra followed the classical mode: his best films all center on the actions of a clearly defined hero. In fact Capra's definition of his central theme in films after *Broadway Bill* could serve as a handbook description for many

1930s films: "A simple honest man . . . can, if he will . . . come up
with the necessary handfuls of courage, wit, and love to triumph
over his environment" (NATT, 186). And clearly the endings of the
Capra films are closed. Though we have noted how tentative or
forced the endings of films like *Mr. Smith* or *Meet John Doe* are
upon reflection, the Capra films do give the viewer a firm sense
that the hero or heroine's problems are resolved by the end of the
film.

Finally, the classical Hollywood style developed a characteristic
system of editing which Capra mastered as few other directors have.
Called "continuity editing," this system aimed at joining shots in
such a way as to prevent any disruption in the story line by preserving the spatial and temporal continuity of the narrative. All the
strategies of continuity editing—establishing shots, the shot/reverse
shot cut, the eyeline match (a character looks off screen, followed
by a shot representing what he sees), among others—were common
in Capra's films. In addition, Capra made special use of the reaction
shot—a close-up of a character's reactions to an event—to guide the
audience's perceptions of the events pictured. Following the rules
of continuity editing, Capra usually used wipes to cut from one
location to another, and he rarely disturbed the linear flow of his
narrative. Only on occasion—Megan's dreams in *The Bitter Tea of
General Yen*, the extended flashback in *Wonderful Life*—did Capra
use dream or flashback sequences, and then they were clearly related to the central character's experience or thoughts. Another
device of continuity editing which Capra frequently used was the
montage sequence, which compresses a long period of time into a
montage of shots, often superimposed. The patriotic montage of
Jefferson Smith's tour through Washington in *Mr. Smith* is a good
example. Capra's films were nearly always edited with an insistent
and skillful pace drawn from the modes of continuity editing; when
that insistent pace waned, as in Capra's later films, the films were
generally much less absorbing for audiences. All in all, Capra clearly
must be considered a master of the dominant system of filmmaking
in Hollywood during the 1930s and 1940s.

What of the cultural values and attitudes expressed in his films?
Stated another way, what is the cultural and historical significance
of the social vision expressed in Capra's films? We might begin to
answer that question by noting what Capra's films were not. When
Andrew Sarris talked about the "populist sentimentality" and "pop-

ulist demagoguery" present in Capra's films, he used a term that has been widely repeated as a way to describe them. Though Jeffrey Richards, the most articulate exponent of this populist interpretation of Capra's films, does offer some good insights into them, particularly those made in the 1930s, his use of the term populist to describe Capra's social vision clouds his analysis. For as Lawrence Goodwyn has recently pointed out, the Populists were a democratic mass movement devoted to fundamental social and economic change in America. In contrast, Capra was more concerned with encouraging more humane behavior in what he perceived as a basically healthy society. The populist interpretation simply doesn't get to the core of Capra's social vision.[5]

When James Agee reviewed *Wonderful Life*, he made a comment that foreshadowed what a number of other critics later observed about Capra's films. "It interests me," Agee commented, "that in representing a twentieth-century town Frank Capra uses so little of the twentieth and idealizes so much that seems essentially nineteenth-century" (FC, 158). Following this, a number of critics have commented on the nineteenth-century roots of Capra's vision (FC, 63, 115, 135, 175), and they clearly have a point: particularly in portraying capitalist villains like Anthony Kirby, Sr., James Taylor, or Potter, Capra was depicting tycoons more common to the late nineteenth century than to the realities of corporate America in his day. Yet I also believe that critics—most of whom have more urban, sophisticated sensibilities than many Americans had in Capra's day—minimize how close Capra's depiction of small-town America was to the memories or—on good days—to past experiences of many of Capra's audience. Small-town life is experienced by a much smaller proportion of Americans today than in 1935, but it has for a long time alternated between the repressiveness of Gopher Prairie in Sinclair Lewis's *Main Street* and the reassuring community spirit of Mandrake Falls in *Mr. Deeds*. As Sinclair Lewis stressed the negative, Capra portrayed the ideal.

To argue about whether Capra's vision is nineteenth or twentieth century, however, is less important than to define its cultural significance. Essentially, I have argued that the core of Capra's vision is a "Christian/American humanism" embodied most clearly in his films between 1936 and 1941. That vision is decidedly humanistic, if by that term we mean one which asserts the dignity of man and the importance of human ideals. It is decidedly antimaterialistic, defending friendship, community, and romantic love over the persistent quest for wealth and power. In its portrayal of women and minorities, it quite accurately reflects dominant American cultural values of the 1930s and 1940s. Women in Capra's films, even the working women, generally seem to desire marriage and family once they fall in love with the hero. (The importance of motherhood becomes more pronounced in Capra's films after World War II.) When minorities are present at all in the Capra films, they play subservient roles: porters (*Mr. Smith*), horse trainers (*Broadway Bill*), janitors (*Meet John Doe*), or maids (*Wonderful Life*). This fact does not indicate any malevolence on Capra's part; it rather indicates the mass media's desire to please as wide an audience as possible. To do so, it often relies on widely shared attitudes and familiar types to prevent upsetting audiences. To generalize, Capra's films portray an image of ideal American middle-class values, embodied by the Capra hero, triumphing over a villain who represents the society's negative values: the ruthless desire to acquire power and wealth. As John Raeburn has observed, Capra's films appeal to audiences because they provide viewers with "a way of looking at middle-class life which does not make it seem banal, sterile, and purposeless, and which invests it with vitality and style" (FC, xii).

This image of middle-class life served an important cultural function in American life in the decade after FDR's election in 1932. It both reflected and helped to shape the reconsolidation of American culture which began in the mid-1930s and solidified during the war years. Though middle-class values, particularly those of individualism and the success ethic, were under siege in the darkest years of the Depression, the country emerged without significant redistribution of wealth and power in part because images like Capra's portrayals of America helped recreate a faith in the system. After that faith had solidified, and Americans—anxious about the Soviet threat after World War II—began to take a much darker, more realistic, and more materialistic approach to human affairs, it is no surprise that Capra's fortunes as a filmmaker should decline. By tempering the threats to the hero in his films after *State of the Union*—in part because he had mellowed, in part because negative portrayals of American tycoons were doubly dangerous in an era of HUAC and postwar prosperity—Capra in effect destroyed what gave his films such power. But even that decline cannot detract from the cultural power and significance of his films between 1932 and 1948.

What place does Capra deserve in American film history? When Andrew Sarris published *The American Cinema* in 1968, he placed Capra just outside his "Pantheon," in his second category, "The Far Side of Paradise." Of the fourteen directors originally in Sarris's Pantheon, eight were foreign-born and one—Robert Flaherty—had few connections with Hollywood. A director like Capra, so firmly and unabashedly American and patriotic, did well to reach Sarris's second level.

Since 1968, however, a revaluation of Capra's work has been underway, partly because his films were more attuned to the personal 1970s than the political 1960s, partly because of the publication of his autobiography, and partly because of the increased availability of his early Columbia films. Sarris himself has written that in looking back over his Pantheon since 1968, Capra is one of three candidates—Preston Sturges and Billy Wilder are the others—whom he might raise into the top echelon. "Further research on Capra's career," Sarris observed, "indicates that of the 36 films he turned out between 1926 and 1961, all but a very few were crafted with unusual skill and sensitivity."[6] Adding that he considers *Wonderful Life* an American masterpiece, Sarris seems to be leaning Capra's way.

My own view is that Capra is, with Chaplin, Lubitsch, Sturges, and Allen, one of the five major directors of American film comedy during the sound era. Each developed a distinctive vision through a number of films. Although Chaplin established himself as a genius during the silent era (and resisted dialogue films until 1940), he deserves his place for successfully adapting his tramp persona to sound films, for challenging fascism (*The Great Dictator*) and postwar complacency (*Monsieur Verdoux*), and for presenting a coda on his career (*Limelight*). Lubitsch's urbane continental sensibility resulted in such comic masterpieces as *Design for Living*, *Trouble in Paradise*, and *To Be or Not to Be*. It's tempting to see Sturges as Capra's antithesis: in *Sullivan's Travels* Sturges satirizes Hollywood's attempts to make films of social consciousness—" like Capra's," a skeptical mogul says. Surely the vision of America developed in films like *The Great McGinty*, *The Miracle of Morgan's Creek*, and *Hail the Conquering Hero* contrasts starkly to Capra's. Influenced by both Chaplin and Keaton, Woody Allen established himself as the major comic filmmaker of the 1970s and 1980s through such films as *Annie Hall*, *Manhattan*, *Hannah and Her Sisters*, and *Crimes and Misdemeanors*. All five directors consistently managed to impress their understandings of the world on their material, and one need only contrast their films on politics—*The Great Dictator, To Be or Not to Be, The Great McGinty, Mr. Smith Goes to Washington,* and *Bananas*—to see how different yet clearly defined their visions were. No other directors of sound comedies in Hollywood have matched their achievements.

But Capra must also be remembered for his masterpiece, *It's a Wonderful Life*, a work central not only to American film but to American culture generally. Lionel Trilling once observed that cultures are characterized by a dialectic of tensions and contradictions and that within any culture "there are likely to be certain artists who contain a large part of the dialectic within themselves." In a sense, writes Trilling, "they contain within themselves . . . the very essence of the culture."[7] Though it is not readily apparent on the surface, Capra was such an artist. He was not simply the aspiring immigrant who made good in America; he also learned, by experiencing the rapid shifts of fortune like being fired by Langdon after directing two successful comedies, how tenuous one's place on the ladder of success can be. Furthermore, Capra experienced internal conflicts arising from the disjunction between his Catholic/humanist moral inclinations—evident in his films from the beginning—and his practical desire to survive and excel in Hollywood. Like many in his culture, Capra was hounded by what William James called "the Bitch-Goddess Success"; also like many others, he felt the contrary pulls of individual achievement and moral responsibility to others.

These tensions, so deeply a part of Capra's experience, found expression in many of Capra's films but most prominently in *It's a Wonderful Life*. For in that film George Bailey, besides struggling against external forces as the other Capra heroes do, also must do battle with himself. Part of the reason for the film's powerful effect on audiences, for its status as a masterpiece of American narrative art, is that it depicts within George Bailey a widespread and persistent American dilemma: is it possible to gratify our personal desires and still maintain a humane compassion for and a sense of responsibility to other human beings? And, ultimately, which is more important?

Surely Capra resides centrally within the long tradition of American artists concerned with what Walter Allen believes to be the "great theme" in American fiction: "the exploration of what it means to be an American." For some time we have had studies of what

Photos: from despair to exhilaration in Capra's masterpiece *It's a Wonderful Life*—a mastery of film style creates a dramatic contrast: (top) George Bailey contemplates suicide on the bridge; (bottom) reunited with his wife Mary (Donna Reed), and daughter Zuzu (Karolyn Grimes), the family responds to the "miracle"

is unique about American fiction; the work of Perry Miller, F. O. Matthiessen, Henry Nash Smith, R. W. B. Lewis, Richard Chase, Leslie Fiedler, and Leo Marx, among others, has helped us understand various preoccupations of our writers. Recently, Robert Carringer has called for more attention to how American film narratives relate to the traditions of American fiction. His essay on the similarities between *The Great Gatsby* and *Citizen Kane* provides a strong beginning for this potentially fruitful area of inquiry.[8]

Placing Capra's work within the traditions described by Chase (*The American Novel and Its Tradition*) or Fiedler (*Love and Death in the American Novel*) would help us understand better how Capra's treatment of his material resembled that of other American artists. I think we would find, among other things, what several critics have suggested: that Capra's films and his approach to comic art resemble that of Mark Twain more than any other American artist (FC, xii–xiii, 182). Not only were both concerned about pleasing a wide, nonelite audience—Twain had his books marketed door-to-door by a subscription firm—but both also combined humor with serious moral concern. Of course, Twain's later skepticism differed markedly from Capra's persistent optimism, but both were master craftsmen, Twain using vernacular language and Capra, cinematic form. Even particular works bear resemblances: William Pechter calls *Wonderful Life* "the *Huckleberry Finn* which gives lie to the *Tom Sawyers*," arguing that both Capra and Twain created fully realized works only once (FC, 182). Lauren Rabinowitz has noted a similar philosophy of determinism at work in *Wonderful Life* and Twain's *Mysterious Stranger*, observing that the resolutions of each work reveal the differences in social vision of Capra and Twain during his final years. To my mind, the most comparable works of these two artists are *Meet John Doe* and *A Connecticut Yankee in King Arthur's Court*. In both, an artist sets out to define and affirm what he sees as his society's unique characteristics; in both, the artists have second thoughts during the process of creation and have difficulty finishing the work.[9]

But another work on American literature—Sacvan Bercovitch's *The American Jeremiad*—can, I think, do a good deal to illuminate the approach and limitations of Capra's work.[10] An important part of Bercovitch's argument is that the idea of America has, since the days of John Winthrop, taken on sacred associations, so that American nationalism and the Christian meaning of the sacred have been combined. From this association has emerged the powerful symbol of America which has helped create a middle-class cultural consensus "unmatched in any other modern culture." It has also helped to shape what Bercovitch sees as a central and ritualistic form of writing in America: the jeremiad. In one form, the jeremiad was a political sermon given by Puritan ministers on important public occasions. In it, the minister would both lament the degenerate behavior of his congregation, often in heightened rhetoric, then issue a call for the congregation to return to the religious and social mission to which they, as Americans and Christians, were called by God. The mode of rhetoric present in these Puritan jeremiads, Bercovitch argues, has extended to many other forms of writing throughout our history—biographies, poems, histories, even novels—and their social effect has undeniably been conservative. Identifying the notion of America with the sacred, according to Bercovitch, "serves to blight, and ultimately to preclude, the possibility of fundamental social change," for anything evil becomes "un-American" and any search for social alternatives turns "into a call for cultural revitalization."[11]

In many ways, I think, Capra's work extends the rhetoric of the jeremiad into the twentieth century and into a new medium, the cinema. This is most evident in *Mr. Smith Goes to Washington* and *Meet John Doe*, films which, as I have argued, combine American and Christian mythology, all embodied in the Capra hero and the values he stands for. Clearly Jefferson Smith and John Doe (once he believes in the speeches he gives) take on the sacred manifestations of "true Americans," while Jim Taylor and D. B. Norton pervert the ideal American values. When Bercovitch argues that *Moby Dick* presents "two modes of individualism, American and false American," and that it upholds the "sacred" American values, he could have as easily been talking about these Capra films. If the jeremiad combines a lament over how some pervert American values with a reaffirmation of those middle-class values, these Capra films clearly fit within the tradition of the jeremiad.[12]

The contention that the jeremiad criticizes evil behavior in order to bring people back to the true sacred path helps us to understand the moral thrust of Capra's films between 1936 and 1948 and thus to clarify the critical confusions about political and social dimensions of Capra's films. These films do present "false Americanism," but only to reaffirm the values of "the ecumenical church of humanism,"

those Christian and American values which Capra inherited from
the traditions of his culture and which he presented in such powerful
narratives. When Capra most closely identifies sacred values with
the symbol of America, he is centrally within the American grain—
and he tends to inhibit social change. When, as in *It's a Wonderful
Life*, American life serves as a background to the film and the
positive values are less closely identified with "Americanism," his
vision is both more powerful and more true, at least to those audiences who refuse to equate the good with the symbol of America.

I began this study by quoting from Walt Whitman's preface to
Leaves of Grass. Since much of what Whitman says illuminates both
Capra and the American tradition, I'll close the same way. In a
famous comment, Whitman wrote, "The United States are essentially the greatest poem." If Capra had been asked between 1936
and 1948 what the greatest setting and subject for movies were, I'm
quite sure he would have said America and Americanism. I hope
I've made it clear that Capra is one of the most talented and effective
interpreters of America to work in the American cinema. But I've
also written this book with the conviction that unless we examine
his (and all) films closely, reflect upon their significance, and connect
them to broader historical and cultural currents, we are in danger
of letting those images dominate us. Such domination is healthy
neither for us nor for our culture.

Notes and References

Preface

1. Cassavetes's comment is quoted on the back cover of *Frank Capra: The Man and His Films*, ed. Richard Glatzer and John Raeburn (Ann Arbor: Univ. of Michigan Press, 1975); Dreyfuss's appears in *Rolling Stone* 282 (January 11, 1979): 90.
2. "Ideology, Genre, Auteur," *Film Comment* 13 (January-February 1977): 46–47.
3. *Name Above the Title* (New York: Macmillan, 1971). Subsequent references to this work will be included in the text in this form: (NATT, page number).

Chapter One

1. John W. Briggs, *An Italian Passage* (New Haven: Yale Univ. Press, 1978), pp. 1–2. See also Andrew Rolle, *The Immigrant Upraised* (Norman: Univ. of Oklahoma Press, 1968).
2. Briggs, p. 10.
3. "Capra's Early Films," in *Frank Capra: The Man and His Films*, pp. 49–50. Bergman repeats the details on p. 70 of the same collection. Hereafter quotations from the anthology will be cited in the text in this form: (FC, pages). See also Joseph McBride, *Frank Capra: The Catastrophe of Success* (New York: Simon and Schuster, 1992), pp. 105–25. Subsequent references to this work will be included in the text in this form: (McB, page numbers).
4. Frank Capra, interview with author at Lake Forest College, Lake Forest, Illinois, March 11, 1978.
5. Leland Poague, *The Cinema of Frank Capra* (New York: Barnes, 1975), p. 234.
6. Ibid., pp. 235–36, and *Name Above the Title*, pp. 57–72.
7. *American Silent Film* (New York: Oxford Univ. Press, 1978), p. 260.
8. "Dialogue on Film," *American Film* 4 (October 1978): 40.

9. Relevant documents in this debate are James Agee's "Comedy's Greatest Era," in *Film Theory and Criticism*, 2nd ed., ed. Gerald Mast and Marshall Cohen (New York: Oxford Univ. Press, 1979), pp. 535–58; Richard Leary, "Capra and Langdon," *Film Comment* 8 (November-December 1972): 18–21; Poague, pp. 120–22; and NATT, 57–72.

10. Everson, pp. 176–77.

11. See note 9.

Chapter Two

1. Robert Stanley, *The Celluloid Empire* (New York: Hastings House, 1978), pp. 45–46.

2. Victor Scherle and William Turner Levy, *The Films of Frank Capra* (Secaucus, N.J.: Citadel Press, 1977), provide more detailed descriptions of the plots of these films. Carney, in *American Vision*, ch. 4, discusses *The Way of the Strong* in some detail.

3. On the transition of Hollywood from silent to sound movies, see Harry Geduld, *The Birth of the Talkies* (Bloomington: Indiana Univ. Press, 1975), esp. chapters 5–7.

4. Scherle and Levy, p. 74.

5. Larry Suid, *Guts and Glory* (Reading, Mass.: Addison-Wesley, 1978), p. 33.

6. Mordaunt Hall, *New York Times*, August 31, 1928, p. 23.

7. Poague, pp. 65–69.

8. *Movie-Made America* (New York: Random House, 1975), p. 175. On the fallen woman film and censorship, see Lea Jacobs, *The Wages of Sin* (Madison: Wisconsin Univ. Press, 1991).

Chapter Three

1. Frank Capra Interview, *American Film*, October 1978, p. 44.

2. Four assessments of Riskin's contributions are by Stephen Handzo, in Glatzer and Raeburn, p. 167; Richard Corliss, *Talking Pictures* (New York: Penguin, 1975), pp. 217–24; Poague, pp. 96–97; and McBride, passim, esp. pp. 289–99 and 334–38.

3. Undated Newspaper Clipping, Fay Wray Collection, University of Southern California, Los Angeles. (Wray was Riskin's wife, and the collection contains many newspaper reviews of films Riskin scripted.)

4. John Raeburn, "*American Madness* and American Values" (FC, p. 57). See also Ed Buscombe, "Notes on Columbia Pictures Corporation 1926–1941," *Screen* 16:4 (Autumn 1975): 65–82.

5. See the profile on Riskin in *Collier's*, March 29, 1941, pp. 21 ff.

6. Poague, p. 152. Poague's whole chapter on *Bitter Tea* has shaped my response to the film.

7. Mordaunt Hall, [Review of *Lady for a Day*], *New York Times*, September 8, 1933, p. 22.

8. Robin Wood used the phrase (and the concept) in his "Ideology, Genre, Auteur."

Chapter Four

1. The standard history of America in the 1930s is William Leuchtenberg, *FDR and the New Deal* (New York: Harper & Row, 1963). On creative American social thought in the 1930s, see Richard Pells, *Radical Visions and American Dreams* (New York: Harper & Row, 1973), esp. pp. 96–150.

2. See Pells, pp. 292–329, and Robert Skotheim, *Totalitarianism and American Social Thought* (New York: Holt-Rinehart, 1971).

3. *Movie-Made America*, p. 196.

4. Among the most important essays on these films are those by Andrew Bergman, Robert Sklar, Stephen Handzo, and William Pechter, all included in Glatzer and Raeburn's anthology. Other essays include Leonard Quart, "Frank Capra and the Popular Front," *Cineaste* 8:1 (1977): 4–7; and Jeffrey Richards, "Frank Capra and the Cinema of Populism," *Film Society Review* 7:6 (1972): 38–46; and 7:9 (1972): 61–71.

5. Discussion, Lake Forest College, March 11, 1978.

6. Schickel, p. 74.

7. Jean-Loup Bourget argues similarly about the political thrust of Capra's films in "Capra et la 'Screwball Comedy,'" *Positif* 133 (December 1971): 47–52. Most of this issue is devoted to Capra.

8. *The Film Criticism of Otis Ferguson,* ed. Robert Wilson (Philadelphia: Temple Univ. Press, 1971), p. 236.

9. *Frank Capra,* New Index Series No. 3 (London: British Film Institute, 1951), p. 18.

10. Wolfe, *Meet John Doe,* esp. pp. 9–13 and 183–93. Capra made comments on the suicide ending in an interview with me, Lake Forest College, March 10, 1978.

11. Though my interpretation differs in emphasis, it stems from reflection generated by Richard Glatzer's interesting essay on *Doe* in FC, 139–48.

12. "Hanging Together: Divergent Unities in American History," *Journal of American History* 61:1 (June 1974): 27.

Chapter Five

1. My account of Capra and the "Why We Fight" series is derived largely from the viewing of the films and study of folders on each film in the National Archives, as well as information from the following sources: Richard Barsam, *Non-Fiction Film* (New York: Dutton, 1973), pp. 181–91; Eric Barnouw, *Documentary* (New York: Oxford Univ. Press, 1974), pp. 144–62; Thomas Bohn, *An Historical and Descriptive Analysis of the "Why We Fight" Series* (New York: Arno, 1977); Richard Dyer MacCann, *The People's Films* (New York: Hastings House, 1973), pp. 152–72; William Murphy, "The Method of 'Why We Fight,'" *Journal of Popular Culture* 1:3 (Summer 1972), 185–96; George Raynor Thompson et al., *The Signal Corps: The Test* (Washington, D.C.: U.S. Govt. Printing Office, 1957) and *The Signal*

Corps: The Outcome (Washington, D.C.: U.S. Govt. Printing Office, 1966). Capra includes his personal account in NATT, 308–67.

2. *The Signal Corps: The Test,* p. 415.

3. MacCann, p. 157; War Department letter to Exhibitors, May 7, 1943, Motion Picture Scripts, 1942–46, Box #31, National Archives.

4. An historical account on the making of *The Negro Soldier* by Thomas Cripps and David Culbert appears in *American Quarterly* 31 (Winter 1979): 616–641.

5. *The Signal Corps: The Outcome,* pp. 556–58.

6. The details on sources are from the motion picture section of the National Archives, in the Signal Corps Motion Picture Case Files, OF, Boxes #1–7.

7. Carl I. Hovland et al., *Experiments on Mass Communication* (Princeton: Princeton Univ. Press, 1949). This book, volume three of the *Studies in Social Psychology in World War Two* series, centers largely on the short- and long-term effects of the "Why We Fight" series.

8. Hovland, pp. 64–65.

Chapter Six

1. Sarris, "Scratch De Mille: New Pillars in the Pantheon," *Village Voice,* July 3, 1978, p. 39; Basinger, *The "It's a Wonderful Life" Book,* p. 3. Wood, "Ideology, Genre, Auteur," p. 49. Other recent insightful treatments of the film include Robert Sklar's "God and Man in Bedford Falls," in Sam Girgus, ed., *The American Self* (Univ. of New Mexico Press, 1981), pp. 211-20; and Robert Ray's treatment of the film in *A Certain Tendency of the Hollywood Cinema* (Princeton, N.J.: Princeton Univ. Press, 1985), pp. 175-215.

2. Unless otherwise noted, the background details about *It's a Wonderful Life* come from my interviews with Capra, March 9-11, 1978. Basinger's book includes a production history of the film, the short story, the final script as shot, and details on the RKO scripts.

3. See Capra's "Breaking Hollywood's Pattern of Sameness," *New York Times Magazine* (May 5, 1946), 18, 57 (also collected in Richard Kozarski's *Hollywood Directors: 1941–76* [New York: Oxford Univ. Press, 1977], pp. 83–89).

4. Letter to the author from Philip Van Doren Stern, May 16, 1978.

5. Interview with Capra, March 10, 1978.

6. *The Films of My Life* (New York: Simon and Schuster, 1978), p. 69.

7. "It's a Wonderful Life," *Cinema Texas* 13 (Fall 1977): 95.

8. Wood, p. 48.

9. See my *American Visions* (New York: Arno Press, 1977), pp. 288–93; and Horney's *The Neurotic Personality of Our Time* (New York: Norton, 1937), p. 287.

10. Wood, p. 49.

Chapter Seven

1. *Variety*, January 8, 1947, pp. 39, 63.
2. Garth Jowett, *Film: The Democratic Art* (Boston: Little-Brown, 1976), pp. 342–50, 475.
3. *America in Our Time* (New York: Doubleday, 1976), pp. 75–98.
4. Poague, p. 61.

Chapter Eight

1. See Scherle, esp. pp. 1–22; Ford's introduction to NATT, pp. ix–x; and Donald Richie, *The Films of Akira Kurosawa* (Berkeley: Univ. of California Press, 1970), p. 45.
2. An English translation of "Cinema/Ideology/Criticism" is included in Bill Nichols, ed., *Movies and Methods* (Berkeley: Univ. of California Press, 1976), pp. 22–30.
3. See Wood's *Personal Views* (London: G. Fraser, 1976), esp. pp. 9–75, 174–88; and Sarris's *Politics and Cinema* (New York: Columbia Univ. Press, 1979).
4. On classical Hollywood, see David Bordwell, Janet Staiger, and Kristin Thompson, *The Classical Hollywood Cinema* (New York: Columbia Univ. Press, 1985); and Robert Ray, *A Certain Tendency of the Hollywood Cinema, 1930–1980* (Princeton, N.J.: Princeton Univ. Press, 1985).
5. Sarris, *The American Cinema*, p. 87; Richards, *Visions of Yesterday* (London: Rutledge and Kegan Paul, 1973), pp. 222–53; Goodwyn, *Democratic Promise* (New York: Oxford Univ. Press, 1976).
6. Sarris, "Scratch DeMille," p. 39.
7. *The Liberal Imagination* (New York: Charles Scribner's Sons, 1950), p. 9.
8. "*Citizen Kane, The Great Gatsby*, and Some Conventions of American Narrative," *Critical Inquiry* 2 (Winter 1975): 325.
9. See Henry Nash Smith, *Democracy and the Novel* (New York: Oxford Univ. Press, 1978), p. 107; Lauren Rabinovitz, "*It's a Wonderful Life*" (see note 7, ch. 6); on Twain and *Connecticut Yankee*, see Henry Nash Smith, *Mark Twain's Fable of Progress* (New Brunswick, N.J.: Rutgers Univ. Press, 1964).
10. (Madison: Univ. of Wisconsin Press, 1978), esp. the preface and chs. 1 and 6.
11. Bercovitch, pp. 176, 4–11, 179.
12. Ibid., p. 192. Significantly, Bercovitch discusses *Connecticut Yankee*, which we might call a jeremiad that turns into an antijeremiad, whereas *Meet John Doe* becomes a forced and unconvincing jeremiad.

Selected Bibliography

FOR A COMPREHENSIVE bibliography of works by and about Frank Capra, see Charles Wolfe's excellent *Frank Capra: A Guide to References and Resources* (Boston: G. K. Hall, 1987). Capra's papers are located in the Frank Capra Archive at Wesleyan University.

Primary Sources

1. Book

Name Above the Title. New York: Macmillan, 1971. An excellent introduction into how Capra perceived himself as a filmmaker, this autobiography is sometimes inaccurate, as McBride's biography (see below) points out.

2. Articles

"Breaking Hollywood's Pattern of Sameness." *New York Times Magazine,* May 5, 1946, pp. 15, 57. Capra defends independent production as a way to avoid conformism in Hollywood films.

"Do I Make You Laugh?" *Films and Filming* (September 1962): 14–15.

"Sacred Cows to the Slaughter." *Stage* (July 1936): 40–41. Capra defends the director in his conflict with producers in the studio era.

3. Interviews

"Capra Today." Interview by James Childs. *Film Comment* (November-December 1972): 22–23.

"Dialogue on Film." *American Film* (October 1978): 39–50.

"Frank Capra." In *The Men Who Made the Movies,* compiled by Richard Schickel. New York: Atheneum, 1975. A partial transcript of the interview Capra did for the PBS television series on Hollywood directors.

GLATZER AND RAEBURN. *Frank Capra,* pp. 16–39 (see below).

Interviews with the author in Lake Forest, Illinois, March 9–11, 1978.

Secondary Sources

1. Books

BASINGER, JEANINE, ET AL. *The "It's a Wonderful Life" Book*. New York: Knopf, 1986. Contains a production history of the film, the shooting script, interviews, and other useful information from the Capra Archive on *Wonderful Life*.

CARNEY, RAYMOND. *American Vision: The Films of Frank Capra*. New York: Cambridge Univ. Press, 1986. Linking Capra to a tradition of American romanticism, Carney, supported by insightful close readings, argues that the power of Capra's films derives from their exploration of "certain prototypical imaginative situations that are deeply ingrained in the American experience" (xi).

GLATZER, RICHARD, AND JOHN RAEBURN, eds. *Frank Capra: The Man and His Films*. Ann Arbor: Univ. of Michigan Press, 1975. A valuable anthology on Capra's life and movies, this collection includes two interviews, biographical sketches, reviews of Capra's films from the 1930s, and critical essays on his films. Particularly helpful are essays by Raeburn, Bergman, Sklar, Glatzer, Handzo, and Pechter.

GRIFFITH, RICHARD. *Frank Capra*. New Index Series No. 3. London: British Film Institute, 1951. This is an early brief study of Capra's films by the critic who called Capra a purveyor of a "fantasy of goodwill."

McBRIDE, JOSEPH. *Frank Capra: The Catastrophe of Success*. New York: Simon and Schuster, 1992. The most thoroughly researched and comprehensive biography of Capra, characterized by a darker portrait of the director than that depicted by critics like Griffith. Although at times unduly hard on Capra, it provides a useful corrective to Capra's autobiography and valuable information about Capra's collaborators.

POAGUE, LELAND. *The Cinema of Frank Capra*. South Brunswick: A. S. Barnes, 1975. This strong study examines Capra's films from the perspective of archetypal comic and romantic structures discussed by Northrop Frye in *Anatomy of Criticism*.

SCHERLE, VICTOR, AND WILLIAM TURNER LEVY. *The Films of Frank Capra*. Secaucus, N.J.: Citadel Press, 1977. This book contains plot summaries of Capra's films and some rare photographs of Capra at work.

WOLFE, CHARLES. *Frank Capra: A Guide to References and Resources*. Boston: G. K. Hall, 1987. An essential annotated guide to works by and about Capra, current through the middle 1980s.

WOLFE, CHARLES, ed. *"Meet John Doe": Frank Capra, Director*. Brunswick, N.J.: Rutgers Univ. Press, 1989. Useful collection on *Meet John Doe* that includes Wolfe's introductory production history of the film, the script (including variant endings), contemporary reviews, and recent critical analyses by Richard Glatzer, Dudley Andrew, and Nick Browne.

2. Articles and Parts of Books

CORLISS, RICHARD. "Capra and Riskin." *Film Comment* 8 (November-December 1972): 18–21.

LOURDEAUX, LEE. *Italian and Irish Filmmakers in America: Ford, Capra, Coppola, and Scorsese,* ch. 2. Philadelphia: Temple Univ. Press, 1990. Lordeaux examines Capra as an ethnic filmmaker whose work is informed by an Italian conception of community and family.

MALAND, CHARLES. "Frank Capra at Columbia: Necessity and Invention." In *Columbia Pictures: Portrait of a Studio,* edited by Bernard Dick, pp. 70–88. Univ. of Kentucky Press, 1992. This essay draws on recent scholarship and Capra's papers at Wesleyan University to discuss Capra's years at Columbia and his relationship to Harry Cohn.

Positif 133 (December 1971), and 317–18 (November-December 1987). Two special issues devoted to Capra that include essays, interviews, and a chronology.

QUART, LEONARD. "Frank Capra and the Popular Front." *Cineaste* 8:1 (1977): 4–7. This essay connects the moral thrust of Capra's films to the antifascist Popular Front attitudes of the late 1930s.

RAY, ROBERT. *A Certain Tendency of the Hollywood Cinema, 1930–1980,* pp. 175–215. Princeton, N.J.: Princeton Univ. Press, 1985. An outstanding close reading of *Wonderful Life* as a crucial postwar American film.

RICHARDS, JEFFREY. *Visions of Yesterday,* pp. 222–53. London: Routledge, 1973. Richards examines the films of Capra, Ford, and Leo McCarey as expressions of the ideology of populism, a perspective that has particularly influenced recent British treatments of Capra.

SARRIS, ANDREW. "Scratch DeMille: New Pillars in the Pantheon." *Village Voice,* July 3, 1978, pp. 39–40. Sarris suggests that Capra may be raised into his pantheon of auteurs.

SKLAR, ROBERT. "The Making of Cultural Myths: Walt Disney and Frank Capra." In *Movie-Made America,* pp. 195–214. New York: Random House, 1975. A discussion of how Capra and Disney created irresistibly engaging mythic images of American life in their movies.

WOOD, ROBIN. "Ideology, Genre, Auteur." *Film Comment* 13 (January-February 1977): 46–51. Urging a "synthetic criticism," Wood perceptively discusses *It's a Wonderful Life* and Hitchcock's *Shadow of a Doubt* as examples of "small town *film noir.*"

Filmography

EACH LISTING indicates if the film is available for 16mm rental and one company that rents it. It also notes if the title may be purchased in videotape (VHS) or laser disc (LD).

FULTAH FISHER'S BOARDING HOUSE (Fireside Productions, 1922)
Producers: G. F. Harris and David Supple
Screenplay: Walter Montague, from Rudyard Kipling's poem
Cinematographer: Roy Wiggins
Cast: Mildred Owens (Anne of Austria), Ethan Allen (Salem Hardieker), Olaf Skavian (Hans)
Running Time: 12 minutes
Premier: April 2, 1922
16mm Rental: Kit Parker Films

THE STRONG MAN (First National, 1926)
Producer: Harry Langdon
Assistant Director: J. Frank Holiday
Screenplay: Hal Conklin, Robert Eddy, and Frank Capra, from a story by Arthur Ripley
Cinematography: Elgin Lessley, Glenn Kershner
Editor: Harold Young
Titles: Reed Henstis
Cast: Harry Langdon (Paul Bergot), Priscilla Bonner (Mary Brown), Gertrude Astor ("Lily" of Broadway), Arthur Thalasso (Zandow)
Running Time: 78 minutes
Premier: September 19, 1926
16mm Rental: Rohauer Collection; VHS

LONG PANTS (First National, 1927)
Producer: Harry Langdon
Screenplay: Arthur Ripley, Robert Eddy
Cinematography: Elgin Lessley
Cast: Harry Langdon (The Boy), Gladys Brockwell (His Mother), Al Roscoe

(His Father), Alma Bennett (The Vamp), Priscilla Bonner (Priscilla),
Frankie Darro (Harry as a boy)
Running Time: 60 minutes
Premier: April 10, 1927
16mm Rental: Rohauer Collection

FOR THE LOVE OF MIKE (First National, 1927)
Producer: Robert Kane
Screenplay: Leland Hayward and J. Clarkson Miller, based on John Mo-
roso's story "Hell's Kitchen"
Cinematographer: Joe Boyle
Cast: Claudette Colbert (Mary), Ben Lyon (Mike), Ford Sterling (Herman
Schultz), George Sidney (Abraham Katz)
Running Time: 73 minutes
Premier: September 1927
16mm Rental: Not available (lost)

THAT CERTAIN THING (Columbia Pictures, 1928)
Producer: Harry Cohn
Screenplay: Elmer Harris
Cinematographer: Joseph Walker
Art Director: Robert E. Lee
Editor: Arthur Roberts
Titles: Al Boasberg
Cast: Viola Dana (Molly), Ralph Graves (A. B. Charles, Jr.), Burr McIntosh
(A. B. Charles, Sr.)
Running Time: 69 minutes
Premier: January 1, 1928
16mm Rental: Kit Parker Films; VHS

SO THIS IS LOVE (Columbia, 1928)
Producer: Harry Cohn
Assistant Director: Eugene DeRue
Screenplay: Elmer Harris and Rex Taylor, from a story by Norman Springer
Cinematographer: Ray June
Art Director: Robert E. Lee
Editor: Arthur Roberts
Cast: Shirley Mason (Hilda Jenson), Buster Collier (Jerry McGuire)
Running Time: 60 minutes
Premier: February 6, 1928
16mm Rental: Kit Parker Films

THE MATINEE IDOL (Columbia, 1928)
Producer: Harry Cohn

Assistant Director: Eugene DeRue
Screenplay: Elmer Harris and Peter Milne, from Robert Lord and Ernest
    S. Pagano's story "Come Back to Aaron"
Cinematographer: Philip Tannura
Art Director: Robert E. Lee
Editor: Arthur Roberts
Cast: Bessie Love (Ginger Bolivar), Johnnie Walker (Don Wilson), Lionel
    Belmore (Col. Bolivar)
Running Time: 66 minutes
Premier: March 14, 1928
16mm Rental: Not available (lost)

THE WAY OF THE STRONG (Columbia, 1928)
Producer: Harry Cohn
Screenplay: William Counselman and Peter Milne
Cinematographer: Ben Reynolds
Cast: Mitchell Lewis (Handsome Williams), Alice Day (Nora)
Running Time: 61 minutes
Premier: June 19, 1928
16mm Rental: Kit Parker Films

SAY IT WITH SABLES (Columbia, 1928)
Producer: Harry Cohn
Assistant Director: Joe Nadel
Screenplay: Dorothy Howell, from story by Frank Capra and Peter Milne
Cinematographer: Joseph Walker
Art Direction: Harrison Wiley
Editor: Arthur Roberts
Cast: Helene Chadwick (Helen Caswell), Francis X. Bushman (John Cas-
    well)
Running Time: 70 minutes
Premier: July 13, 1928
16mm Rental: Not available (lost)

SUBMARINE (Columbia, 1928)
Producer: Harry Cohn
Assistant Director: Buddy Coleman
Screenplay: Dorothy Howell, from story by Norman Springer
Cinematographer: Joseph Walker
Cast: Jack Holt (Jack Dorgan), Dorothy Revier (Bessie), Ralph Graves (Bob
    Mason), Clarence Burton (submarine commander)
Running Time: 93 minutes
Premier: August 28, 1928
16mm Rental: Kit Parker Films

THE POWER OF THE PRESS (Columbia, 1928)
Producer: Jack Cohn
Assistant Director: Buddy Coleman
Screenplay: Sonya Levien, from story by Frederick A. Thompson
Cinematographer: Chet Lyons
Art Direction: Harrison Wiley
Editor: Frank Atkinson
Cast: Douglas Fairbanks, Jr. (Clem Rogers), Jobnya Ralston (Jane Atwill),
    Mildred Harris (Marie)
Running Time: 62 minutes
Premier: October 31, 1928
16mm Rental: Not available

THE YOUNGER GENERATION (Columbia, 1929)
Producer: Jack Cohn
Screenplay: Sonya Levien, from a story by Fannie Hurst
Cinematographer: Ted Tetzlaff
Editor: Arthur Roberts
Dialogue: Howard J. Green
Cast: Jean Hersholt (Papa Goldfish), Rosa Rosanova (Mama Goldfish), Lina
    Basquette (Birdie), Ricardo Cortez (Morris), Rex Lease (Eddie Lesser)
Running Time: 75 minutes
Premier: March 4, 1929
16mm Rental: Kit Parker Films

THE DONOVAN AFFAIR (Columbia, 1929)
Producer: Harry Cohn
Assistant Director: Tenny Wright
Screenplay: Howard J. Green and Dorothy Howell, from Owen Davis's
    play
Cinematography: Teddy Tetzlaff
Art Direction: Harrison Wiley
Editor: Arthur Roberts
Cast: Jack Holt (Inspector Killian), Dorothy Revier (Jean Rankin), Agnes
    Ayres (Lydia Rankin)
Running Time: 83 minutes
Premier: April 11, 1929
16mm Rental: Not available

FLIGHT (Columbia, 1929)
Producer: Harry Cohn
Assistant Director: Buddy Coleman
Screenplay: Frank Capra, from story by Ralph Graves
Cinematography: Joseph Walker (aerial photography by Elmer Dyer)

Art Director: Harrison Wiley
Sound: John Livaldary and Harry Blanchard
Editors: Ben Pivar, Maurice Wright, and Gene Milford
Cast: Jack Holt ("Panama" Williams), Lila Lee (Elinor), Ralph Graves ("Lefty" Phelps)
Running Time: 110 minutes
Premier: September 18, 1929
16mm Rental: Kit Parker Films

LADIES OF LEISURE (Columbia, 1930)
Producer: Harry Cohn
Screenplay: Jo Swerling, from Milton Herbert Gropper's play, *Ladies of the Evening*
Cinematographer: Joseph Walker
Art Director: Harrison Wiley
Sound: John P. Livadary, Harry Blanchard
Editor: Maurice Wright
Cast: Barbara Stanwyck (Kay Arnold), Ralph Graves (Jerry Strong), Lowell Sherman (Bill Standish), Marie Prevost (Dot Lamar), George Fawcett (Mr. Strange)
Running Time: 98 minutes
Premier: April 5, 1930
16mm Rental: Kit Parker Films

RAIN OR SHINE (Columbia, 1930)
Producer: Harry Cohn
Assistant Director: Sam Nelson
Screenplay: Dorothy Howell and Jo Swerling, from a play by James Gleason, who also wrote the novel
Cinematography: Joseph Walker
Art Director: Harrison Wiley
Music: Bakaleinikoff
Sound: John P. Livadary and E. L. Bernds
Editor: Maurice Wright
Cast: Joe Cook (Smiley Johnson), Louise Fazenda ("Princess"), Joan Peers (Mary Rainey), Tom Howard (Amos K. Shrewsbury), Clarence Muse (Nero), Alan Roscoe (Dalton)
Running Time: 87 minutes
Premier: August 10, 1930
16mm Rental: Kit Parker Films

DIRIGIBLE (Columbia, 1931)
Producer: Harry Cohn
Assistant Director: Sam Nelson

Screenplay: Jo Swerling, from a story by Commander Frank Wilber Wead, USN
Cinematography: Joseph Walker
Aerial Photography: Elmer Dyer
Sound: E. L. Bernds
Editor: Maurice Wright
Cast: Ralph Graves (Frisky Pierce), Jack Holt (Jack Bradon), Fay Wray (Helen Pierce), Hobart Bosworth (Louis Rondele), Roscoe Karns (Sock McGuire), Clarence Muse (Clarence)
Running Time: 100 minutes
Premier: April 4, 1931
16mm Rental: Kit Parker Films

THE MIRACLE WOMAN (Columbia, 1931)
Producer: Harry Cohn
Screenplay: Jo Swerling, from the play *God Bless You, Sister*, by John Meehan and Robert Riskin
Cinematography: Joseph Walker
Editor: Maurice Wright
Cast: Barbara Stanwyck (Florence Fallon), David Manners (John Carson), Sam Hardy (Hornsby), Beryl Mercer (Mrs. Higgins), Charles Middleton (Simpson)
Running Time: 87 minutes
Premier: July 20, 1931
16mm Rental: Kit Parker Films

PLATINUM BLONDE (Columbia, 1931)
Producer: Harry Cohn
Screenplay: Jo Swerling (adaptation) and Robert Riskin (dialogue), from a story by Harry Chandler and Douglas Churchill
Cinematographer: Joseph Walker
Editor: Gene Milford
Cast: Loretta Young (Gallagher), Robert Williams (Stew Smith), Jean Harlow (Anne Schuyler), Walter Catlett (Bingy), Louise Closser Hale (Mrs. Schuyler), Halliwell Hobbes (Smythe), Reginald Owen (Dexter Grayson)
Running Time: 90 minutes
Premier: October 31, 1931
16mm Rental: Kit Parker Films; VHS

FORBIDDEN (Columbia, 1932)
Producer: Harry Cohn
Screenplay: Jo Swerling, from story by Frank Capra
Cinematography: Joseph Walker

Editor: Maurice Wright
Cast: Barbara Stanwyck (LuLu Smith), Adolphe Menjou (Bob Grover), Ralph Bellamy (Al Holland), Dorothy Peterson (Helen Grover), Halliwell Hobbes (florist)
Running Time: 83 minutes
Premier: January 15, 1932
16mm Rental: Kit Parker Films

AMERICAN MADNESS (Columbia, 1932)
Producer: Harry Cohn
Asst. Director: Charles Coleman
Screenplay: Robert Riskin, from his story
Cinematographer: Joseph Walker
Art Director: Stephen Goosson
Editor: Maurice Wright
Cast: Walter Huston (Thomas Dickson), Pat O'Brien (Matt Brown), Kay Johnson (Mrs. Dickson), Constance Cummings (Helen), Sterling Holloway
Running Time: 76 Minutes
Premier: August 15, 1932
16mm Rental: Kit Parker Films

THE BITTER TEA OF GENERAL YEN (Columbia, 1933)
Producer: Harry Cohn
Assistant Director: Charles C. Coleman
Screenplay: Edward Paramore, from the novel by Grace Zaring Stone
Cinematographer: Joseph Walker
Art Director: Stephen Goosson
Music: W. Frank Harling
Editor: Edward Curtis
Cast: Barbara Stanwyck (Megan Davis), Nils Asther (General Yen), Walter Connolly (Jones), Toshia Mori (Mah-Li), Gavin Gordon (Bob Strike), Lucien Littlefield (Mr. Jackson)
Running Time: 89 minutes
Premier: January 6, 1933
16mm Rental: Kit Parker Films

LADY FOR A DAY (Columbia, 1933)
Producer: Frank Capra
Assistant Director: Charles C. Coleman
Screenplay: Robert Riskin, from the story "Madame La Gimp," by Damon Runyon
Cinematographer: Joseph Walker
Art Director: Stephen Goosson

Costumes: Robert Kalloch
Editor: Gene Havlick
Cast: Warren Williams (Dave the Dude), May Robson (Apple Annie), Guy
    Kibbee (Judge Henry G. Blake), Glenda Farrell (Missouri Martin),
    Walter Connolly (Count Romero), Jean Parker (Louise), Barry Norton
    (Carlos Romero), Halliwell Hobbes (butler), Samuel S. Hinds (mayor),
    Hobart Bosworth (governor)
Running Time: 88 minutes
Premier: September 13, 1933
16mm Rental: Not in distribution; VHS, LD

IT HAPPENED ONE NIGHT (Columbia, 1934)
Producer: Frank Capra
Assistant Director: Charles C. Coleman
Screenplay: Robert Riskin, from "Night Bus," by Samuel Hopkins Adams
Cinematography: Joseph Walker
Art Director: Stephen Goosson
Costumes: Robert Kalloch
Music: Louis Silvers
Editor: Gene Havlick
Cast: Clark Gable (Peter Warne), Claudette Colbert (Ellie Andrews), Wal-
    ter Connolly (Alexander Andrews), Roscoe Karns (Shapely), Jameson
    Thomas (King Westley), Ward Bond (Bus Driver)
Running Time: 105 minutes
Premier: February 23, 1934
16mm Rental: Kit Parker Films; VHS, LD

BROADWAY BILL (Columbia, 1934)
Producer: Frank Capra
Screenplay: Robert Riskin, from the story by Mark Hellinger
Cinematography: Joseph Walker
Editor: Gene Havlick
Cast: Warner Baxter (Dan Brooks), Myrna Loy (Alice), Walter Connolly
    (J. L. Higgins), Clarence Muse (Whitey), Raymond Walburn (Colonel
    Pettigrew), Margaret Hamilton (Edna), Douglas Dumbrille (Eddie
    Morgan), Jason Robards, Sr. (Arthur Winslow)
Running Time: 90 minutes
Premier: November 21, 1934
16mm Rental: Not in distribution

MR. DEEDS GOES TO TOWN (Columbia, 1936)
Producer: Frank Capra
Assistant Director: C. C. Coleman

Screenplay: Robert Riskin, from Clarence Budington Kelland's story "Opera Hat"
Cinematographer: Joseph Walker
Art Director: Stephen Goosson
Costumes: Samuel Lange
Music: Howard Jackson
Sound: Edward Bernds
Special effects: E. Roy Davidson
Editor: Gene Havlick
Cast: Gary Cooper (Longfellow Deeds), Jean Arthur (Babe Bennett), Lionel Stander (Cornelius Cobb), Walter Catlett (Morrow), Douglas Dumbrille (John Cedar), George Bancroft (MacWade), Raymond Walburn (Walter), H.B. Warner (Judge Walker), Franklin Pangborn (tailor), Mayo Methot (Mrs. Semple), Margaret Seddon and Margaret McWade (Amy and Jane Faulkner, the "pixilated" sisters)
Running Time: 115 minutes
Premier: April 12, 1936
16mm Rental: Kit Parker Films; VHS

LOST HORIZON (Columbia, 1937)
Producer: Frank Capra
Assistant Director: C.C. Coleman
Screenplay: Robert Riskin, from James Hilton's novel
Cinematographer: Joseph Walker (Aerial photography by Elmer Dyer)
Art Direction: Stephen Goosson
Set Direction: Babs Johnstone
Costumes: Ernst Dryden
Music: Dimitri Tiomkin
Music Direction: Max Steiner
Special Effects: E. Roy Davidson and Ganahl Carson
Editor: Gene Havlick, Gene Milford
Technical Advisor: Harrison Forman
Cast: Ronald Colman (Robert Conway), Jane Wyatt (Sondra), Edward Everett Horton (Alexander P. Lovett), Thomas Mitchell (Henry Barnard), John Howard (George Conway), H.B. Warner (Chang), Sam Jaffee (High Lama), Margo (Maria), Isabel Jewell (Gloria Stone)
Running Time: 118 minutes
Premier: February 27, 1937
16mm Rental: Kit Parker Films; VHS, LD

YOU CAN'T TAKE IT WITH YOU (Columbia, 1938)
Producer: Frank Capra
Assistant Director: Art Black

Screenplay: Robert Riskin, based on George S. Kaufman and Moss Hart's play
Cinematographer: Joseph Walker
Art Direction: Stephen Goosson
Costumes: Bernard Newman and Irene
Music: Dimitri Tiomkin
Musical Direction: Morris Stoloff
Editor: Gene Havlick
Cast: Jean Arthur (Alice Sycamore), Lionel Barrymore (Grandpa Vander-hof), James Stewart (Tony Kirby), Edward Arnold (Anthony Kirby, Sr.), Spring Byington (Penny Sycamore), Mischa Auer (Kolenkhov), Ann Miller (Essie Carmichael), Dub Taylor (Ed Carmichael), Samuel S. Hinds (Paul Sycamore), Donald Meek (Poppins), H.B. Warner (Ramsey), Halliwell Hobbes (Mr. DePinna), Mary Forbes (Mrs. Anthony Kirby), Eddie Anderson (Donald), Lillian Yarbo (Rheba), Harry Davenport (judge)
Running Time: 127 minutes
Premier: August 23, 1938
16mm Rental: Films, Inc.; VHS

MR. SMITH GOES TO WASHINGTON (Columbia, 1939)
Producer: Frank Capra
Assistant Director: Arthur S. Black
2nd Unit Director: Charles Vidor
Screenplay: Sidney Buchman, based on Lewis R. Foster's story "The Gentleman from Montana"
Cinematographer: Joseph Walker
Montage Effects: Slavko Vorkapich
Art Direction: Lionel Banks
Costumes: Kalloch
Music: Dimitri Tiomkin
Musical Director: M. W. Stoloff
Sound: Ed Bernds
Editors: Gene Havlick and Al Clark
Cast: James Stewart (Jefferson Smith), Jean Arthur (Clarissa Saunders), Claude Rains (Senator Joseph Paine), Edward Arnold (Jim Taylor), Thomas Mitchell (Dizz), Eugene Pallette (Chick McGann), Guy Kib-bee (Gov. Hopper), Beulah Bondi (Ma Smith), Porter Hall (Sen. Monroe), H.B. Warner (majority leader of Senate), Astrid Allwyn (Susan Paine), Ruth Donnelly (Emma Hopper), William Demarest (Bill Griffith), Grant Mitchell (Sen. McPherson), H. V. Kaltenborn (himself)
Running Time: 125 minutes
Premier: October 19, 1939
16mm Rental: Kit Parker Films; VHS, LD

MEET JOHN DOE (Warner's, 1941)
Producer: Frank Capra
Assistant Director: Arthur S. Black
Screenplay: Robert Riskin, from a story by Richard Connell and Robert Presnell
Cinematographer: George Barnes
Montage Effects: Slavko Vorkapich
Art Direction: Stephen Goosson
Costumes: Natalie Visart
Music: Dimitri Tiomkin
Musical Director: Leo F. Forbstein
Sound: C. A. Riggs
Special Effects: Jack Cosgrove
Editor: Daniel Mandell
Cast: Gary Cooper (Long John Willoughby), Barbara Stanwyck (Ann Mitchell), Edward Arnold (D. B. Norton), Walter Brennan (The "Colonel"), James Gleason (Henry Connell), Spring Byington (Mrs. Mitchell), Rod La Rocque (Ted Sheldon), Regis Toomey (Bert Hansen), Warren Hymer (Angelface), Sterling Holloway (Dan), Gene Lockhart (Mayor Lovett), J. Farrell MacDonald (Sourpuss Smithers)
Running Time: 135 minutes
Premier: May 3, 1941
16mm Rental: Kit Parker Films; VHS, LD

ARSENIC AND OLD LACE (Warner Brothers, 1942, release 1944)
Producer: Frank Capra
Assistant Director: Jesse Hibbs
Screenplay: Philip G. and Julius J. Epstein, from Joseph Kesselring's play.
Cinematography: Sol Polito
Art Director: Max Parker
Music: Max Steiner
Editor: Daniel Mandel
Special Effects: Byron Haskin, Robert Burks
Cast: Cary Grant (Mortimer Brewster), Priscilla Lane (Elaine Harper), Raymond Massey (Jonathon Brewster), Peter Lorre (Dr. Einstein), Josephine Hull (Abby Brewster), Jean Adair (Martha Brewster), Edward Everett Horton (Mr. Witherspoon), John Alexander (Teddy Roosevelt Brewster), James Gleason (Lt. Rooney)
Running Time: 118 minutes
Premier: September 23, 1944 (Filmed 1941–42)
16mm Rental: Swank; VHS, LD

"WHY WE FIGHT" SERIES
Part I: **PRELUDE TO WAR** (1942)

Producer: Frank Capra
Director: Frank Capra
Script: Anthony Veiller, Eric Knight
Music: Alfred Newman
Narration: Walter Huston
Editor: William Hornbeck
Running Time: 53 minutes
16mm Rental: Kit Parker Films; VHS

Part II: **THE NAZIS STRIKE** (1943)
Producer: Frank Capra
Directors: Frank Capra, Anatole Litvak
Script: Eric Knight, Anthony Veiller, Robert Heller
Music: Dimitri Tiomkin
Narration: Walter Huston, Anthony Veiller
Editor: William Hornbeck
Running Time: 42 minutes
16mm Rental: Kit Parker Films; VHS

Part III: **DIVIDE AND CONQUER** (1943)
Producer: Frank Capra
Directors: Frank Capra, Anatole Litvak
Script: Anthony Veiller, Robert Heller
Music: Dimitri Tiomkin
Editor: William Hornbeck
Running Time: 58 minutes
16mm Rental: Kit Parker Films; VHS

Part IV: **THE BATTLE OF BRITAIN** (1943)
Producer: Frank Capra
Director: Anthony Veiller
Script: Anthony Veiller
Music: Dimitri Tiomkin
Narration: Walter Huston, Anthony Veiller
Editor: William Hornbeck
Running Time: 54 minutes
16mm Rental: Kit Parker Films; VHS

Part V: **THE BATTLE OF RUSSIA** (1944)
Producer: Frank Capra
Director: Anatole Litvak
Script: Anatole Litvak, Anthony Veiller, Robert Heller
Music: Dimitri Tiomkin
Narration: Walter Huston, Anthony Veiller
Editor: Walter Hornbeck
Running Time: 80 minutes
16mm Rental: Kit Parker Films

Part VI: **THE BATTLE OF CHINA** (1944)

Producer: Frank Capra
Directors: Frank Capra, Anatole Litvak
Script: Anthony Veiller, Robert Heller
Music: Dimitri Tiomkin
Narration: Walter Huston, Anthony Veiller
Editor: William Hornbeck
Running Time: 64 minutes
16mm Rental: Kit Parker Films

Part VII: **WAR COMES TO AMERICA** (1945)
Producer: Frank Capra
Director: Anatole Litvak
Script: Anatole Litvak, Anthony Veiller
Music: Dimitri Tiomkin
Narration: Walter Huston, Anthony Veiller
Editor: William Hornbeck
Running Time: 70 minutes
16mm Rental: Kit Parker Films; VHS
Capra was also credited as producer for several other films done by the
War Department and Army Pictorial Service: **THE NEGRO SOL-
DIER** (1944), **KNOW YOUR ENEMY: GERMANY** (1945), **KNOW
YOUR ENEMY: JAPAN** (1945), and **TWO DOWN, ONE TO GO**
(1945). He also received directoral credit for the last film and shared
credit with Joris Ivens for **KNOW YOUR ENEMY: JAPAN.**

IT'S A WONDERFUL LIFE (Liberty Films, 1946)
Producer: Frank Capra
Assistant Director: Arthur S. Black
Screenplay: Frances Goodrich, Albert Hackett, and Frank Capra, based
on Philip Van Doren Stern's story "The Greatest Gift." Additional
scenes by Jo Swerling
Cinematography: Joseph Walker and Joseph Biroc
Art Director: Jack Okey
Set Directions: Emile Kuri
Costumes: Edward Stevenson
Music: Dimitri Tiomkin
Sound: Richard Van Hessen and Clem Portman
Special Effects: Russell A. Cully
Editor: William Hornbeck
Cast: James Stewart (George Bailey), Donna Reed (Mary Hatch), Lionel
Barrymore (Potter), Thomas Mitchell (Uncle Billy), Henry Travers
(Clarence Oddbody), Beulah Bondi (Mrs. Bailey), Ward Bond (Bert),
Frank Faylen (Ernie), Gloria Graham (Violet), H. B. Warner (Gower),
Todd Karns (Harry Bailey), Samuel S. Hinds (Mr. Bailey), Tom Fadden
(tollhouse keeper)
Running Time: 129 minutes

Premier: December 23, 1946
16mm Rental: Kit Parker Films; VHS, LD

STATE OF THE UNION (Liberty Films, 1948)
Producer: Frank Capra
Associate Producer: Anthony Veiller
Assistant Director: Arthur S. Black, Jr.
Screenplay: Anthony Veiller and Myles Connolly, from the play by Howard
    Lindsay and Russell Crouse
Cinematography: George J. Folsey
Art Directors: Cedric Gibbons and Urie McCleary
Music: Victor Young
Costumes: Irene
Editor: William Hornbeck
Cast: Spencer Tracy (Grant Matthews), Katharine Hepburn (Mary Mat-
    thews), Van Johnson (Spike McManus), Angela Lansbury (Kay Thorn-
    dyke), Adolphe Menjou (Jim Conover), Charles Lane (Blink Moran),
    Irving Bacon (Buck Swenson), Lewis Stone (Sam Thorndyke), Margaret
    Hamilton (Norah)
Running Time: 121 minutes
Premier: April 30, 1948
16mm Rental: Swank; VHS, LD

RIDING HIGH (Paramount, 1950)
Producer: Frank Capra
Assistant Director: Arthur Black
Screenplay: Robert Riskin, Melville Shavelson, and Jack Rose, from Mark
    Hellinger's story (remake of Capra's 1934 film **BROADWAY BILL**)
Cinematographer: George Barnes and Ernest Laszlo
Art Directors: Hans Dreier and Walter Tyler
Set Decorator: Emile Kuri
Costumes: Edith Head
Music: Johnny Burke and James Van Heusen
Vocal Arrangements: Joseph J. Lilley
Musical Director: Victor Young
Editor: William Hornbeck
Cast: Bing Crosby (Dan Brooks), Colleen Gray (Alice Higgins), Charles
    Bickford (J. L. Higgins), William Demarest (Happy McGuire), Ray-
    mond Walburn (Professor Pettigrew), Margaret Hamilton (Edna),
    James Gleason (racing secretary), Percy Kilbride (Pop Jones), Ward
    Bond (Lee), Douglas Dumbrille (Eddie), Gene Lockhart (J. P. Chase)
Running Time: 112 minutes
Premier: April 12, 1950
16mm Rental: Films, Inc.

HERE COMES THE GROOM (Paramount, 1951)
Producer: Frank Capra
Associate Producer: Irving Asher
Assistant Director: Arthur S. Black, Jr.
Screenplay: Virginia Van Upp, Liam O'Brien, Myles Connolly from a story by Robert Riskin and Liam O'Brien
Cinematography: George Barnes
Art Directors: Hal Pereira, Earl Hedrick
Music: Songs by Johnny Mercer, Hoagy Carmichael, Jay Livingston, and Ray Evans; Musical Direction by Joseph J. Lilley
Editor: Ellsworth Hoagland
Cast: Bing Crosby (Peter Garvey), Jane Wyman (Emmadel Jones), Alexis Smith (Winifrid Stanley), Franchot Tone (Wilbur Stanley), James Barton (Pa Jones), Robert Keith (George Degnan), Jacques Gencel (Bobby), Beverly Washburn (Suzi), Walter Catlett (McGonigle), H. B. Warner (Uncle Elihu)
Running Time: 113 minutes
Premier: September 20, 1951
16mm Rental: Films, Inc.; VHS

BELL SYSTEM SCIENCE SERIES
Number I: **OUR MR. SUN** (Frank Capra Productions, 1956)
Producer: Frank Capra
Script: Frank Capra
Research: Jeanne Curtis
Cinematography: Harold Wellman
Animation: United Productions of America
Editor: Frank P. Keller

Number II: **HEMO THE MAGNIFICENT** (FCP, 1957)
Producer: Frank Capra
Script: Frank Capra
Research: Nancy Pitt
Cinematography: Harold Wellman
Animation: Shamus Culhane Productions
Editor: Frank P. Keller

Number III: **THE STRANGE CASE OF THE COSMIC RAYS** (FCP, 1957)
Producer: Frank Capra
Script: Frank Capra, Jonathon Latimer
Research: Nancy Pitt
Cinematography: Harold Wellman, Ellis Carter
Animation: Shamus Culhane Productions

Editors: Frank P. Keller, Raymond Snyder

Number IV: **THE UNCHAINED GODDESS** (FCP, 1958)
Producer: Frank Capra
Director: Richard Carlson
Script: Frank Capra, Jonathon Latimer
Research: Nancy Pitt
Cinematography: Harold Wellman
Animation: Shamus Culhane Productions
Editor: Frank P. Keller

A HOLE IN THE HEAD (United Artists, 1959)
Producer: Frank Capra
Assistant Directors: Arthur Black and Jack R. Berne
Screenplay: Arnold Schulman, based on his play
Cinematographer: William H. Daniels '
Art Director: Eddie Imazu
Set Decoration: Fred MacLean
Costumes: Edith Head
Music: Nelson Riddle (Songs: "High Hopes" and "All My Tomorrows," by
    Sammy Cahn and Jimmy Van Heusen)
Music Direction: Arthur Morton
Sound: Fred Lau
Editor: William Hornbeck
Cast: Frank Sinatra (Tony Manetta), Edward G. Robinson (Mario Manetta),
    Eddie Hodges (Ally Manetta), Eleanor Parker (Mrs. Rogers), Carolyn
    Jones (Shirl), Keenan Wynn (Jerry Marks), Thelma Ritter (Sophie
    Manetta)
Running Time: 120 minutes
Premier: July 15, 1959
16mm Rental: Swank; VHS

POCKETFUL OF MIRACLES (United Artists, 1961)
Producer: Frank Capra
Associate Producers: Glenn Ford and Joseph Sistrom
Assistant Director: Arthur S. Black
Screenplay: Hal Kanter and Harry Tugend, based on screenplay **LADY
    FOR A DAY**, by Robert Riskin, and short story "Madam La Gimp,"
    by Damon Runyon
Cinematographer: Robert Bronner
Art Directors: Hal Pereira and Roland Anderson
Set Decorators: Sam Comer and Ray Moyer
Costumes: Edith Head and Walter Plunkett

Music: Walter Scharf (Song: "Pocketful of Miracles," by Sammy Cahn and
James Van Heusen)

Choreography: Nick Castle

Sound: Hugo Grenzback and Charles Grenzbach

Editor: Frank P. Keller

Cast: Glenn Ford (Dave the Dude), Bette Davis (Apple Annie), Hope
Lange (Queenie Martin), Peter Falk (Joy Boy), Thomas Mitchell (Judge
Blake), Edward Everett Horton (Butler), Ann-Margret (Louise), Snub
Pollard, Benny Rubin, Doodles Weaver

Running Time: 136 minutes

Premier: December 18, 1961

16mm Rental: Swank; VHS, LD

Index

Adventures of Huckleberry Finn, The (Twain), 131, 184
Adventures of Tom Sawyer, The (Twain), 185
Advise and Consent, 158
Agee, James, 36, 179
Albert, Eddie, 166
Alexander Nevsky, 123
Allen, Walter, 182
Allen, Woody, 182
Allies, 123, 125, 126, 128
All the President's Men, 108, 158
Altman, Robert, 39, 177
American Cinema, The (Sarris), 181
American cultural consensus, revival of in late 1930s, 35, 89–90, 114, 156, 180; solidification of in late 1940s, 156, 180. *See also* Capra, Frank, and consensus nationalism; Popular Front
American liberalism after World War II, 156–57
Annie Hall, 182
Army Morale Branch (later renamed Special Services) 119, 120–21
Army Signal Corps, 117, 118, 119, 120, 121
Arnold, Edward, 103, 111
Arthur, Jean, 93, 95, 106
Auteur criticism, 20, 175–76
Autobiography in Capra's films. *See* Capra, Frank, submerged autobiography
Axis Powers, 123, 125, 128

Ball, Walter, 27
Barrymore, Lionel, 135

Baxter, Warner, 86
Bellamy, Ralph, 57, 58
Bells of St. Mary's, The, 148
Bell System Science Series, 166–67. *See also* Capra, Frank, Works: Documentary Films
Bercovitch, Sacvan, 184–85
Bergman, Andrew, 24, 82
Best Man, The, 171
Best Years of Our Lives, The, 155
Bicycle Thieves, The, 133
Biroc, Joseph, 121, 135
Brandt, Joe, 40
Brennan, Walter, 111
Briskin, Sam, 40, 133
Buchman, Sidney, 106, 134
Burch, Noel, 176

Cahan, Abraham, 45
Cahiers du Cinéma, 19, 176
Candidate, The, 158
Capra, Frank, ambivalence about success ethic, 22–23, 141–43, 160, 182; and anti-Communism after World War II, 157; and audiences, 92–93, 177, 184; childhood, 21–22; and comedy, 92–93, 136; and consensus nationalism ("the ecumenical church of humanism"), 91, 92, 96–97, 99, 102, 109, 114, 152–53, 158, 179–80, 182, 184–86; education, 22; and film style, 41–42, 107–109, 125–27, 148–51, 177–78, *see also* Music in Capra's films; Editing in Capra's films; and Classical Hollywood style; immigration to America, 21; and

212

independent production, 109, 132, 161; and Langdon, 28, 29, *30*, 31–37 passim; moral approach to filmmaking, 20, 33, 66, 91–93, 104, 156, 182; religious views, 91–92; reversals of fortune during career, 22–23, 37, 40, 152–53, 171–72; and Riskin collaboration, 64–65; submerged autobiography in films, 95, 113–14, 152–53, 158

WORKS: DOCUMENTARY FILMS

Battle of Britain, 122, 125, 126
Battle of China, 122, 125, 126, 127
Battle of Russia, 122, *123–24*, 125, 126, 127
Divide and Conquer, 122, 125
Hemo the Magnificent, 166
"Know Your Ally" films, 122
"Know Your Enemy" films, 122
Negro Soldier, The, 122
Our Mr. Sun, 166–67
Prelude to War, 117, 121, 125, 126, 127
Strange Case of Cosmic Rays, The, 166–67
Tunisian Victory, 122
Two Down and One to Go!, 122
Unchained Goddess, The, 166–67
War Comes to America, 122, 123, *124*, 125, 127
See also "Why We Fight" series

WORKS: FEATURE FILMS

American Madness, 40, 42, 63, 64, 66, 69, *70–74*, 78, 82, 138, 168
Arsenic and Old Lace, 118–19
Bitter Tea of General Yen, The, 63, 74–78, 101, 104, 178
Broadway Bill, 64, 66, *83–86*, 157, 161, 163, 177
Dirigible, 43, 46, 47, *49–52*, 54, 60, 63
Flight, 43, 46, *48–49*, 51, 52
Forbidden, 43, 52, 57–58, 65, 69–70, 136
For the Love of Mike, 39–40
Fultah Fisher's Boarding House, *25–26*, 33, 175
Here Comes the Groom, 64, 157, *164–66*

Hole in the Head, A, 31, 157, *167–70*
It Happened One Night, 23, 27, 42, 63, 64, 65, 66, 67, 79–*84*, 90, 91, 165
It's a Wonderful Life, 27, 34, 63, 74, 103, 110, 114, 121, *131–53*, 155, 157, 171, 178–86 passim; and American cultural history, 138–40; autobiographical elements in, 152–53; casting, 135; collaborators, 135; comedy in 144–45; conflicts, external and internal, 140–43; cultural significance of, 151–52; parallels to other Capra films, 138; screenplay, 134–35; segmentation of narrative, 137–38; source, 132–34
Ladies of Leisure, 42, 52–53
Lady for a Day, 63, 64, 66, 78–79, 86, 157, 168, 170
Long Pants, 28, 35–37, 95
Lost Horizon, 64, 65, 90, 93, *98–101*, 108, 112, 171
Meet John Doe, 27, 42, 43, 54, 56, 57, 64, 69, 76, 90, 91, 104, *109–14*, 117, 118, 138, 164, 171, 185
Miracle Woman, The, 52, *54–57*, 60, 63, 67, 94
Mr. Deeds Goes to Town, 42, 43, 65, 69, 74, 90, 91, *93–98*, 102, 106, 114, 117
Mr. Smith Goes to Washington, 27, 63, 69, 74, 90, *104–109*, 124, 158, 160–61, 164, 171, 178, 185
Platinum Blonde, 43, 52, 64, 65, *66–69*, 70, 78, 85, 86
Pocketful of Miracles, 64, 78, 79, 157, 167, *169–71*, 175
Power of the Press, 43
Rain or Shine, 52, *53–54*
Riding High, 64, 157, *161–64*
Say It With Sables, 43
So This is Love, 41, *42–43*
State of the Union, 26, 74, *157–61*
Strong Man, The, 28, *30–35*, 40, 54, 65, 86, 91, 114, 168
Submarine, 41, 43, 46, *47–48*, 49, 51, 52, 161
That Certain Thing, *41–42*, 58
Way of the Strong, The, 43

You Can't Take It With You, 23, 26, 42, 90, 101–104, 106, 107, 138, 171

Younger Generation, The, 44–46, 47, 60, 165

See also American cultural consensus; Langdon, Harry; Riskin, Robert

Capra, Frank, Jr., 64
Çapra, Helen Howell, 40
Capra, Lucille, Reyburn, 64, 152
Capra, Salvatore, 20, 22
Capra, Sarah Nicolas, 20
Carmichael, Hoagy, 164
Carringer, Robert, 184
Casablanca, 118
Chaplin, Charles, 28, 29, *Circus, The,* 29, 41; *City Lights,* 32; *Easy Street,* 34; *Gold Rush, The,* 29; *Great Dictator, The,* 160, 181, 182; *Kid, The,* 29; *Limelight,* 170, 181; *Modern Times,* 180; *Rink, The,* 145
Chase, Richard, 184
Churchill, Winston, 126
Circus, 171
Citizen Kane, 58, 86, 133, 184
Classical Hollywood style, Capra's use of, 25–26, 58, 107–109, 177–78. *See also* Capra, Frank, film style
Cohn, Harry, 37, 40, 79, 98, 101, 129
Cohn, Jack, 40
Colbert, Claudette, 40, 79, 86
Cold War, 115, 156, 161, 181
Columbia Pictures, 19, 37, 58, 79, 98, 109, 152
Communism, 91, 102
Confessions of a Nazi Spy, 124
Connecticut Yankee in King Arthur's Court, A (Twain), 114, 184
Connolly, Myles, 66, 112
Connolly, Walter, 79
Cook, Joe, 53, 54
Cool Million, A (Nathaniel West), 110
Cooper, Gary, 95, 110
Coppola, Francis Ford, 39
Corman, Roger, 28
Crosby, Bing, 157, 163, 164
Crowther, Bosley, 131
Cukor, George, 20

Dawn Patrol, 46
Decline of Hollywood after World War II, 155–56
DePalma, Brian, 39
Depression, 63, 67, 69, 70, 73, 78, 82, 87, 138, 180
Design for Living, 181
Dewey, Thomas, 161
Documentary film. *See* Capra, Frank, documentary films; "Why We Fight" series
Dovzhenko, Alexander, 58
Dwan, Allen, 175

"Ecumenical church of humanism." *See* Capra, Frank, and consensus nationalism
Eddy, Bob, 27
Editing, in Capra's films, 27, 48, 49, 108, 126–27, 150–51, 178. *See also* Capra, Frank, film style; Classical Hollywood style
Edwards, Blake, 175
Edwards, Harry, 28
Eisenhower, Dwight D., 99
Eisenstein, Sergei, 177
Ellington, Duke, 124
Epstein, Julius and Philip, 118
Everson, William K., 28, 35

"Fallen women" films, 57, 58
Falk, Peter, 171
Fascism, 89–90, 91, 102, 110, 118. *See also* Nazis
Ferguson, Otis, 86, 101
Fiedler, Leslie, 184
Fields, W. C., 35, 145
Film criticism, 175–77; auteur criticism, 19, 175–76; cultural criticism, 176–77; ideological criticism, 176–77; synthetic criticism, 177
film noir, 146–47
Film style. *See* Capra, Frank, film style; Classical Hollywood style; Editing in Capra's films; Music in Capra's films
Film Technique (Pudovkin), 27
Fireside Studios, 25
Fitzgerald, F. Scott, 131

Flaherty, Robert, 121, 123, 124, 181
Ford, Glenn, 168
Ford, John, 22, 41, 132, 135, 175
Frankenheimer, John, 39
Franklin, Benjamin, 22
Friedkin, William, 175
Front Page, The, 58, 66, 67
Furthman, Jules, 112

Gable, Clark, 79, 86
Gabriel Over the White House, 158
Genteel tradition, 35, 114
Gershwin, George, 124
Giannini, A. H., 40, 70
Godfather, The, 46
Goldwyn, Samuel, 155
Gone With the Wind, 90
Goodrich, Frances, 134–35
Goodwyn, Lawrence, 179
Grant, Cary, 118
Grant's Tomb, 95, 158
Graves, Ralph, 48, 49, 52
Gray, Colleen, 163
"Greatest Gift, The" (Stern), 132–34
Great Gatsby, The (Fitzgerald), 131, 184
Great McGinty, The, 181, 182
Griffith, D. W., 26, 48
Griffith, Richard, 24, 104
Gropper, Milton Herbert, 52

Hackett, Albert, 134–35
Hail the Conquering Hero, 181
Hal Roach Studios, 27
Hamilton, Alexander, 73
Handzo, Stephen, 65, 107, 131, 135, 153
Harlow, Jean, 67, 69
Hart, Moss, 101
Hathaway, Henry, 172
Hays Code, 93
Hays Office, 57
Hearts of Age, The, 26
Hecht, Ben, 64
Heisler, Stuart, 121, 122
Hepburn, Kathryn, 159
Hester Street, 46
Higham, John, 114
Hilton, James, 98, 101, 121
Hitchcock, Alfred, 119

Hitler, Adolph, 125, 126, 127
Hodges, Eddie, 167
Hodgson, Geoffrey, 156
Hollywood Ten trials, 156
Holt, Jack, 48, 49
Hoover, Herbert, 140
Hornbeck, William, 121
Horney, Karen, 151
House Un-American Activities Committee. *See* HUAC
HUAC (House Un-American Activities Committee), 156, 180
Hubbard, Elbert, 24
Hurst, Fanny, 45
Hurwitz, Leo, 124
Huston, John, 121, 132
Huston, Walter, 70, 117, 121

Ideology, Capra's. *See* Capra, Frank, consensus nationalism
Immigration to America, theories of, 21–22
It Can't Happen Here (Sinclair Lewis), 110
It Happened One Christmas, 133

Jenkins, George, 108
Jeremiad tradition, and Capra's films, 184–86

Kaufman, George S., 101
Keaton, Buster, 28, 29, 145
Kern, Jerome, 124
Kesselring, Joseph, 118
Keynes, John Maynard, 73
Keystone Studios, 27–28
Kibbee, Guy, 78, 79
King, Henry, 175
Kipling, Rudyard, 25
Knight, Eric, 121
Korean War, 165
Kubrick, Stanley, 175
Kurosawa, Akira, 175

Ladies of the Evening, 52
Langdon, Harry, 23, 28, 29–37, 58
Lansbury, Angela, 159
Lastfogel, Abe, 167, 170

Leaves of Grass (Whitman), 186
Lewis, R. W. B., 184
Lewis, Sinclair, 110, 179
Liberty Films, 132, 155, 161
Lies My Father Told Me, 46
Litvak, Anatole, 121, 122
Lloyd, Harold, 29
Lorentz, Pare, 124
Lorre, Peter, 119
Lowry, Malcolm, 33
Lubitsch, Ernst, 181
Lucas, George, 39
Lumet, Sidney, 39

McCarey, Leo, 148
McCarthy, Joseph, 165
McGowan, Bob, 27
McPherson, Aimee Semple, 54
Main Street (Sinclair Lewis), 179
Manhattan, 182
Mankiewicz, Herman, 64
Marooned, 172
Marshall, General George C., 119, 120,
    121, 135, 129
Marx, Leo, 184
Massey, Raymond, 119
Matthiessen, F. O., 184
Mayer, Louis B. 79
Meehan, John, 54
Mein Kampf (Hitler), 125
Menjou, Adolphe, 57, 157
Mercer, Johnny, 164
Metro-Goldwyn-Mayer (MGM), 79
Miller, Perry, 184
Miracle of Morgan's Creek, 181
Moby Dick (Melville), 185
Montague, Walter, 25
Motion Picture Academy of Arts and Sci-
    ences (the Academy), 19, 90
Murnau, F. W., 41
Muse, Clarence, 163
Music in Capra's films, 58, 81, 84, 96,
    104, 108, 113, 123, 124, 142, 145, 150,
    157, 163, 164, 165, 168
Mussolini, Benito, 127
Mysterious Stranger, The (Twain), 184

Name Above the Title (Capra), publica-
    tion of, 172

Narrative conventions of late 1930s films,
    93–94; hero, 93; heroine, 93–94; ritual
    humiliation, 94; ritual victory, 94
Nashville, 177
Native Land, 124
Nazis, 89, 110, 120, 123, 124, 126. *See
    also* Fascism
New Deal legislation, 89, 98
Newman, Alfred, 121, 124
Niebuhr, Reinhold, 156

O'Brien, Liam, 164
O'Brien, Pat, 70
Odets, Clifford, 134
One Flew Over the Cuckoo's Nest, 63
Osborn, Brigadier General F. W., 119,
    121
Our Gang comedies, 27, 41
Our Hospitality, 29

Paramore, Edward, 74
Paramount Studios, 155, 158, 161
Pascal, Blaise, 171
Pechter, William, 143, 145, 146, 184
Peckinpah, Sam, 175
Penn, Arthur, 39, 175
Poague, Leland, 28, 30, 51, 76, 157
Popular Front, 89, 156, 161. *See also*
    American cultural consensus; Fascism;
    New Deal legislation
Potemkin, 133
Prokofiev, Sergei, 124
Pudovkin, Vsevolod, 27

Rabinovitz, Lauren, 142, 184
Rachmininov, Sergei, 124
Raeburn, John, 74, 180
Rashomon, 133
Reed, Donna, 135
Richards, Jeffrey, 179
"Rich Boy, The" (Fitzgerald), 131
Riefenstahl, Leni, 120
Rimsky-Korsakov, Nicholas, 124
Ripley, Arthur, 28, 35, 36
Rise of David Levinsky, The (Cahan), 45
Riskin, Robert, 54, 55, 57, 64–65, 69, 74,
    79, 84, 104, 109, 135, 165
Ritt, Martin, 175
Roaring Twenties, The, 124

Robinson, Edward G., 168
Robson, May, 78, 79, 86
Rocky, 43
Roman Holiday, 161
Roosevelt, Franklin Delano, 70, 89, 94, 98, 181
Rosebud syndrome," 86–87
Rules of the Game, 133

St. Francis of Assisi, 167
Santayana, George, 35
Sarris, Andrew, 131, 176, 178, 181
Schulman, Arnold, 167
Scorsese, Martin, 39
Screen Directors Guild, 19, 90, 129
Screwball comedies, 82
Sennett, Mack, 27–28
Shaffner, Franklin, 171
Shakespeare, 42, 165
Shostakovich, Dmitri, 124
Silent film comedy, 28–29
Sinatra, Frank, 157, 167
Sklar, Robert, 57, 90, 93
Smith, Al, 140
Smith, Henry Nash, 184
Spanish Civil War, 98
Special Services. *See* Army Morale Branch
Stagecoach, 133
Stanwyck, Barbara, 52, 54, 56, 57, 75, 93, 110
Stern, Philip van Doren, 133–34
Stevens, George, 121, 132
Stevenson, Robert, 121
Stewart, James, 106, 107, 135, 148–50
Stimson, Henry, 124
Stock Market Crash, 89
Story of Adele H, The, 57
Stravinsky, Igor, 124
Streetcar Named Desire, A, 166
Sturges, John, 172
Sturges, Preston, 181
Surles, General Alexander, 122
Swerling, Jo, 52, 54, 57, 67, 134–35

Talkies, introduction of, 43–44
Tchaikovsky, Peter Ilyich, 123–24
Third Man, The, 73
Thomas, Marlo, 133
Thompson, George, 120

Thoreau, Henry David, 95
Thurmond, Strom, 161
Tiomkin, Dimitri, 108, 121, 122, 135
To Be or Not to Be, 181, 182
Tojo, General Hideki, 127
Tramp, Tramp, Tramp, 28, 29, 30
Trilling, Lionel, 182
Triumph of the Will, 120
Trouble in Paradise, 181
Truffaut, François, 19, 58, 135
Truman, Harry, 161
Trumbo, Dalton, 134
Twain, Mark, 131, 184

Vidal, Gore, 171
Vidor, King, 41
Von Sternberg, Joseph, 75
Von Stroheim, Erich, 26
Vorkapich, Slavko, 108

Wagner, Richard, 124
Walker, Joseph, 52, 135
Wallace, Henry, 126, 161
Walsh, Raoul, 175
Walt Disney Studios, 123, 126
Wanger, Walter, 74
Warner Brothers, 43, 44, 109, 118
Webster, Daniel, 108
Welles, Orson, 26
West, Jessamyn, 161
West, Nathaniel, 110
Whitman, Walt, 186
"Why We Fight" series, *119–29;* analysis of, 122–27; Capra's involvement with, 119–22; scholarship on, 189; effect on audiences, 127–28; sources for footage and music, 123–24. *See also* Capra, Frank, Documentary films, for individual films
Wilder, Billy, 181
Williams, Robert, 66, 86
Wilson, Woodrow, 138
"Wings trilogy," 46–52
"Winter Dreams" (Fitzgerald), 131
Winthrop, John, 185
Wood, Robin, 131, 146, 153, 176–77
World War I, 23, 35, 64
World War II, 93, 106, 117–29 passim, 130, 132, 137, 138, 180
Wray, Fay, 51

Wright, Frank Lloyd, 101
Wyler, William, 20, 121, 132, 135, 155,
    161, 175

Young, Loretta, 66
Young Mr. Lincoln, 176

Zanuck, Darryl, 121